Education Policy Research

ALSO AVAILABLE FROM BLOOMSBURY

Partnerships in Education Research, Michael Anderson and Kelly Freebody

Challenging the Qualitative-Quantitative Divide, Barry Cooper, Judith Glaesser, Roger Gomm and Martyn Hammersley

State and Education Policy, edited by Helen M. Gunter

Networking Research, Patrick Carmichael

Education Policy Research

Design and Practice at
a Time of Rapid Reform

EDITED BY
HELEN M. GUNTER, DAVID HALL
AND COLIN MILLS

B L O O M S B U R Y
LONDON • NEW DELHI • NEW YORK • SYDNEY

Bloomsbury Academic

An imprint of Bloomsbury Publishing Plc

50 Bedford Square	1385 Broadway
London	New York
WC1B 3DP	NY 10018
UK	USA

www.bloomsbury.com

First published 2014

British Library Cataloguing-in-Publication Data
A catalogue record for this book is available from the British Library.

ISBN: HB: 978-1-4725-1439-4
PB: 978-1-4725-0909-3
ePub: 978-1-4725-1278-9
ePDF: 978-1-4725-1225-3

Library of Congress Cataloging-in-Publication Data
Education Policy Research : design and practice at a time of rapid reform /
edited by Helen M. Gunter, Dave Hall and Colin Mills.
pages cm
ISBN 978-1-4725-1439-4 (hardback) – ISBN 978-1-4725-0909-3 (paperback)
1. Education–Research. 2. Education and state. 3. Educational change. I. Gunter, Helen M.
LB1028.E259 2014
370.72 – dc23
2014008255

Typeset by Integra Software Services Pvt. Ltd.
Printed and bound in India

CONTENTS

FOREWORD

Michael W. Apple

Over the past number of years, I have been fortunate enough to spend a good deal of time at the University of Manchester. It is an institution that deserves its reputation. The faculty members and post-graduate students there who have been engaged in long term efforts to bring critical analyses to bear on the realities of educational policies and practices have been particularly impressive to me. Under the leadership of Helen Gunter, David Hall and others, a tradition has been established at Manchester that makes it one of the most notable places for research on the intricate dynamics of power in schools and other educational institutions and on how these dynamics are built, experienced and at times interrupted. *Education Policy Research: Design and Practice at a Time of Rapid Reform* is the result of a number of these ongoing research projects.

In the introductory chapter of this fine book you are about to read, Helen Gunter, David Hall and Colin Mills remind us that these are 'dark times'. Indeed, this book comes at a time when there is (again) a severe economic crisis not only in the United States and England but in many regions of the world. At the same time, partly as a response to this crisis, there is a resurgence of rightist sentiments. White male anger is growing; many working-class people are being pulled under the umbrella of retrogressive movements; empire is being threatened; openly expressed racism is resurgent; and anti-immigrant sentiment is turning ugly. And for large numbers of people, the previously settled understandings of one's 'rightful' place in the world and its hierarchies are now under severe threat.

For conservative governments in England, in Australia, in major cities and entire states in the United States, and in so many other places, the crisis, the impoverishment and the loss of identifiable people's possibilities, can only be solved by the religion of the market. Shrink the state, remove the safety net, establish market discipline, fire public employees, make people more insecure by removing the right to affordable health care, slash pensions, cut funding for education, lay off teachers, engage in what is best thought of as 'management by stress', and I could go on enumerating the areas of pain. In Stephen Ball's words, 'The public sector must be remade in order to respond to the exigencies of globalization and to play its part in the economics of global competition. Individual and institutional actors and their dispositions and responses are tied to the fate of the nation in the global economy' (Ball, 2008, p. 15). Education is clearly not immune to these intense pressures.

I purposely have used the term 'religion' in the previous paragraph, since the positions pushed forward often seem to be immune to counter-factuals. It is as if the glasses that are worn by those who hew to the positions associated with the neo-liberal agenda make all of the pain invisible. Education policy is one of the arenas in which the limitations of these glasses are particularly evident.

Part of the reason for such invisibility is that within dominant groups, there seems to be something of an epistemological fog, an almost willful opacity. Most of these groups know least about what the lives of so many millions of people are actually like, especially but not only in slums and poor rural areas, about housing in them, about education, about the services they need and (almost always) don't get, and so on. The lack of knowledge provides an epistemological veil (Davis, 2006). What goes on under the veil is a secret and must be kept from public view. To know is to be subject to demands. Thus, the very lack of Foucault's panoptican constitutes a form of control.[1]

But it is not only neo-liberalism's veil on which we need to focus our attention. All of this is coupled with a neo-conservative cultural agenda involving a restorative project. Bring 'traditional' and 'real' knowledge, values, and (particular, not everyone's) religious commitments back to the centre of what should be the core of a society and of people's identities. Re-establish the hierarchies that are associated with this knowledge and these values and this religion. Fight against the 'pollution' brought in by the values, knowledge, religion and indeed the very body of the *Other*, of the 'constitutive outside' that gives meaning to our lives when we oppose the source of such pollution.

In the face of the neo-liberal and neo-conservative positions that circulate so widely both nationally and internationally, there is a growing body of literature in education that critically examines the conceptual and ideological underpinnings and the ethical, political and empirical realities of the major educational reforms that are currently travelling throughout the world. As I show in *Educating the 'Right' Way* (Apple, 2006), we cannot understand why these policies have such power unless we go more deeply into the creative ways in which the Right has worked at changing our commonsense so that the meanings of key words that have what might be called 'emotional economies' are radically transformed (Williams, 1985).

---

[1]This is an important conceptual and political point. I hope that it causes some of those within the postmodern education research community who are uncritically wedded to Foucault as a theorist of new forms of control to raise questions about whether *the absence of knowledge* and the absence of the panoptican may be equally as important when we are talking about massive structural inequalities and the blindness of the neo-liberal agenda.

The 'thick democracy' of full participation is being replaced by the 'thin democracy' of markets and consumption practices. Education is one of the prime sites for this strategy as it too is being commodified. Choice in a competitive market replaces the collective creation and recreation of our fundamental institutions. Words such as democracy, equality, and freedom become eviscerated, drained of their critical histories and of the social movements that established them as key elements in the formation of more progressive social and educational policies (Foner, 1998).

As I have also documented, in order to do justice to the complicated ideological assemblage behind the movement towards thinner versions of democracy, we also need to direct our attention to a wider set of conservative groups. So far, I have mentioned two of the groups. However, within the complicated alliance of *conservative modernization* are four groups: neo-liberals, neo-conservatives, members of an upwardly mobile fraction of the professional and managerial new middle class who are committed to audits and very limited forms of 'evidence' and in an increasing number of nations, authoritarian populist religious conservatives (Apple, 2006). It is also important to recognize that there are not only multiple groups and tendencies within this conservative alliance, but there are also multiple relations of power that are being fought out – not only class relations but those of gender, sexuality, race and religion (see, for example, Apple, 2010; Apple, Au and Gandin, 2009; Apple, Ball and Gandin, 2010).

So far I have talked mostly at an abstract level. But let me again stress that these larger ideological movements are having profound effects on the specifics of educational policies and on the daily realities of teaching, curriculum and evaluation in schools all over the world. I have had intense discussions with researchers at universities, with activists in social and educational movements and with teachers and administrators in schools, about the kinds of policies that have been put in place in education and in so much else. The dominance of testing and reductive models of accountability is pronounced. The English and Australian equivalents of Teach for America, and the attacks on teacher education in general, are growing. The calls for a focus on 'hard' rather than 'soft' subjects and a call to return to 'real curricula', and to rigorously police the teaching of them, are visible both in the government and in the media. Performance pay for teachers has either been instituted or is on the agenda. Privatization, marketization, competition, choice – these and other similar rhetorical devices are being marshalled to convince the public that what exists in teaching, curricula, evaluation, leadership and so much else is uniformly 'bad'. They must be replaced with neo-liberal, neo-conservative and managerial policies and reorganized around the technologies and ideologies of audit cultures so that the emphasis is on the constant production of evidence that one is doing 'the right thing'. The state and its forms are being transformed. New arenas for profit-making are being created. Not only are schools and pupils being commodified but so too are knowledge and policy themselves

(Ball, 2007, 2012; Burch, 2009; Apple, 2013; Gunter, 2014). What may be among the most disheartening facts is that some of the support for many of these policies has come and continues to come from supposedly more progressive political parties such as the Democratic Party in the United States and the Labour Party in both England and Australia.

In its project of instituting 'thin' forms of democracy, neo-liberalism(s) need to destabilize the opposition to its project. One of the most effective strategies has been a process of disarticulation and rearticulation (Gandin and Apple, 2003). As I noted, words with an emotional economy such as 'democracy' and 'justice' are to be taken from their origins in progressive movements, emptied of their previous meanings, and then filled with new meanings, all the while keeping the words themselves in circulation. Thus, through long-term and creative ideological work in the media and elsewhere, 'thick' meanings of democracy grounded in full collective participation are replaced by 'thin' understandings where democracy is reduced to choice in a market. These are not simply linguistic transformations, although that is important. These new understandings are accompanied by major shifts in identity. Subjectivities are slowly but ultimately radically transformed. What it means to be responsive and effective and the ways in which such things are evaluated are rationalized and used to (re)organize the state and to bring the norms of the private into the public. And once again, schools often sit at the very centre of these 'reforms'.

Of course, this is not a one-way process. These changes are resisted and mediated. Indeed, there have been and are times when and places where progressive movements and policies can win back these concepts and establish more thickly critically democratic norms and institutional forms. The policies in Porto Alegre, Brazil, involving the Citizen School and especially participatory budgeting provide ample evidence that progressive alliances can themselves engage in successful disarticulations and rearticulations that are lasting (Gandin and Apple, 2012). Popular and academic journals and books are filled with accounts of counter-hegemonic teaching and curricula that make a real difference in the lives of students and communities. More detailed pictures of these kinds of successful practices are constantly being published, giving us a sense of possibility in a time of rightist attacks (see Gutstein, 2006; Apple and Beane, 2007; Schultz, 2008; Watson, 2012; Swalwell, 2013).

The arguments I make above are important to the honest and insightful research described in the chapters in *Education Policy Research: Design and Practice at a Time of Rapid Reform*. My claims are grounded in a recognition of the importance of two interconnected projects – one 'deconstructive' and the other 'constructive'. The first asks us to engage in research that 'bears witness' to what is actually happening in schools and universities, in communities, in government offices and in all of the institutions that are affected by current policies. The second, more constructive project requires something else. It asks us to act as *critical secretaries*, to give accounts of the spaces, possibilities and actually existing programs that provide articulate defenses of and gains in more critically democratic actions inside and outside of education (Apple, 2013).

These two projects require powerful, nuanced and caring research of various kinds. The chapters included here are examples of such research, since both of these projects are more than a little visible in this book. That fact in and of itself would be enough to make this volume so carefully edited by Gunter, Hall and Mills a worthy contribution. But *Education Policy Research: Design and Practice at a Time of Rapid Reform* speaks to another set of issues, those surrounding how we are to more fully understand the complex workings of our educational institutions and what counts as evidence in making claims about them. Let me say more about this.

Our ordinary language points to the complex histories that are embodied in the words we use to understand our institutions. Take a word that has a good deal of rhetorical power in the world of educational policy and research right now – *accountability*. As it is currently mobilized in education, accountability (too often) refers to a limited set of measurement practices such as the results of students on standardized tests. In this way of thinking about what counts as a good teacher, a good administrator and a good school, numbers tell us everything of importance that we need to know.

Not only does this mode of understanding radically reduce the complexities associated with the act of education, it also evacuates another robust meaning of the concept of accountability itself. Our language already carries within it another meaning, one that is present when we ask someone to 'give an account' of what happened or is happening in a social situation, institution or practice. Here, what is called for is not only numbers – some of which may at times indeed be important – but a narrative, a thicker story of what is both social and personal. It asks for a narrative that resists the act of epistemological reduction. Rather it is based on a sensitivity to complexity, to experience, to voice, to giving more not less.

In many ways, these differences mirror the distinction between thin and thick democracy that I noted earlier. In a time of neo-liberalism and the accompanying demands of audit cultures, thin versions of democracy map on to thin epistemological evidentiary commitments. But thick democratic understandings are grounded in thicker epistemological commitments. What counts as 'evidence' and as 'powerful research' is then considerably broader. It does not shun complexity, contradiction, real people's experiences and narratives, and epistemological tensions. Rather it makes them core parts of what needs to be opened up and illuminated. *Education Policy Research: Design and Practice at a Time of Rapid Reform* embodies this sense of complexity, contradiction, experience, voice and epistemological tension in important ways. The book does this by revivifying two things: the importance of research that is connected to the lives of real people in real schools, organizations and communities; and the importance of multiple voices and actors engaging in such research.

The book also asks the reader to constantly take seriously a series of questions. What is research for? Who should it benefit? What is the role of the researcher in an age of neo-liberal, neo-conservative and managerial agendas and the reconstruction of the public sphere? Who is the researcher? I have discussed these questions at much greater length in *Can Education Change Society?* And it is gratifying to see how my own work has helped frame a number of the contributions in this book. But what is even more gratifying is to see how my and others' arguments have been extended and used in the accounts this book provides.

One of the marks of a valuable book is whether it illuminates the realties we face in ways that allow us to see these realities better, to give us insights into the 'whats and whys' of our current situations. Gunter, Hall, Mills and their colleagues have produced such a book. In the process, they have 'given us an account' of life in educational institutions that contributes to the building of better theories, better descriptions, better research, better policies and better practices.

References

Apple, M.W. (2006), *Educating the 'Right' Way: Markets, Standards, God, and Inequality, 2nd ed.* New York: Routledge.

Apple, M.W. (ed.) (2010), *Global Crises, Social Justice, and Education.* New York: Routledge.

Apple, M.W. (2013), *Can Education Change Society?* New York: Routledge.

Apple, M.W., Au, W. and Gandin, L.A. (eds) (2009), *The Routledge International Handbook of Critical Education.* New York: Routledge.

Apple, M.W., Ball, S. and Gandin, L.A. (eds) (2010), *The Routledge International Handbook of the Sociology of Education.* New York: Routledge.

Apple, M.W. and Beane, J.A. (eds) (2007), *Democratic Schools: Lessons in Powerful Education, 2nd ed.* Portsmouth, NH: Heinemann.

Ball, S. (2007), *Education plc.* New York: Routledge.

Ball, S. (2008), *The Education Debate: Politics and Policy in the 21st Century.* Bristol: Policy Press.

Ball, S. (2012), *Global Education, Inc.: New Policy Networks and the Neo-liberal Imaginary.* New York: Routledge.

Burch, P. (2009), *Hidden Markets.* New York: Routledge.

Davis, M. (2006), *Planet of Slums.* New York: Verso.

Foner, E. (1998), *The Story of American Freedom.* New York: Norton.

Gandin, L.A. and Apple, M.W. (2003), 'Educating the state, democratizing knowledge', in Apple, M.W., Aasen, P., Kim Cho, M., Gandin, L.A., Oliver, A., Sung, Y.-K., Tavares, H., and Wong, T.-H. (eds), *The State and the Politics of Knowledge.* New York: RoutledgeFalmer, 193–219.

Gandin, L.A. and Apple, M.W. (2012), 'Can critical democracy last: Porto Alegre and the struggle for thick democracy in education'. *Journal of Education Policy,* 27: 621–39.

Gunter, H. (2014), *Educational Leadership and Hannah Arendt*. London: Routledge.

Gutstein, E. (2006), *Reading and Writing the World with Mathematics*. New York: Routledge.

Schultz, B. (2008), *Spectacular Things Happen Along the Way: Lessons from an Urban Classroom*. New York: Teachers College Press.

Swalwell, K. (2013), *Educating Activist Allies*. New York: Routledge.

Watson, V. (2012), *Learning to Liberate: Community-based Solutions to the Crisis in Urban Education*. New York: Routledge.

Williams, R. (1985), *Keywords*. New York: Oxford University Press.

ACKNOWLEDGEMENTS

Working together as an editorial team, as well as with our colleagues and our students and former students, has been a joy. We talked a great deal about the book at the lively seminars and meetings we have as a critical community, eager to look closely at the current contexts of schooling and education in which we live and work.

We support each other in our writing and in our ongoing studies. Such critical scholarship and collaboration is at a premium these days, and we appreciate how fortunate we are. We gave our writers an open brief, asking them to describe and to analyse their work in ways that may resonate with others and also to encourage others who may be starting on the kinds of critical work that we undertake.

We know that our writers have very busy lives. Many of them are starting out in academic life and that brings with it its own pressures and uncertainties these days. However, they met our challenges and we think that their voices come through. Their 'data sing', as Dimitriadis says in his series introduction to Jean Anyon et al's book (2009, p. vii). She and her colleagues published their inspiring accounts as *Theory and Educational Research* in 2009, and is cited by many of our writers here.

We owe many debts. First, as editorial group, we acknowledge each other's help and support. Then we are thankful to our writers, who tolerated the many tight deadlines and the pressures and have 'taken flight'. We are sure that many of them will have important careers and professional trajectories in the field of scholarship. We have learned so much from them. We know that they are indebted to all the people who have been involved with and supported their research. This is varied but includes supervisors, research participants, funders and their families.

We are thankful to our colleagues, Francis Arnold, Alison Baker, David Barker, Kasia Figiel and Rosie Pattinson, at Bloomsbury Press. They have been supportive and encouraging, particular thanks to Alison, who led the book 'take off', and Kasia, who helped us steer the book 'landing'. Our colleagues in The Manchester Institute of Education, University of Manchester, have had their ears bent by us and have given us support and time. Helen, David and Colin would like to thank their families for handling our absence while we typed and checked references in the run up to Christmas. Colin would like to acknowledge the support of Andy

Fleetwood and Neil Hubbard, who bailed him out with much-valued administrative and technical support when it was needed.

As we point out in our Introduction, theorizing and asking questions is sometimes a risky business. Our colleagues have done all that and have done important work that shines through these pages. Our biggest hope is that it inspires conversations and much more 'holding tight and letting go'.

NOTES ON CONTRIBUTORS

Michael W. Apple is Professor of Education in The Manchester Institute of Education, University of Manchester, UK, and John Bascom Professor of Curriculum and Instruction and Educational Policy Studies at the University of Wisconsin, Madison, USA.

Paul Armstrong graduated with a PhD from The Manchester Institute of Education, University of Manchester, in 2014. His research interests are about the emerging practice and cultural influence of school business managers in England. He also holds a master's in Educational Research from the same institution. He currently holds Research Associate positions at the University of Nottingham's School of Education, exploring policy enactments in schools in England and Hong Kong, and the Institute of Education in London, exploring young school leaders in London, New York and Toronto.

Maureen E. Cain graduated with an EdD from The Manchester Institute of Education, University of Manchester, in 2011. Her research interest is the development of primary school leaders in their professional practice. Her background as a primary school head provided experiences of leading school improvement in different schools. She also worked as a National College education consultant, training and facilitating the development and assessment of leaders for national accreditation. Maureen continues to work with schools and their leadership teams, using her doctoral research framework to guide teachers' intellectual enquiry for professional development, personal growth and improved provision for students.

Patricia M. Davies graduated with an EdD from The Manchester Institute of Education, University of Manchester, in 2013. She is currently head of computer studies at a private independent school in south-east England. Her doctoral research is about student participation in school ICT policymaking. She is also interested in student leadership and student voice.

James R. Duggan graduated with a PhD from The Manchester Institute of Education, University of Manchester, in 2012. He is now Research Assistant at the Education and Social Research Institute, Manchester Metropolitan University, UK. His research interests are in policy enactment, leadership, collaboration and more generally in the constraints and limitations of managerial forms of organizing in the public sector.

Carl Emery is a doctoral student and part-time lecturer in The Manchester Institute of Education, University of Manchester, UK. His research is focused on the rise of social and emotional learning (SEL) within education, and he is particularly interested in national identities, policy development, discourse and power dynamics associated with SEL across England and Wales. Carl is the joint author of *Children's Social and Emotional Wellbeing: A Critical Perspective* (2012).

Cate Goodlad is Lecturer in The Manchester Institute of Education, University of Manchester, UK, and also programme director for the MA Education (Teach First Leadership). She completed a PhD in 2010 at the University of Sheffield. Her research interests include education policy and issues of equity and access, with particular reference to the experiences of adult learners.

Helen M. Gunter is Professor of Education Policy in The Manchester Institute of Education, University of Manchester, UK. Her research is focused on education policy with specific attention on knowledge production in educational leadership. Her most recent books include: *Leadership and the Reform of Education* (2013) and *Educational Leadership and Hannah Arendt* (2014).

David Hall is Professor of Education Policy and Practice in The Manchester Institute of Education, University of Manchester, UK. His research has focused upon the contemporary working lives of education professionals with a particular interest in the development of professional identities during periods of rapid reform. His research has been funded by organizations including the Joseph Rowntree Foundation, the Department of Education and the Economic Social Research Council for which he recently completed as Principal Investigator of a project focusing upon teacher perceptions of leadership. He has published in a range of international journals including *Journal of Education Policy, Oxford Review of Education, Educational Review* and *International Journal of Leadership in Education*. David is currently Head of The Manchester Institute of Education, UK.

John Hull graduated with an EdD from The Manchester Institute of Education, University of Manchester, in 2008. His research concerned inter-school collaboration. He was a member (2001–2004) of the Leadership Development Unit within the University, commissioned by DCSF to support inter-school collaborations. A former secondary head, John led three schools in Yorkshire and was head teacher associate in Sheffield's School Effectiveness

Service (2000–2004). He was an advisor in the Greater Manchester Challenge (2008–2010), drawing on strategies studied in his EdD. He now teaches in The Manchester Institute of Education on MA (Teach First Leadership) and MA (Leadership and Improvement) programmes.

Steven Jones is a Senior Lecturer in The Manchester Institute of Education, University of Manchester. His research background is in English Language and Linguistics, but he also writes about international Higher Education systems. Dr Jones is particularly interested in how socio-economically disadvantaged young people conceptualize post-compulsory education and interpret the advice and guidance they receive. He investigates the student experience, from application to graduation, and how it is influenced by educational background. Dr Jones has conducted research for the Sutton Trust and Joseph Rowntree Foundation and collaborates with the government-funded Employers and Education Taskforce.

Colin Mills is Senior Teaching Fellow in The Manchester Institute of Education at the University of Manchester, UK, where he teaches and researches as well as co-ordinates the part-time master's degree in Educational Leadership. He has worked as a deputy head teacher of a primary school and as a local authority advisory teacher and has published widely in the areas of primary schooling and literacy. He has taught at the Universities of Exeter, Worcester and at Birmingham City University. His interests now focus on two specific areas: on the work of consultants in schools and the relationships between privatizations and the pedagogies and practices in schools; and on the implications of new forms of governance on primary schools and leadership.

Ruth McGinity is Lecturer in Educational Leadership and Policy in The Manchester Institute of Education, University of Manchester, UK. Her doctoral research has been funded by an ESRC CASE studentship and is an ethnographic study of localized policy processes in a secondary school during a period of rapid educational reform in England. The aim of her research is to both provide an empirical account of localized policymaking and to explain how and why certain policy processes are engaged with, prioritized, resisted, rearticulated or rejected and the ways in which such processes are influenced by political, economic and cultural conditions which have been developed as part of a modernizing policy discourse framed at both national and international levels.

Stephen Rogers graduated with a PhD in 2012 from The Manchester Institute of Education, University of Manchester, UK. His thesis was awarded BERA's best doctoral dissertation prize for 2013. Stephen is a part-time lecturer at the University of Manchester, and his research interests are in public policy, the philosophy of education, social justice and student voice issues.

Harriet Rowley was awarded her PhD in 2013 from The Manchester Institute of Education, University of Manchester, UK. Her doctorate is concerned with the role of schools in combating the effects of social disadvantage. Presently, Harriet is Research Assistant at Manchester Metropolitan University where she is researching School Direct and, more broadly, policy changes in Initial Teacher Education.

Maija Salokangas was awarded her PhD in 2013 from The Manchester Institute of Education, University of Manchester. She is a Lecturer at Trinity College Dublin. Her doctoral research concerned governance in a chain of academies from the perspective of a case-study academy.

INTRODUCTION

Working Towards Critical Research

Helen M. Gunter, David Hall
and Colin Mills

Introduction

We present accounts of thinking and doing research about educational issues in sites where educational provision is being designed and engaged with. Researchers at different stages in their careers narrate stories about their experiences of entering into and working with educational professionals and students regarding important educational questions. The brief we gave our authors was to describe their experiences of doing educational research, to explain the processes they have gone through in thinking with and through social science theories and to critically examine why research matters. These are tough but necessary accounts of researcher experiences, not least because the realities of doing research are rarely talked about, and both social science theorizing and educational research are under threat as irrelevant. Our contributions will not only confront such charges directly, but will also illustrate in their accounts of ordinary practice why, and how, educational research located in the social sciences matters to the day-to-day activities within educational organizations. And they will demonstrate how research has a role to play in thinking strategically and doing strategy at organizational and system levels.

The authors, and ourselves as editors, are all current or recent members of The Manchester Institute of Education at the University of Manchester, UK, and, as a community of researchers who have formal appointments as students and staff, we wanted to show how a range of projects developed in one site could illuminate the richness and vitality of the research process. In doing this, we are not making any unique claims because educational researchers in other places will be able to show parity with and extensions to this contribution. But we are writing at a time when education as a field of study – for and about practice – is in danger because it is seen as dangerous. We hope that our declaration of research practice will encourage other researchers to make explicit their work, not only in order to support methodological development but also to show scholarly activism in action.

While much could be written about the design and delivery of the various projects reported here, we wanted to put more emphasis on the vernacular realities of doing a project. That kind of emphasis not only uncovers learning and development. It also shows how the contributions our colleagues offer here goes beyond the official report or thesis into the experiences of those within research networks and partnerships. The book is essentially a counter-weight to the neat and tidy how-to-do-it methodology books and a forthright reply to demands to be instrumentally relevant in order to apply findings to bring about immediate technical improvements, that may not be advances in learning. We speak loudly about the interplay between ideas and action, and as such we work towards the exposure of processes of thinking with ideas by the self and with others as a means of understanding the doing and importance of research that is not only about education but is itself educational.

We begin this opening chapter by framing the context in which our authors have developed, agreed and completed their projects. Their voices will be loudest in these stories. But we do need to engage with how their revealed sense of agency and its deployment need to be located within enduring social injustices within our current political, economic and cultural times. Importantly, we are dealing with such issues in ways that may not be as confident or as complete as the publication process bestows on authors, we are all at different stages in our development as researchers.

Research in dark times

Arendt (1993) characterized the twentieth century as 'dark times', where she charted and explained totalitarian darkness:

> all this was real enough as it took place in public; there was nothing secret or mysterious about it. And still, it was by no means visible to all, nor was it at all easy to perceive it; for until the very moment when catastrophe overtook everything and everybody, it was covered up not by realities but by the highly efficient talk and double-talk of nearly all official representatives who, without interruption and in many ingenious variations, explained away unpleasant facts and justified concerns.

When we think of dark times and of people living and moving in them, we have to take this camouflage, emanating from and spread by 'the establishment' – or 'the system', as it was then called – also into account. If it is the function of the public realm to throw light on the affairs of men by providing a space of appearances in which they can show in deed and word, for better or for worse, who they are and what they do, then darkness has come when this light is extinguished by 'credibility gaps' and 'invisible government', by speech that does not disclose what is but sweeps it under the carpet, by exhortations, moral and otherwise, that, under the pretext of upholding old truths, degrade all truth to meaningless triviality. (p. viii)

We think this describes well the predicament that educational researchers find themselves in at the current time, and in saying this we agree with Arendt that this is not a rarity in the history of ideas. But describing and understanding the particular form of contemporary darkness not only requires us to show how Arendt's analysis resonates with us, but also what is distinctive about the current situation.

At a time in England where there has been major financial reinvestment in education under the New Labour governments (1997–2010) and education has been protected at a time of disinvestment in public services by the current Coalition government (2010–) and major political investment through identifying the importance of education, it seems odd and downright dangerous to be raising concerns about what is unfolding. A positive case can be made that successive governments over the past thirty years have recognized the need for higher standards from publicly funded education, and have responded productively to parental and corporate demands for reform (e.g. DES, 1985; DfEE, 1997). In doing so, governments have generally recognized and continued the reforms of their predecessors. Vibrant politicking about national standards has enabled 'newness' to be constructed through comparisons with the government that has left office. The solutions generated tend to be based on centralized regulation through performance regimes of data and measurement, combined with decentralization of the school as an 'independent' business in a competitive market place. These phenomena are well documented by our colleagues and by those whose writings we – and our contributors – have learned from in their postgraduate study (Ball, 2007; Gunter, 2012a). Following Arendt, the case we would like to make is that the catastrophe that is unfolding in English education as a result of this approach is one that is being done *in public*. Although it is all presented as seemingly common sense, it is taking publicly funded education away from the public and our publics. What is distinctive for our project, compared with Arendt's set of essays, is that we are focusing on the ordinariness of research, and researchers who experience acclaim through university accreditation and localized feedback from professionals, children and parents for their research but are simultaneously facing exclusion and, possibly, vilification. Let us say some more about this situation.

Knowledge production and educational change are central to these matters, and our argument is that the former has been captured by political pragmatism in alliance with neo-liberal and neo-conservative interests. The latter has therefore been framed as technical and functional in regard to aims, processes and outcomes. The problem that had to be tackled is that publicly funded education has been too successful. This is difficult for those who want to access it for capital accumulation and/or who want to limit the ideas that children have access to. It seems to us that the enemies of public education are hiding in plain sight. They are popularizing notions and strategies that are restoring the powerful to power, and are embedding the economizing of public services into how problems are imagined and addressed. Research in western style democracies is showing how this is a global phenomenon, and how new businesses, markets and a managerial class are emerging through a discourse of necessity and vitality (Saltman and Gabbard, 2011; Ball, 2012; Gunter, 2012a,b; Spring, 2012).

We recognize the demands of political office and the need to make a case for election and re-election. Our study of education policy over the last thirty years illustrates for us that the rhetoric is firmly located in functional claims about change, not least the need to remove dysfunctions as a means of securing the four 'Es': economy, effectiveness, efficiency and excellence. Policymakers from a range of political ideologies are seemingly enthralled by the competition of global economic survival and so have accepted and popularized neo-liberal arguments about the economizing of education as the means of producing a work-capable workforce. At the same time traditional beliefs are emoted regarding the power structures within the curriculum, pedagogic process and subject knowledge, as illustrated by an emphasis on 'basics', punishments, and school uniform. Such beliefs have been captured by neoconservative interests in families, communities and groups, and have been allied with neoliberal calls for 'freedom' from the maligned so-called 'provider capture' of professional expertise. As Apple (2001) has argued education must be done 'the right way', and the political right has not only controlled the media and messages about education but has spoken in ways that are seen to respond to the aspirations and fears of parents and communities.

The knowledge production processes have therefore been concerned with defining problems in ways that provide solutions that can be scaled up and universally implemented. This has enabled knowledge decisions about the canon, methodologies and researchers to be based on functional utility and normative believability. Utility is concerned with close-to-practice delivery in ways that can be measured for performance requirements for the individual, organization and system, and winning professionals over by making values-based links to children, their learning and their future. The readability of the simplifications is enhanced through the packaging and repackaging of ideas. Even if a policy fails, it is framed as a matter of delivery (not least sabotage by those who are contracted to deliver). A burgeoning managerial class has grown within public services, and certainly in education, where the emphasis is on securing the localized delivery of solutions to the problem of teaching and learning. This managerial class is supported by an industry of private consultants who bring popular ideas about tactical solutions to busy managers. An emphasis has been put on the reworking of professional standards and practice, as well as on the terms and conditions of service. All this has enabled the remodelling of the profession as enthusiastic users of pre-packaged solutions. Increasingly, the training and accreditation of teachers is being replaced through the appointment of either non-qualified or speedily accredited personnel who are required to implement learning and behavioural packages. Support for handling dysfunctional implementation is through a combination of performance management (not least capability procedures and removal) and the purchase of consultancy, as is documented in both the US and English-based accounts (Koyama, 2010; Mills, 2011).

This framing of knowledge production and educational change has become woven into both the funding and the discourses around research and the research community. For example, New Labour (1997–2010) governments invested heavily in major reforms in which commissioned research to support policy was key to their claims of evidence-informed policies. At the same time, educational research was the focus of political attention and was found wanting in comparison with medical research (Hillage et al., 1998). Investment was made in systematic reviews of the literatures in order to support the building of a more coherent evidence base. While the education research community addressed this through robust debate and fired back with evidenced claims (e.g. Rudduck and MacIntyre, 1998; Ribbins et al., 2003), it impacted in a number of problematic ways. First, commissioned research enabled researchers in higher education, think tanks and private businesses to generate significant income streams and contribute to policy development as 'on the sofa' government intellectuals. Second, such projects legitimized government interventions into the research design and analysis process on the basis of quality delivery and relevant findings. Third, the positioning of researchers as entrepreneurs created a direct relationship between projects, product development and consultancy services. The discourses were inflected with a language of the 'modern' and 'new', along with demands for relevance and getting on board (see DfEE, 2000). Our research shows the ways in which this operated in regard to the field of school leadership (Gunter, 2012a; Hall, et al., 2013) and literacy policy (Mills, 2011), where policy-determined research became big business and educational researchers could simply not 'afford' not to be involved, either financially or symbolically. More importantly much critical analysis was done outside of the academy through investigative journalism (e.g. Beckett, 2007; Mansell, 2007). There are also heartening and encouraging calls for a new ethics of educational research that illuminates the integrity of practice that is truly 'evidence-based' (Ellis and Moss, 2013).

The response of successive governments to independent research and critical analysis is crucial. The approach taken has tended to be to defend, ignore, ridicule and/or denounce. For example, in response to a letter about reforms to the National Curriculum signed by 100 Professors of Education in *The Independent* (20 March 2013), the Secretary of State for Education Michael Gove replied: 'sadly, they seem to be more interested in valuing Marxism, revering jargon and fighting excellence' (Gove, 2013, unpaged). Importantly, Gove (2013) has exploited the situation through claiming that the 'reds out from under the bed' means that Universities are not safe places to train teachers. This is not the first time that those who seek to raise alternative evidence and arguments have been positioned in this way, and this has happened to parents and children who continue to challenge, for example, the academies programme. Being located as a public sector professional at the moment is difficult, confusing and fear inducing. Seeking to engage in debate through raising ideas and evidence may be seen as disloyal to people who may lose their jobs when teacher training graded as outstanding by the government is closed down by the government.

In spite of this, pluralism does endure. This book is a contribution to the need to value a range of projects and positions regarding methodologies and claims. Such pluralism continues to expose the hubris of politicians and the damage done by intellectuals trapped in the Whitehall village, and to generate a range of alternative approaches to educational issues. We have ourselves made contributions to this but in this book we would like to position ourselves as editors with our co-authors as scholarly activists. We think that Apple (2010) is correct when he identifies the privileges and responsibilities of researchers, and how the interrelationship between ideas and action needs to be exposed and articulated. The necessity to develop such a voice not only enables what has always gone on to be recognized but to also do more of this. Not least because we have taken seriously Tamboukou's (2012) argument that researchers have withdrawn to the library, and, while library work is vital, it is not the only space we would want to position ourselves in. Through research undertaken with partners (in the library, in classrooms, in offices, homes, community meeting places), we would like to strengthen the contribution of educational research to the educational experiences of adults and students. We would like to show the productive complexity of the research process. This means that knowledge production is not only about functionality (and we think educational effectiveness and improvement are important). It is also about criticality, social and otherwise. By this we mean the need to critically begin research with the realities of people and their lives, and to commit to working for a socially just public education system. In doing so, we are seeking to make the ordinary visible with the potential for democratizing knowledge production through the interplay between codified ideas in libraries and espoused ideas in researcher and respondent narratives. This is not easy. We do risk exposing such research to negative attention. However, we are working at a time when we would evidence the necessity of demonstrating and making claims for a historically rooted and valid approach to how major educational issues are engaged with.

Educational research as a flickering light

even in the darkest of times we have the right to expect some illumination, and that such illumination may well come less from theories and concepts than from the uncertain, flickering, and often weak light that some men and women, in their lives and works, will kindle under almost all circumstances and shed over the time span that was given them on earth. (Arendt, 1993, p. ix)

This quotation from Arendt enables us to locate the accounts in this book as being focused on shedding some light onto educational issues through and about the research process. We would want to say more about this through articulating an example.

School dinners are a major issue in the educational process in England. The contribution of a nutritious meal during the school day is recognized as being integral to effective learning and to working for a more equitable society. Recently, the quality of food, and the link with the rise in obesity, has been opened up to scrutiny, and the internationally renowned chef Jamie Oliver has challenged policymakers at national, local and school level to confront this and work differently through his TV programme *Jamie's School Dinners* in 2005. Research has shown a positive impact on eating habits, but Jamie Oliver has criticized government policy for not requiring Academies to meet the same standards of nutrition as in maintained schools (Campbell, 2012). In the midst of the ongoing discourse about nutrition and health, a primary school pupil, Martha Payne, hit the headlines in April 2012 through the blog she wrote with the help of her father. Her project was to photograph her school dinner each day, describe her thoughts about the food and give it a rating. This hit the headlines, received praise from Jamie Oliver, and through media interest about the *NeverSeconds* blog, the link to *Mary's Meals* meant that more than £120,000 was donated to the building of a new kitchen for a school in Malawi. At the same time, political controversy arose as Martha was told to terminate her project by the Local Authority because of how it was being used by the media to threaten the employment of kitchen staff. Continued publicity and concerns about the politics of social media led to the ban being rescinded.

This is just one case amongst many regarding education that hits the headlines every year. We would like to use it as an example of how research matters.

Our starting point is that clearly Martha is doing some research and using social media to publicize her results. She obtained permission to do this project in school. What is interesting is how students as researchers is an important aspect of educational research, and how student voice can connect with this case to illustrate the pedagogic importance of student enquiry and analysis. Such projects show that the edifice of elite adult dominance of education does not come tumbling down through student research activism. Importantly, the astonished media accounts seem to suggest that primary school students are not capable of such an approach, and the success of the project is very much dependent on the novelty effect. At the same time the politics of research means that there is a bigger picture to take into account, not least the limited funding for school meals, the low pay and limited training of the kitchen staff and the gendered assumptions about women's kitchen labour. The duty of the local authority as an employer needs to be taken into account, and it seems that the relationship between the project and people's jobs is integral to project design. A final point that we need to take into account is how this project links to the 'big society' drive to enable the development of philanthropy in the UK: the emphasis is on people giving money through inspirational stories, with a clear message that if a child can exercise agency in this way then so can you.

Educational research (as well as other social science research) has the potential to both undertake such projects with children and schools, and to also problematize as well. The media reports suggest a rollercoaster of events for Martha and her family, with benefits such access to learning opportunities has generated, and that without the project she might not have had: working with a parent on the project; meeting and working with a range of people, including those in Malawi; together with both positive and negative publicity that generates feedback and debates. What is interesting is that in all of the media attention there is no link to the curriculum or professional practice, and we are mindful that scholarly activism, particularly located within school-university partnership projects, could have approached the idea of student projects differently.

Scholarly activists are concerned with building partnerships to develop disciplined enquiries into all aspects of activity. For example, staff could be undertaking postgraduate study — the university where they are registered could run sessions within the school, with researchers in residence. In addition the organization such as a school could be a site for projects where there is co-operation regarding project design and delivery. Importantly, the partnership could work on joint projects, which included the staff and students as researchers. This is not a new phenomenon, and educational researchers have worked on action research and other types of projects over many decades (e.g. Fielding, 2006; Thomson and Gunter, 2006), and have developed collaborative dissemination events and publications (e.g. Czerniawski and Kidd, 2011; Wrigley et al., 2012). For us the Martha Payne case illustrates the need for research skills, process and integrity issues to be integral to the curriculum in schools (and in teacher training), and for partnerships with outside researchers to be enabled to support and develop this. The first question is: who do children and parents turn to for support when they want to develop their ideas and projects? And, the second interconnected question is: how well prepared are professionals in enabling and preparing such projects (not least in ways that enable all staff to be involved, and in ways that recognize research integrity issues in a social media world)?

These are important questions that need to be examined in ways that draw on social theory. The Martha Payne example illustrates the way that power works in our societies: the role and position of the child, the parent, the teacher, the cook, the union representative, the local authority official, the journalist and the celebrity chef. Importantly, the case illustrates the interplay between agency and structure, not least how the agency of the school student and the parent have been enabled through power structures within the media, and those of the kitchen staff have through the unions and local authority personnel. The theories and thinking tools from the social sciences that can be used in research partnerships enable new perspectives to be generated. For example:

Close-to-practice theorizing could be undertaken by using Thomson's (2010b) work on 'virtual school bags'. The life experiences of children are brought to school with them, and so we might ask questions about what Martha Payne brought that is similar to and different from other children in her class, and how the curriculum might provide such opportunities for all children.

Mid-range theorizing could be undertaken by using Foucault's (1994) thinking tool of discourse. The discourses around student voice could be examined in relation to that of those staff who prepare children's food, and so we might ask questions about silences and power relationships, and how the curriculum might generate understandings about how children and workers are spoken to and about.

Grand-narrative theorizing could be undertaken by using Apple's (2013a) work on whether the school can change society. The purposes of education and the relationship between child, parent and professional could be examined, and so we might ask questions about experiences, status and credentials and how the curriculum might generate explanations about how and why the school and home are places of learning. Pedagogy should not only be about how students are taught but also about what they are taught and how they make sense of it in relation to the lived experiences.

Scholarly activism is about the recognition and undertaking of intellectual work. Following Connell (1983) we would recognize that reading, thinking, talking are labour processes whereby tools (pen, computer, desk) are deployed to interplay ideas and action. Importantly, we would not only want such practice to be 'work' in the Arendtian (1958) sense of crafting something that has durability and a contribution beyond the creator's mortality but also to be action whereby we engage with others as publics. In doing this we are inspired by Anyon and her colleagues' (2009) accounts of using theory to think and do research with, particularly the dramatic and convincing shift away from applying theory as a 'fit' with data, towards a productive conversation between research, theory and action. So the current common sense urgencies of effectiveness, efficiency, economy and excellence need to be engaged with through how the underlying conceptualizations are developed, contested and promoted – who wins and who gains by such ideas, and how are actions shaped through this.

The contribution of this book

eyes so used to the darkness as ours will hardly be able to tell whether their light was the light of a candle or that of a blazing sun. (Arendt, 1993, pp. ix–x)

As editors and authors we do not know whether what is about to unfold will be hidden in the shadows or potentially illuminating though engagement, but we set out to provide a resource that can be read and thought about in a range of ways. We are a group of research contemporaries who work and study in one university, though some of us have gained employment elsewhere and some of us already have full time jobs alongside part time study. We are located in the Critical Education Policy and Leadership (CEPaL) thematic research group at Manchester, and are networked nationally through the CEPaL's research interest group within the British Educational Leadership Management and Administration Society (BELMAS) and internationally through various networks including the Leading Education and Democratic Schools (LE@Ds) community from various European countries (see http://www.seed.manchester.ac.uk/subjects/education/research/cepal/). We do not claim to have any new or different research experiences to our colleagues in other sites of educational research in higher education in the UK and internationally, but what we have done in this instance is to work on research purposes, rationales and narratives in such a way that we are ready to talk this through in ways that enable fellow researchers to relate to, and contribute to, debates about the place of educational research in partnerships between higher education and other educational organizations.

We present eleven chapters written by people who have proactively designed their research projects, where funding may not have been provided or has been limited. Some are employed within the context in which they are researching (e.g. Davies, Goodlad and Hull), some have been appointed to research projects where they are embedded within the context in which they are researching (e.g. Duggan, McGinity, Rowley, Salokangas), while some know about the context but at the time of the research were employed outside of it (e.g. Armstrong, Cain, Emery, Jones, Rogers). Each have been asked to tell a story about their experiences of doing research and what this means for their position as researcher. In doing so we wanted to move beyond the insider-outsider binary, to consider the interplay between the lives, working lives and projects that these researchers are involved in, and how they have come to understand what this means. For some, it is reflecting on the meaning of access and partnerships, and how this actually works in real life and over time; for others, it is about the people they have met and learned from and it is about confronting dilemmas and tensions that can be life changing. All are concerned with border issues: entrances and exits, expected and constructed identities, with prior knowledge that journeys through the entrances and generates expectations and with acquired knowledge that exits a site with relational understandings.

The book can be read cover to cover, but also can be dipped into and out of. To facilitate this we have organized the chapters into interconnected clusters or sections that begin with embeddedness (Duggan, Davies, Rowley, Salokangas), move on to confront the insider-outsider interplay (Armstrong, Cain, Emery, Goodlad and Hull) and end with issues of theorizing (McGinity, Jones, Rogers). Our authors have not drawn strict borders around their thinking, and so while we have organized them, there is much in the chapters that could rework this order.

In summary, the chapters cover the following:

Paul Armstrong graduated with a PhD in 2014, and as an outsider to the sites where he undertook his study into school business managers he focuses on relational trust. He uses the literatures about trust to develop an understanding about what it means to be trusted as a researcher, and how trust is developed and sustained during the lifetime and beyond the particular project. Our responsibility to our respondents is not just a technical ethical issue but is a longer-term commitment based on respect and integrity.

Maureen Cain graduated with an EdD Education in 2011 and her thesis project is based on research into the development of primary school leadership. Her professional knowledge as a former primary school headteacher and NCSL trainer underpins her knowledge of the professional community that she researched with in four schools. By focusing on the professional experiences of one of her respondents, she shows how her own learning that had been located in the official government discourses about leadership radically developed through the interplay between her data and new ideas from the literatures.

Patricia Davies graduated with an EdD Education in 2013 and her thesis project is based on her professional work as a teacher and leader in a high school. Building on an action research project with children as researchers and policymakers in school, she reports on her experiences of doing research within her own employment context. Importantly, she reveals the complexities involved in working with a range of people in designing and enacting change through student research. She is frank about the challenges of this, not least how she learned to construct and deploy multiple identities.

James Duggan graduated with a PhD in 2013 and his thesis project is based on an embedded ethnographic study of planned improvements to Children's Services known as the Stockborough Challenge. He outlines the aims and events within this major initiative, and in telling the story of a failed project, he is able to reflexively consider the contribution of the research at a time of major national reforms that made professional practice impossible through the demands of managerial rationalities.

Carl Emery is in the process of completing his PhD and his project is centred on social and emotional well-being in education. He focuses on his emerging and changing identities as a professional and as a researcher, where he tells the story of an epiphany in regard to his positioning in the field. Through this story he provides an account where he realizes how research has enabled him to realize what he was doing, and how he made a momentous decision to change his professional role.

Cate Goodlad and John Hull teach on the MA Education programme for Teach First participants. They both have doctorates, and have taken the position that research about and for professional learning is integral to programme development and the learning partnerships between the University and professionals. Those of us who have worked with professionals over time have known the value that they put on the intellectual and practical work that postgraduate research helps to develop. The data confirms how master's work not only builds resilience but how such productive dispositions are integral to educational change.

Steven Jones is a senior lecturer and has a doctorate. As an experienced researcher he has recently shifted direction from linguistics to develop a new project about school to university transition with a focus on equity. Deploying Bourdieu's thinking tools he is able to raise questions about himself as elite researcher in an elite university, and what this means in the data collection process with school students. He knows and understands the rules of the higher education game, and how they are being recodified in ways that could exclude the very students he has been working with. Social theory develops perspectives, and helps in handling the complexity and tensions that his research has revealed.

Ruth McGinity is in the process of completing her PhD and has been an embedded ethnographic researcher in a high school for three years. She identifies her entrance into a university–school research partnership and what it means to work collaboratively on various projects, and she then focuses on how her own project developed over time. Importantly, she focuses on how the 2010 Academies Act was engaged with by the school, and how her research shifted from being a contribution to localized policymaking to providing an account of academy conversion.

Stephen Rogers graduated with a PhD in 2012 having undertaken a critical policy scholarship of the New Labour personalization in education policy. Drawing on MacIntyre's philosophical thinking, he brings new insights to the issue of student voice and the challenges of headship, particularly at a time of rabid audit and performativity. Interestingly, he uses virtue ethics to interrogate his data and through this reveals how professionals and children are concerned about the 'goods of excellence'. He goes further in using MacIntyre to critique research, identifying the need for independent judgement but also mutuality and reciprocity.

Harriet Rowley graduated with a PhD in 2013 having undertaken an embedded ethnographic project into the strategic and operational role of Weston Housing Trust and the establishment of Weston Academy. She examines the partnership between the Trust and The Manchester Institute of Education, and her role as a doctoral researcher in charting and examining the development of the academy. By making her aspirations contribute to research for social justice explicit, she not only shows the importance of value systems but also the challenges she faced when those values were marginalized.

Maija Salokangas graduated with a PhD in 2013 having undertaken an embedded ethnographic project within an academy. She not only makes visible the travelling researcher journeying between the university and the school but also across national borders as she has moved from Finland to England to take up the studentship. Seeking to understand systems and practices through the eyes of a 'legal alien', she raises questions about what it means to be an outsider, and how those who are located in the English context need to take up the position that she has adopted in order to more authentically understand what can be regarded as normal.

All of the authors are seeking to work through and develop a form of scholarly activism, and integral to this is the process of thinking out loud through writing and developing a voice about the experience of doing research.

PART ONE
Embedded Researchers

CHAPTER ONE

Embedded Research: Contextualizing Managerialization in a Local Authority

James R. Duggan

Introduction

I undertook my doctoral research as an embedded researcher on the Stockborough Challenge, a local authority initiative to improve collaboration within Stockborough Children's Services (Duggan, 2012). As my research progressed, I came to feel considerable unease about my findings, and I acknowledged this in my thesis:

> Research is a strange thing: not listening to someone as they talk is impolite; listening to someone intently and responding appropriately is polite; listening to someone intently and then spending three or more years talking to many of their colleagues to 'fact' check what they said and reading extensively to critically engage with what they were saying seems to me a particular form of malice. So thanks to all those working at 'Stockborough Children's Services' for taking time out from their earnest attempts to improve the lives of the children and young people they work with every day. (Duggan, 2012, p. 8)

While researching the Stockborough Challenge, I frequently felt like a photographer at a wedding in which one of the partners had been jilted at the altar, busily taking pictures of an unhappy event. In this chapter, I explore the implications of researching a largely unsuccessful local authority initiative. I also discuss the implications of small-scale, doctoral-level embedded research which seeks to engage with, and change the policy agenda of, the managerialized public sector. I conclude by analysing some of the factors that I judged to have constrained, limited and contributed to the failure of the initiative I studied.

Embedded research

Embedded research describes an arrangement whereby researchers join non-academic organizations in order to conduct mutually beneficial research projects (McGinity and Salokangas, 2012; Duggan, 2014). *My* role as an embedded researcher was to produce knowledge which informed the development of the Challenge, while writing my PhD thesis on the initiative. For my role – to uncover evidence in order to inform the Challenge – to have any meaning, or impact, the initiative needed to remain open and changeable. But, before my research began, it was increasingly orientated towards a fixed series of enactments of national policy. As I go on to explain, the Challenge was defined and focused in ways that became distant from my research. Therefore, my study existed in a negative space, a seemingly redundant process within the context of the embedded research relationship.

Once the possibility of informing the Challenge had passed, I began to consider what type of influence or impact my research could have. Previous commentators on embedded research into policy have observed that although evaluation is aimed at influencing policy decisions, it rarely does. Instead, such work often contributes to a process of 'enlightenment' when it 'challenges old ideas, provides new perspectives and helps to re-order the policy agenda' (Weiss, 1999, p. 470). Aiming to add to the accumulation of knowledge through my endeavours seemed like an eminently worthwhile aim as I set out on my research journey. However, by the time I completed my research, the policy agenda had moved on to such an extent that the specific policy context to which my research related when I began had become the equivalent of an evolutionary cul-de-sac. I want here to make the claim though that my findings were more significant in a wider and more general sense.

I think the pace of change within the initiative was indicative of the ongoing *managerialization* of the public sector (e.g. Pollitt, 2007), something I go on to define in this chapter as researching in a 'transient vacuum'.

The influence of the managerialization of the public sector was evident both in national policy and at the local level, in terms of the identification of managerial technologies (e.g. cultural change) and subjectivities (e.g. leadership) as ways of representing and engaging with the task of improving collaboration. There is a literature on the unintended and perverse consequences of managerial reforms to the public sector (e.g. van Thiel and Leeuw, 2002; Hood and Peters, 2004). Thus, the enlightenment I hoped to achieve was extending the evidence base of the *failures* and *constraints* of applying management approaches in the public sector – managerialism – to the specific case of collaboration in children's services. In the next section, I go on to give some of the contextual background to the Challenge as well as to explain some of my main findings.

The Stockborough Challenge

There is insufficient space here in relation to the purpose of this chapter to describe the Stockborough Challenge in full detail (see Duggan, 2012). Instead, I want to present a series of key issues that are worth foregrounding in order to understand how an initiative about public sector change became managerialized. The discussion of these issues draws on evidence from data gathered from interviews with key personnel involved with the Stockborough Challenge, as well as from reviews of national and authority-level policy documents.

The Challenge began as a local-level initiative to understand what changes would be necessary in terms of the organization of children's services so as to implement successfully New Labour's *Every Child Matters* (ECM) agenda (DfES, 2003). A common feature of the Challenge was the managers' orientation to national policy, and the way in which they sought to anticipate, interpret and enact guidance from Whitehall, as was described in *Bringing Together*, a long document providing the rationale for greater collaborative working in Stockborough Children's Services that drove much of the work:

> The national aspiration for joined up leadership and management is now becoming clear. However, it will be for local partners to put this into practice taking account of the local context. (Stockborough Challenge, 2007, Section 3.36)

In my research, I identified two phases of the Stockborough Challenge that I term *Challenge One* and *Challenge Two*. They were defined by different representations of the problem of collaboration (Bacchi, 2009), relating to two different phases in national policy.

Challenge One

Stockborough Challenge One emerged, in September 2007, towards the end of the period when the ECM agenda was relatively undefined, in comparison to later guidance. In the *Bringing Together* document introduced above, the managers repeatedly explained that they did not know what collaborative working meant in practice but that they would figure it out through a 'conversation', or consultation, between the managers and professionals. Distributed across this document, were a range of ideas or concepts, such as the enhanced forms of leadership that the Challenge would use to improve collaborative working. In general, the approach was for the managers to understand what collaboration was and develop appropriate structures, roles and relationships to facilitate collaborative working. This open approach to understanding and engaging in collaboration made a lot of sense to me, and it was something towards which I thought I could contribute. I had the time, resources and skills to provide relevant findings from the research literature. I had time to collect, analyse and communicate evidence from across the organization in a coherent and informative way. Thus, I saw it as my remit to understand, define and critically engage with concepts and ideas around collaboration to inform the Stockborough Challenge.

However, *Challenge One* was discontinued due to a range of factors, from the looming reality of the 'credit crunch' and public sector cuts, to personnel changes and the newer leadership choosing to align the Challenge with the re-articulation of national policy that instructed senior managers to engender cultural change (DSCSF, 2007). These factors led to the shift to the second phase of the Challenge.

Challenge Two

The focus of *Challenge Two* was on fostering cultural change in order to develop a culture that was conducive to collaboration in children's services and, in particular, the Children's Trust (DCSF, 2008a,b), a national policy that was an important 'driver' in local policy. A central priority of *Challenge Two* was the introduction of targets, a feature of the performance-accountability regime that was presenting contrary incentives to different professionals and organizations. This new kind of priority tended to *prevent* collaboration. There was conflict for the professionals involved in that some of them tried to resist the 'pull and push' of targets that appeared (to them) to obscure the 'real needs' of the children they worked with, as well as preventing collaborative working. There were parts of the initiative that were undeveloped, but the Stockborough Challenge was finally discontinued due to (yet again) a change in policy direction from a collaborative culture within children's services towards the commissioning of external support so as to drive towards nationally imposed targets. An external advisor to Stockborough Council explained:

> It's strange how you have these things called Children's Trusts, and they had one in Stockborough but they didn't know they had one, and then they were drip fed the guidance, and then there was a moment when they said 'oh, it's about commissioning'. (Interview: External Advisor)

What I found significant was that the managers developing the Challenge did not *clarify* what collaboration was; neither did they make specific just what collaborative working looked like. Perhaps this concern was based on my self-identified function of conversing between the concepts employed in the Challenge and those in the literature. Nevertheless, I was struck by the following admission by the director of the Challenge,

> What we do not yet know is quite what we are hoping to achieve through the big thinking and the small starts, what the partnership working of 2013 will look actually look like, and how we will get to the point at which we know. (Stockborough Challenge 2007, Section 1.5)

Reconfiguring my research task: Viewing 'failure' positively?

Only three months into my fieldwork phase, the initiative was discontinued. So, without the opportunity to inform its future development, I was left with the option of seeking how best to draw on my findings and analyses in order to be able to contribute to the literature and, more ambitiously, to inform the policy agenda. Thus, very early in my research, I was continuously wondering about the nature of my findings.

It quickly became apparent that an uncharitable and superficial – but essentially valid – view of the Stockborough Challenge was that the senior managers failed to adequately conceptualize collaboration, nor to propose ways in which the initiative would help professionals in the practical tasks of working collaboratively. In my research, therefore, I sought to develop a new and more appropriate way of conceptualizing collaboration, bridging policy, research and practice (Duggan, 2012).

Describing the Challenge as a 'failure' was uncomfortable to me, due to the negative cultural connotations. It also reflected negatively on the managers and professionals in Stockborough. More than this, it seemed unfair and beside the point! The failure of managers to define collaboration and to specify the Challenge was maybe less important than the nationally defined and driven managerial context that informed and constrained how the managers and professionals interpreted and engaged with the challenge of improving collaboration at the local level. Some of these issues are explored in the next section.

Researching in a 'transient vacuum'

The 'transient vacuum' is presented here as a metaphor for the spaces that emerge within the managerialism and neo-liberalization of the public sector, and the challenges of conducting critical research with the aim of informing the development of an initiative, while also contributing to policy. Like several of my colleagues who contribute to this book, I understand managerialism as the application of business rationalities and practices to the public sector with the consequential re-articulation of behaviours, expectations, values and beliefs along business lines (Clarke and Newman, 1997). Neo-liberalization is taken to mean an ideological and class project to subsume society and social relations within the market (Harvey, 2007). Emery, in this publication, applies those notions to his work in the field of social and emotional learning.

'Transience' denotes the temporal, spatial and dynamic aspects of public sector reforms. The public sector in England has been the site of considerable re-organization or 're-disorganization' (Pollitt, 2007) since the 1980s. What characterizes this kind of re-organization/re-disorganization is hyperactive change at a rapid pace, as well as the introduction of new structures and organizations, with a typically abrupt end of initiatives, and the introduction of more re-form. The Stockborough Challenge exemplified many of these features of transience. It was developed in response to the ECM agenda in England which were in turn based on ideas developed in Vermont (Garrett, 2009). This nomadic policy articulation was also evident in Scotland's *Getting It Right for Every Child* (Scottish Executive, 2006). This policy transfer and proliferation tends to happen in spite of the concerns about the limitations and absences of such policy 'travel'.

Indeed, the common culture and leadership of Stockborough *Challenge Two* was indicative of ongoing re-articulations of managerialism in response to the apparent failure of New Public Management (NPM) (Clarke and Newman, 1997; Clarke et al., 2000; Exworthy and Halford, 2002). Researchers have identified a trend, labelled *post-NPM*, for leadership campaigns focused on common and converging cultures in order to remedy the negative effects of NPM in the public sector (Christensen and Lægreid, 2008, 2011).

The focus of the Challenge was a roving and transient problem, following the priorities of national policy. First, the concern was to understand and improve collaboration; then it became about cultural change; finally, the initiative was discontinued when, among other factors, national policy switched to commissioning – as described above.

A further significant factor was the transience of the *key personnel* involved in developing the Challenge. The initiative started in September 2007. The original author of the Challenge retired in November 2008. For a while, a key supporter became acting-Director of Children's Services. He left the authority in the summer of 2009, followed by the Director of the Challenge in November 2009. Then, the leading Challenge 'champion', an energetic head teacher who had pioneered the initiative in a school, also left. It is perhaps unhelpful to attribute these changes to any particular trend such as managerialism. Professionals have always retired and resigned to take up better opportunities elsewhere. But the public sector has become a site of considerable instability, with staff working on short-term contracts, and continually moving on (Easen et al., 2004). In addition, the shifting nature of managerial identities and entrepreneurialism has resulted in individuals continually moving on for career advancement (Ball, 2003; Pollitt, 2007).

The 'vacuum' which I identify relates to the intangible and hard-to-describe experience of researching an initiative where the 'centre did not hold', in terms of there being no *clear and coherent focus at the local level linking concepts, people, organizations and activities*. There was no sense that the real agency was with the *local* authority. Rather, the actions of the managers were in effect attempts to interpret and enact *national* policy through the Challenge, as best they could. This local-national disjuncture is represented in the shift from *collaboration* to *commissioning*.

There was also a series of disconnections between the language of policy and professionals' substantive understandings of what these things *were* as well as what was required to enact them. There were various words in national policy and the local policy of the Challenge that described 'collaboration', such as 'partnership' or 'joined-up working', but, as was acknowledged by the director of the Challenge, practitioners did not know what collaborative working would look like or how they would develop their knowledge and their skills.

In addition, there was a troubling feeling within the Challenge that there was a lack of substance to the initiative. The Stockborough Challenge had begun with the aim of figuring out ways of collaboration, but it became a cultural change campaign associated with the development of the Stockborough Children's Trust. The Challenge was utilized by the managers as they interacted with *other* policies at the national level (e.g. the *Building Schools for the Future* funding stream) as well as at local levels (e.g. the Stockborough Council's corporate transformation).

That shift in policies and priorities is not hard to understand nor are the issues relating to the multiple and representational uses of the Challenge. But the issues about knowing the words for collaboration, yet not knowing how to do it, interested me, and became significant concerns within my research. After a good deal of reading, I came to understand the disjuncture between words and the ability to enact them in terms of forms of contextualized and re-contextualized managerial knowledge.

Managerialism and knowledge

Flybjerg (2001) observes that the fields of policy analysis, management, planning and organization are now dominated by rational, de-contextualized and rule-based approaches to making decisions. These approaches often exclude experience and situated, intuitive or contextualized knowledge. Furthermore, management thinking and its application in the public sector is informed and predicated in terms of managerialism, an ideology that asserts the rights and legitimacy to manage as well as the universal *applicability* of management strategies and tools in public and private organizations and projects (Fergusson, 2000).

Research documents the influence of both management approaches and managerialism in New Labour's public sector reforms and in educational and children's services policy (Newman, 2001; Gunter et al., 2012). In driving public sector reform, New Labour adopted particular approaches, such as 'deliverology' (Barber, 2008), that sought to define practitioners' actions and meanings from the centre, thereby closing the scope for local interpretations (Bevir, 2005). One of the consequences of this adoption was that the intersection between policy and practitioners in education, as Smyth (1998) identifies, constructed teachers and other professionals as 'ventriloquists', implementing with compliance the rational, technocratic and managerial reforms without the space, time or legitimacy to disrupt, resist, question or dialogically engage with directives.

Both 'de-contextualized knowledge' and 'ventriloquism' help in understanding how the managers in Stockborough could speak the language of collaboration, yet not know how to re-organize children's services to improve collaborative working. Furthermore, the continual shift in the Challenge from *collaboration* to *commissioning* was illustrative of the centralization, from the local level to the national, of the representation and interpretations of problems, such as how to improve collaboration. The 'vacuum' was therefore, at least in part, the feeling of researching in a context where ventriloquists spoke a language of and acted upon de-contextualized concepts, articulated and inscribed in documents by national policymakers, all of which was disconnected or laid upon the local context of professionals seeking to work together to improve the lives of the children and young people they worked with.

So, with reference to the ways in which managers' roles, relationship to policy and forms of knowledge changed, it is possible to defend the problems and apparent 'failures' experienced in the Stockborough Challenge. Rather than labelling such phenomena as failures, it would be more appropriate to emphasize the constraints imposed on public sector workers by managerial rationalities. With this in mind, I returned to the task of how to contribute to the literature by articulating my findings about *how* the managerialized representations and change processes obscured and constrained the task of the enactment of policy.

In short, I considered my research as a further case detailing the failure of managerialism in the public sector – but at this point, I began to connect the critique I was developing with previous scholarship dealing with failure and ideological projects.

Failure and the neo-liberal project

I have been purposely using the word 'failure' throughout this chapter because of the characterization of the endemic incompetence of the public sector worker. The 'discourses of derision' (Ball, 1990) is a cornerstone of the neo-liberal argument for the continued re-organization of society along market principles (Johnston and Kouzmin, 1998). The Stockborough Challenge could be placed within this cynical discourse, detailing the failure of the public sector, and therefore forming a part of the imperative for reform. This way of looking at reform views policy initiatives as 'transient vacuums'. If the Challenge was an example of a failed managerial process, there is a view that, rather than being an unintended or unfortunate consequence of managerial/reformist reforms, that failure is an integral and purposive component of the neo-liberalization of the public sector. Some critics go further. Mirowski, for example, describes the working of the, 'neo-liberal playbook: attack the legitimacy of government, assume power, impose various neo-liberal market/government "reforms", wait for failures, rinse, repeat' (Mirowski, 2013, unpaged).

Pollitt (2007) provides an alternative, more descriptive view, arguing that the constant change in and re-disorganization of the UK public sector, especially in the English context, is a product, of the high priority of public service outcomes, the ability of administrations to instigate reform, as well as the disruptive and complex consequences of making changes. The frequency of change makes it difficult to determine what the effects of change are and what works. That frequency also reduces the effectiveness of the public sector through churn and disruption. These factors provide the context to understand why reforms frequently end in failure.

Back to the Challenge

If I label the Stockborough Challenge initiative a failure, what is it that I judge to have failed? Should I locate the explanation with the actions of the managers in Stockborough, based on an inference that public sector managers elsewhere fail, or that private sector managers would have done a better job? Indeed, what does it mean to label the Challenge as a failure? The managers, at least from my viewpoint, did not figure out how to do collaboration better. But perhaps that was not the priority or the only goal. Furthermore, it was arguably the continual change in policy orientation – collaboration, cultural change, Children's Trusts and commissioning – that prevented any focused and sustained engagement with one task.

It is significant that there was a lack of evidence on many dimensions of improving collaboration and the particular approach promoted by policy. Previous writers document the lack of evidence or conceptual clarity on collaboration in both research (Canavan et al., 2009) and policy (Clarke et al., 2008). For example, the Audit Commission (2008) reviewing the Children's Trust policy, which became part of the focus of Challenge Two, found that there was no evidence to support the formation of the Trusts, nor for the subsequent shifts in the form of cultural change. More generally, there is a lack of evidence on which managerialism is based (Pollitt, 1995, 2007; Pollitt and Bouckaert, 2003). There is an abundance of examples where the application of managerial or privatized dynamics in the public sector has been counterproductive, or of dubious benefit (Pollock et al., 2002, 2007) or created perverse consequences (Ravitch, 2011).

Yet, in the short but eventful time since the research was conducted, the Right, in the form of the Conservative–Liberal Democrat coalition, has forged ahead with the rapid and substantive outsourcing and privatization of the public sector, including local councils, children's services and education. For example, the One Barnet transformation programme is in the process of outsourcing all council services to private contractors (Barnet London Borough, 2010). Free schools and academy chains are 'free' from local authority controls, and so are able to innovate to drive up standards in education (Gove, 2012).

It is fair to say that there are different standards of permissible failure for the traditional public sector (professionalized, unionized and public) in comparison to managerialized forms of the public sector (managerial, marketized and outsourced). The quote below is taken from *Tory Modernization 2.0*, a publication by the Conservative pressure group *Bright Blue*. In the chapter 'Accelerating education reform', the author writes,

> Sometimes, however, markets can be unfair and inefficient, and government has a positive role to play in redressing this: indeed, if you believe in markets, you need to be prepared to make them work, not just leave them to fail. (Shorthouse, 2013, p. 61)

This idea that markets can fail but the idea of the market, or at least a different form of *the* market, as the taken-for-granted solution to problems is a fundamental tenet of neo-liberalism (Mirowski, 2013). Indeed, within the context of the reform of the public sector, including the Stockborough Challenge, the acknowledged failure of NPM and the managerial project in the public sector was engaged with by post-NPM strategies. That was a re-articulation of the managerial project drawn from the same tradition of managerial thinking with a greater emphasis on leadership. An alternative approach could have been to realize that managerial approaches in the public sector *are* inappropriate. Yet, it seems unthinkable in the contemporary 'centre' and 'centre-right' discourse to propose that any apparent failure in the public sector should be engaged with by a meaningful and substantive focus on professional values and practice or on democratic accountability.

I am left with the sense that this is fundamentally not about evidence of the failure or success of managerial reforms, but rather an ideological project, and the way in which this consensus has been articulated, reinforced, re-articulated and defended. Maybe such a claim can be brought about by doctoral research?

A role for critical policy research

So, what role can such small-scale, embedded research perform in engaging with, and abating, this shift towards the manager and the market? It is contrary to logic that research should not be carried out. Research investigates and explores the limitations of policies. It produces evidence-based work from which to criticize and recommend policies. The field is not short on critique of managerial and neo-liberal reforms. Indeed, researchers have pointed out the limitations of these reforms on a near-industrial scale for years (e.g. Gerwitz, 2001; Ball, 2003, 2008). Yet, the re-organization of public services under New Labour focusing on 'choice' and 'quasi-markets', as well as on the out-right privatization under the Conservative-Liberal Democrat coalition has continued apace. So *how* can doctoral or academic research be done differently?

A starting point can be found within Apple's (2006) *Interrupting the Right* strategy. There, he argues that the Right was not always so powerful. Moreover, the Left can learn from the purposeful and ruthless ways in which neo-liberal advocates rearticulated the 'common sense' of the age. Indeed, there are a number of books that detail how this strategy was executed (Mirowski, 2013; Peck, 2013). A central feature of Apple's argument is that *the Left must change the way it communicates, as the Right has learned to speak to the everyday concerns of the person in the street.*

Thus, critical research can essentially stay the same, but the post-research dissemination can lead to a more activist stance, challenging neo-liberal *doxa* in the public and media spheres. As a newly minted PhD, I could grow into such a role, with practice and dedication. But I think such a strategy would miss something out.

Dunleavy et al. (2005) identify a two-tier process in the rise to prominence of New Public Management (NPM), a central driver in the managerialization of the public sector. There were three themes of NPM: the disaggregation of public sector bureaucracies; the introduction of competition; and the incentivization of employees. Crucially these higher-order concerns were underpinned by,

> a prolific second tier of NPM-badged or NPM-incorporated ideas, a whole string of specific inventions and extensions of policy technologies that continuously expanded the NPM wave and kept it moving and changing configuration. (Dunleavy et al., 2005, p. 5)

These technologies, varying from performance-related pay to the purchaser-provider split, were imported from business and other cognate fields and applied in the public sector. In doing so, business rationalities, assumptions and practices were imported.

Returning again to the Challenge, it was the identification with national policy of the managers that may have been the key to the processes. The application of roles, tools and technologies which were broadly managerial, and predominantly focused on motivating individuals to change, came to replace and obscure *Challenge One's* initial aim of understanding collaboration and developing appropriate facilitative conditions. However, the Challenge was indicative of a broader shift from NPM to post-NPM, which reflected the shift from management tools to a greater emphasis on leadership and cultural change in order to support new forms of collaborative working.

During the transition from NPM to post-NPM, there was a significant moment when national policymakers acknowledged the critique, or perhaps just the limitations, of NPM tools in the public sector. They sought to find new technologies and tools that were amenable to working and managing in collaborative contexts. It is perhaps of little surprise that the solution for the failure of management tools was to select a different formulation of management tools. In the case of the Challenge, this was found to lead to similar limitations in supporting collaborative working.

Agendas for change; roles for researchers...

If those opposed to the managerialism and to the consequences of neo-liberalism within the public sector are to learn from history, then the development of critique, and the articulation of the key themes of democracy, equality and professionalism, will have to be complemented by the identification of *new* tools and technologies. These tools and technologies need to be both consonant with the critique and also useful to practitioners. However, it is not an easy task to identify how these tools and technologies will be developed in national and international policy spheres without the financial support of government or global edu-businesses (Ball, 2012).

One possible project is for practitioners and embedded researchers to develop, test and share tools and technologies in collaborative ways, through online and networked communities, according to agreed protocols and procedures. There are spaces to do this within the managerialized educational context in England. An example is the growth of the strong *Co-operative School Movement*. There is scope to create new pedagogies and practices, centred on more co-operative values. Of course, a real challenge will be for *practitioners* to find the time to develop, record and share these alternative ways of working. At the same time, they will have to ensure that that they do not fall foul of the performance-accountability regime.

A role for embedded researchers is to support and to broker these processes of practitioner-developed technologies and these modes of organizing. These tasks will require both funded and 'underground' research, in order to facilitate the sharing and the spreading of co-operative, pro-democratic and professional-focused practices and ways of working.

CHAPTER TWO

Student Action Research: Fluidity and Researcher Identities

Patricia M. Davies

Introduction

One of the concerns of educational research is the influence of the identity of the researcher on the data and findings of a study. It is well agreed that the role a researcher plays in the field will have some impact on the conclusions he or she draws. These themes are well rehearsed within this book by my colleagues who were working as 'outsiders' (e.g. Rogers and Jones) and by those who had some kind of quasi-contractual associations with their research sites (e.g. Duggan and Rowley). However, the intricacies of conducting research at one's place of work tend to be glossed over by traditional writings on research methodology, particularly those on educational leadership. As a doctoral student between 2007 and 2013, I was introduced to two distinct notions used to represent researcher identity: *insider* and *outsider*. I draw on the work of my colleagues such as that of Emery, in this book, so as to use those notions to explore aspects of my research. Several researchers present researcher identity as singular and static (Brannick and Coghlan, 2007; Anderson and Herr, 2009; Corbin Dwyer and Buckle, 2009). Some use the term 'insider' to refer to a researcher who is also a member of the group being researched. For example, Robson (2011) refers to research done by teachers about their school or classroom as insider research. Hodkinson (2005) equates insider research to ethnography, participant observation and action research. Others broaden this definition to include individuals with privileged access to participants or knowledge pertaining to the researched subject (Thomson and Gunter, 2011).

My experiences as a doctoral researcher while I was, at the same time, a head of department in a school have caused me to examine the dichotomous insider-outsider perspective. Reflecting on the interactions that took place while I was conducting research at my place of work, I am aware of times when I had to assume multiple identities, which themselves shifted according to the situations I was in. With no structures to solidify my position, it was often up to me to determine whether I was an insider, or an outsider, or both simultaneously; or something else somewhere along the insider-outsider continuum.

Exploring fluidity

This chapter explores this fluidity (Bauman, 2000) in my identity as a researcher through an analysis of my doctoral project. Reflection on this project provides both a means of making sense of the dynamics and dilemmas, as well as a way of understanding of the continuities in the social relations that developed during the research. It has changed my view of myself as a researcher. In addressing this issue, I have used my research diary to recount episodes encountered during the project. This diary analysis enables me to recall processes that were unfamiliar, complex and changing. I often had to act purely on my own judgement, and quite often, on the spot. Following Thomson and Gunter (2011), I argue that the insider-outsider binary, although helpful as political categories in which researchers may be classified, actually can limit the understandings of what those writers term as the 'messy research practice' (p. 17) within schools. To further the debate on this under-researched methodological issue, I discuss how this fluid identity has led to, in Bauman's (2000) terms, my emancipation and individuality as a researcher.

The chapter has three main parts. First, I describe the site of my doctoral research, providing the background to, and the development of, a student-led project which I facilitated. In the second part, I discuss the changes in my identity resulting from interactions with my colleagues and student participants throughout the project, using Bauman's (2000) notion of fluidity. Finally, I offer an examination of the lessons learned from the turbulence of this period. For, while the research generated substantive theoretical findings, and practical solutions, this turbulence was also an important part of my training as a doctoral researcher.

The Acorn Project at Oaktree

Situated on almost 130 acres of luxurious countryside in south-east England, Oaktree High (a pseudonym) is the senior division of one of four private independent schools owned by the same organization. At the time my research was being conducted, its student population of 500, aged from 14 to 19, was predominantly of international background and from affluent families. The sixty teachers at the school were also of international background. School administrators within the division included a principal, an assistant principal, an academic dean, an assistant academic dean, a college counsellor and a personal counsellor. In order to graduate with a high school diploma, students at the school must study core subjects including English, mathematics, modern languages, science, social studies, physical education and life skills. Other subjects, such as art, Information and Communications Technology (ICT), drama and music, are elected.

Despite the claims of the student-centred teaching approach purported on its website, participation in school decision-making by students at Oaktree High was not unlike that of their counterparts within the state sector. These students may be seen from the outside as privileged due to their socio-economic backgrounds and attendance at a fee-paying independent school (Reay et al., 2001). But, within the context of the school system, and because of the way power works, I identified that they were largely excluded from opportunities to participate in school leadership, except as followers.

My thinking began with a literature search conducted during my first year of doctoral studies. I noticed that few of the studies relating to school educational technology decisions involved students directly. Instead, their views were made known through proxy informants: teachers, principals and ICT co-ordinators. Students made more use of ICTs than most school staff, utilizing them in all aspects of their lives, and often stretching their use beyond the confines of assigned tasks. Yet, they are excluded from decisions about school ICTs. In my second year of postgraduate studies, I conducted an empirical study at the school, examining students' views about the access to, and the uses of, school ICTs. The findings revealed that the students were themselves aware that they were *marginalized* when it came to decisions about ICTs used for learning at the school. Exploring ways of involving students in school ICT-leadership became the impetus for my doctoral project.

I went on to facilitate a student-led research project, which I call the Acorn Project. It involved twenty-five students enrolled in an ICT course I taught. These students worked with staff at the school to devise policy statements about ICTs for advancing teaching and learning, for recommendation to the school's Senior Management Team (SMT). The project became central to the course and lasted eight months. Students involved in the project framed my understanding of student leadership, and I studied this phenomenon over thirty-three months using case-study methodology. Data were collected using participant interviews, analysis of school documents and unstructured observations. My doctoral research investigates the role of these students in leading learning with ICT from the perspective of a researching practitioner, an insider who was also interested in examining the consequences of student involvement in school-ICT policymaking. Initially, I saw myself simultaneously as an insider – because I was an employee at the school – and as an outsider – because I was acting as a researcher within the school. These roles were distinct and clear, and I planned to take measures to minimize their influence on my research through a process of reflexive awareness.

Social interactions and identity dynamism

The social interactions that took place during this project were of two main types: facilitating and observing the Acorn Project, and interviewing the participants involved in the project. Throughout the project, I observed how the student participants interacted with staff during the consortium meetings. I later conducted separate interviews with some of the consortium staff, and group interviews with the students. These exchanges alerted me to the changes, fluidity and uncertainty I experienced as I tried to establish myself as a professional researcher. I was also attempting to grasp an understanding of what the research itself was uncovering. Early in life, I had learned to internally negotiate a complicated sense of identity dynamism stemming from the concrete realities of both personal and collective experiences. But these occurred only in brief encounters. This struggle to define and embrace my research position, and to negotiate how I wanted to be seen, began with the setting up of the project – and continued for much longer than its eight-month duration! The dynamism in my identity was unpredictable, sometimes disturbing my carefully planned processes of research. I present and analyse some of these changes in my identity as well as in my identification of the researcher's role/s by examining some key encounters I had during the project. I term these as *encounters with students*; *encounters with staff* (my colleagues); and phenomena that I label *even stranger encounters*.

Encounters with students: 'dust in the wind'?

The Acorn Project began with students documenting their daily experiences of school ICTs over one week. It gave them the opportunity to understand the project from their own perspective, and to commit to the work. Through the data in their diaries, and subsequent class discussion, these students argued that ICT had primacy in their lives. Yet, at school, they felt excluded from classroom and school-ICT decisions. One student commented, 'We are the ones who make the most use of ICTs available at the school – computers, printers and the software provided – but nobody asks us; we are just dust in the wind.' I began to empathize with the students. I understood the scenes they had recorded in the diaries, describing classrooms with no computers for them to use and teachers who refused to allow them to use their own computers in classes. I made sense of their frustration, expressed through their gestures and intonations. This made me question whether I really was, and could remain, an *outsider* to the project. The young people were not inanimate objects that I could manipulate and measure: they were human. Added to that, they were students for whom I had a duty of care. I began to realize how important it was for them to trust me if I was to take them on a journey that would lead to their recognition as learners with strong ICT needs. In particular, being another adult within the school, I knew that it was necessary to convince them that I *would* take their contribution seriously and treat them differently.

The week of the student diary-data collection marked a period of reconnaissance in what became a student-led action research project. The findings from the diary data documented the reasons why students were disadvantaged: (i) slow network connections that resulted in missed learning opportunities; (ii) teachers' lack of skill and background necessary for using ICT effectively in the classroom; (iii) the dominance of a teacher-led approach to using ICT in classrooms. We discussed how changes to school ICTs could be brought about to alleviate these setbacks. It was decided that they would lead the project on devising recommendations on school-ICT policy, recommendations which would be forwarded to the SMT. It was at this point they decided to involve staff at the school because they agreed that the involvement of adults was likely to strengthen *their* voices.

During the first meeting of the consortium, which took place about a month later, the students presented the findings from their diaries and elaborated their concerns about school ICTs. They also shared principles as to *why* they felt the project was necessary. These principles included the following points. ICT has primacy in the lives of young people. There is a need for change in the way ICTs are used in classrooms. Students wanted to collaborate with staff on improving learning with ICT at the school. I felt divided throughout. First, I had formed a strong bond with these students, sharing their concerns. Second, as an employee of the school I was an insider, though the staff participants, when faced with the challenging things the students had to say, did *not* see me as neutral or loyal! They might have assumed that the students were indirectly expressing my views by asking who is responsible for making ICT decisions at the school, and *where* this knowledge comes from and *why* students are not consulted.

The consortium met regularly throughout the project, with the students serving as researchers and the adults taking on the roles of 'critical friends'. Students collected data in three more action research cycles. First, they surveyed the entire student body at Oaktree High about their experiences with school ICT. They analysed the data, and they then presented their findings to the consortium. In the next cycle, the students were asked to survey a random sample of staff at the school because they too used school ICTs. Once the staff data had been analysed, the consortium agreed that in the final action research cycle, the students should research the ICT practices at other independent schools. As the project progressed, the power differences of traditional teacher-student relationships between the staff and student participants diminished, giving way to more trusting relationships based on a shared vision. Each group began to demonstrate a genuine desire to work together for the common good.

I was never really concerned with how these students viewed my relationship with them because I assumed that they trusted me. I had helped them to articulate their ICT needs and to develop new relationships with some of their teachers, who were now willing to help them bring about changes to school-ICT decision-making. However, as their teacher I had to assign them exercises, which I marked. This sometimes caused tensions as even though they were clearly motivated about the project, being typical teenagers, they did not always get their work done! Frequently, I had to make on the spot decisions about which hat to put on: my *teacher* hat – requiring that I become to them an outsider – or my *co-researcher* hat – requiring me to be an insider to them. But our relationship was not always that straightforward. There were times when I also had to be an *inquisitor* questioning them about their data analysis techniques, or a *confidant* listening to their latest grievances about being marginalized.

During a class session when the students were reflecting on the project, one said, 'You gave us the idea and we took it and ran with it.' This indicated that these students might not have been seeing me in a single role, or even in the dual roles of insider and outsider. Instead, I occupied different positions within their sphere of interaction. Over time, I drew closer to being a person they could trust – one who gave them ideas that they could extend. Hence, their knowledge grew out of mine. It was as if I had started a relay, which they completed – 'we took it and ran'. But the handing over process had involved a struggle, which led to my relationships with them spanning the entire insider–outsider gamut and to much dynamism in my identity. In some of our encounters I had to assume more than one identity: inquisitor, teacher, co-researcher, friend and confidant – sometimes all at once.

Encounters with staff: Handling potential distrust

The end of the Acorn Project marked the start of my case-study interviews with participants. Two rounds of interviews were conducted with staff and three with the students. The aim was to elicit participants' views about the project, its reach and its significance, as well as its potential for student involvement in school-ICT decision-making. Interviewing my colleagues brought on feelings of ambivalence. I could neither assume that they were not sophisticated enough to know what was going on nor could I distance myself from the research (Platt, 1981). Asking them about the ways in which they used ICT in their classes was odd. I tried to make it appear as though

I had not been commissioned by school administrators to find out which teachers were not using the ICTs provided in their classrooms. I informed participants about my research objectives and their involvement in it – according to BERA guidelines – and made sure that I received their consent in advance.

Yet, one of the staff participants remained unconvinced and requested anonymity. She told me she wanted to speak openly but needed reassurance of her anonymity above what I had provided in the consent form. Following my first interview with her, I wrote in my research diary, 'I'm not sure why she seems filled with so much distrust.' During the second round of staff interviews, it was easier for her to divulge her opinions about the project and the school to me as she had decided to resign. But there was still much tension in the dialogue: she asked plenty of questions, including when the findings would be published, and where, and which administrators would be given access to the report. The other teachers were much more reticent in their responses, even though I did my best to find something common within our backgrounds upon which to 'anchor' the interviews (Platt, 1981). Relations with staff who were not members of the consortium grew strained as the project progressed. The faculty lounge would fall silent whenever I walked in, most probably out of ignorance about the project rather than to signal the arrival of a whistle-blower. My colleagues – even those who were good friends – no longer saw me as one of them but rather as an outsider. As there had never been a student voice project previously at the school, many of them viewed the project with suspicion. The anxiety of the staff may have reflected the political situation at the school. So I was excited when, at the end of the project, one of the student researchers proposed that they should do a presentation to the whole school about their research. I felt that having the details of the project finally be made known to all, and by the students, would vindicate me.

However, the administrators I interviewed endeavoured to know what the teachers had told me. They kept their doors open to me, and one told me, 'You are welcome to stop by at any time so we can discuss this further.' On two separate occasions, I was encouraged to divulge what the teachers I interviewed had told me. While interviewing the administrators, I had pointed out that teachers would only subscribe to Oaktree's student-centred learning approach if their voices were being heard. They had asked how this could be done. In reporting the teachers' needs, which included being provided with clear guidelines on how to request new ICTs, and training on pedagogies for using classroom ICTs, I tried to be very professional by sounding more like a negotiator – not implicating anyone but just stating the facts. At their request, further meetings were held with administrators during which I was more like a consultant within the school; I became someone with the knowledge on how to improve teaching and learning with ICT at the school. They used this information to implement the changes for teachers.

My new identity as *consultant* was, however, short-lived and the teachers I had interviewed knew what I had done. In further discussions with staff participants, I had to argue in my defence, telling them that I believed it is the school's responsibility to train teachers and explaining why I passed on the information. The identity pendulum was once again oscillating widely – consultant, researcher, confidant, colleague – and now a *mole*.

Even stranger encounters: 'doing this for ourselves'

The encounters recounted above were part of the regular interactions I had with participants of the project, but there were two incidents with the students that were different. These stayed in my mind and, upon analysis, revealed qualities in the students that made me think about and understand student leadership more deeply. The first episode took place soon after the students had completed designing the questions that were going to be used in the all-school student survey. They forwarded the questionnaire to me to review. Five of the questions required Likert-scale responses from participants: 'Give the best response that applies to you for each of the following statements – strongly agree, agree, disagree, strongly disagree.' The statements related the access to or ways in which ICTs were used in lessons, for example: 'I prefer lessons which allow me to use a computer independently.' In my feedback to the students, I pointed out that the questions were unclear. Even though students might prefer to use a computer independently in one subject, there might be others in which they did not. I asked them to rewrite each statement separately to address each of the five core subjects within the curriculum. They got my point but were upset, judging from the uproar that ensued. They argued that this would increase the amount of work they would have to do in analysing the data fivefold. Instead of each student giving one response to each of the five questions, he or she would now have to give five responses per question, one for each subject. I was surprised at seeing the students so angry. This was clearly not the time for the teacher in me to emerge and insist that they get on with it. Nor did I want to cajole them by allowing them to proceed with collecting useless data. I was also aware that an incorrect decision could lead to the termination of the project. I sat listening to the students yell out their opinions, not knowing how to proceed and searching for an identity to match the situation at hand. Then a voice spoke. 'Look guys, we are not doing this for Ms Davies; we are doing this for ourselves. She's just helping us to do things right.' It was the project leader, Phil. He had summed up the whole essence of the project in a way that I could not. The group calmed down and he went on to explain to them how the task could be divided up efficiently. At this point, I felt as though I was standing behind him, like a child seeking refuge from an angry mob.

The second incident centres on a question one of the students asked while they were developing the questionnaire used for surveying staff at the school. She said, 'How would we know that what they tell us in the survey results is true?' Another student promptly added, 'Some teachers will lie, you know.' My initial reaction was animosity. I had to decipher quickly whether or not I was included in the 'they' – teachers who tell their students untruths. After a few thoughtful moments, I decided that this was unlikely to be the case since the students remained enthusiastic about the project. However, their remarks raise serious questions about the levels of trust that operate between students and their teachers in classrooms, not least the students' confidence that teachers are competent enough to use ICT in teaching. I decided to start a discussion on the relationship between researchers and their participants. I explained gently that their relationship with the teachers – who were their participants – should be just like that between them and me. I also worked with them on designing the participant information sheet for the teachers who took part in the survey, which, I told them, was important for helping staff to understand the importance of their participation.

Both of these incidents are illustrative of students' critical thinking that often goes undetected and is not assessed within the traditional setting of schools. Within the context of my research, they helped me to see the students differently and to understand my relationship with them better. Any prior doubt about their commitment to the project soon vanished, and I had full assurance that these students were capable of leading the consortium to a successful conclusion. They had demonstrated that they could be critical, transformative, educative and ethical (Foster, 1989). As a group, they had taken a leadership approach based in a shared culture and involving a careful interplay between knowledge and action. That would challenge the status quo, while working for the good of all – staff and students. Yet, I had not found this out by consulting any text. Instead, my understanding of this had been pieced together through the frequent interactions with the student participants.

Emancipation and individuality

Acting as a researcher within the school setting, one can experience increasingly remote situations that are quite different from those described in standard texts. There are traditionally no patterns, codes or rules provided for doctoral students to use as stable orientation points in the field. Rather, I was faced with an array of conflicting life choices on my own, which I had to deal with in increasing isolation. This lack of structure gave rise to a certain kind of freedom, or emancipation, which Bauman (2000) refers to as *liberation* – the freedom to choose whether to be an outsider or an insider; freedom to decide how to present myself and how I wished to be positioned. But, Bauman also asks, 'Is liberation a blessing, or a curse? A curse disguised as blessing, or a blessing feared as curse?' (p. 18). As I discovered, being a researcher within the familiar setting of one's place of work raises an important question. How do I take on these new responsibilities without the traditional guidance of a supervisor? As my research progressed, I often felt isolated and preoccupied with private issues relating to my identity, even though my research was being conducted in the interest of the school, and taking place within the public setting of the school. At times, I questioned all that I had learned that had shaped my understanding. I became increasingly fluid, transient, uncertain and changeable.

The importance to me of these encounters includes the self-critical activity advocated in reflective practice and critical pedagogy. These encounters provided a creative avenue 'to arrest or slow down the flow, to solidify the fluid, to give form to the formless' (Bauman, 2000, p. 82), which I have also found liberating. Without liberation, the research process would still be incomplete because I would never have attained such a radical disengagement from the processes, structures and systems of the school that once bound me within. Instead, I am now positioned to be critical, in constructive ways – free to step outside the organization to which I belong, and examine it through an objective lens, asking salient questions pertaining to its goals, processes and aspirations. This all involves a level of comprehension of that which is already known: a re-education of the substance of things. In my case, this translated into a struggle for freedom.

Conclusion

The 'messy, continuously shifting relationships' (Thomson and Gunter, 2011, p. 18) are illustrative of the complexity, emancipation and individuality of my research identity, and make it possible for me to challenge views of identity as dichotomous. Narratives that offer this perspective are often about research from which the researcher is removed. My research took place within the school where I worked, so my research identity was being constructed in dynamic conversations with others and within the political structures and power relations that existed at the school. It therefore appeared fixed 'only when seen, in a flash, from outside' (Bauman, 2000, p. 83). This identity was not something I came into a situation with, inherent, internal and waiting to be revealed. Instead it was fluid. It was continually under construction, being reinvented and changed in my encounters with others as circumstances changed.

These insights are similar to the insights offered by other contributors to this book who have been my colleagues on doctoral programmes. They help me to understand some of the new dimensions of identity which I will take with me as I embark on a career as an educational researcher. Being able to see identity not just through the naturalized categories of insider and outsider but through practice as exemplified in my everyday professional work, has been crucial to my learning. For, this view of identity has potential for my future ambitions as a policy researcher not least the act of what Jackson and Mazzei (2012) have taught my colleagues and myself to call 'thinking with theory'. Accessing theoretical understandings such as Bauman's on the fluidity of identity has made a vital contribution to my understanding of what lies beneath the surface when research is conducted within schools.

CHAPTER THREE

Navigating Research Partnerships as a Critical Secretary

Harriet Rowley

Introduction

In this chapter, I reflect upon my experiences of doing a PhD as part of a Development and Research partnership between a team of academics at The University of Manchester and the executive board of Weston Academy. I start by explaining why Weston Academy was a particularly distinctive and interesting research site due to the sponsorship of the school by the local social housing provider. I go on to draw comparisons between Weston Academy and the community-oriented school approach. I identify how the vision of the school offered a potentially powerful model to tackle intractable problems which have traditionally beset schools and their communities in deprived areas. In a similar vein, I will explain the rich potential of the Development and Research partnership from a research perspective as an opportunity for academics to use their knowledge and skills on a practical level.

In the spirit of this book, I seek to make problematic some of my experiences. I show how the navigation of the research partnership was far from easy at times. At times, I questioned the value of the partnership as well as the worth of the research I was conducting. In confronting the research as a critical scholar, recognizing the importance of what has been defined as 'bearing witness to negativity' (Apple, 2013a, p. 41)

and channelling the 'sociological spirit' (Burawoy, 2005, p. 261), I end
with a consideration of the importance of self-reflection, in the sense of
developing my practice as a researcher, and also in the sense of questioning
who I am, and what I hope to achieve in the future.

The rich potential of Weston Academy

Weston Academy opened in September 2008, joining together two schools
previously labelled as 'under-performing'. The schools were located on the
edge of a large conurbation in the North of England. As was the case with
many schools converting to Academy status during the New Labour years,
Weston Academy was located in a deprived area where the community
was plagued by a range of social and economic problems. The predecessor
schools struggled to contend with how these issues permeated through the
school walls and their negative impact upon students' educational outcomes.
Weston Academy's leaders set out to change this, freeing the schools from
local authority control and starting afresh as a singular institution. Under
new management, the academy could break with the old and use its new
found freedom to drive innovative practice. What was most distinctive
about Weston Academy was the sponsor. Weston Housing Trust was the
largest social housing landlord operating in the area. They considered their
aims as being more than managing the bricks and mortar. For them, the
school provided a vehicle for continuing their regeneration efforts, creating
a sustainable community by offering a range of area-wide services.

Although the links between housing and schooling are not often made,
the sponsorship of Weston Academy by the local social housing provider
can in many ways be considered as an 'ideal partnership' (Rowley and
Dyson, 2011). There was a significant overlap between the areas where the
trust provided housing and where the school recruited its students. Despite
the differing core business of each service provider, both were forced to deal
with similar aspects of a range of social and economic issues. However,
neither housing nor education providers have traditionally considered the
implications of their policies for one another. Instead, they have tended to
become trapped in a vicious cycle where the decline of the area and the
decline of the school are mutually reinforcing, meaning that any substantial
impact to community members' lives is difficult to achieve (Power and
Mumford, 1999).

Weston Academy therefore was rich in potential: the joining together
of the two service providers offered a real chance to tackle the effects of
deprivation in a more holistic and powerful way. As Martin Rayner, the Chief
Executive of Weston Housing Trust explained in an interview in late 2008:

> We see providing a school with a good reputation for educational
> standards as central. For us though, it's not just about improving learning

but creating a sort of 'community hub' where everyone can benefit. We see the Academy as not just improving educational chances but life chances; improving employability, aspirations, health and general wellbeing of our residents and others living in Haleton. (Interview, 2008)

A number of parallels can be drawn between what they hoped to achieve and the community-oriented school approach which can be traced back to William Morris' Cambridge Village Schools, over 100 years ago. The community-oriented school movement is a broad church. A range of terms is used to describe them; the aims and rationales behind the approach also differ (Dyson and Raffo, 2007). Despite this ambiguity, schools that adopt the model are commonly located in deprived areas and typically involve a reconfiguration of services which by themselves are regarded as 'failing'. A more coherent and 'joined up' approach is seen as necessary (Dryfoos, 1994; Dyson et al., 2002; Crowther et al., 2003; Cummings et al., 2004; Dyson and Raffo, 2007). There has in the past been an advocacy for the 'joined up' approach (for example, see Children's Aid Society, 2001), and it has been asserted that community-oriented schools have the potential to 'make a major contribution to solving some of the most intractable problems that have traditionally beset disadvantaged communities and their schools' (Dyson and Raffo, 2007, p. 299).

The development and research partnership

It perhaps comes as no surprise that the executive board of Weston Academy were keen to track the impact of their ambitious venture. The initiative offered a site for researchers interested in how the effects of deprivation can be mediated. The Centre for Equity in Education at the University of Manchester housed a number of such researchers who had established a range of Development and Research Partnerships. In return for access to interesting data collection opportunities, teams of academics could practically apply their knowledge. Furthermore, the research carried out was expected to be used to inform development while the academics provided critical friendship in an effort to be supportive yet challenging (Ainscow, 2002). In the case of the partnership with Weston Academy, the team of academics was expected to track the development of the Academy over a three-year period using a range of data collection techniques; to meet regularly with the executive board members of the school to discuss the evidence; and to reflect upon the progress of the school as well as deliberate upon future directions. A key element of the partnership was the sponsorship of a doctoral studentship of which I was the holder.

Prior to starting work on a PhD, I had been a teacher and youth worker in deprived parts of the North-east of England. Despite enjoying the interaction and work that I did with these communities, I became frustrated with the barriers I came up against – in terms of what I saw as inflexible structures inhibiting partnership work. The centrally devised policies were often ill-equipped to deal with the dynamics of individual contexts. There was limited community engagement. After studying for my master's degree, and conducting some action-research projects, I became increasingly interested in combining theoretical understanding of the effects of inequality with understandings of policy responses. I welcomed the opportunity to carry out a case study of the implementation of change. This approach presented a real opportunity for different professionals and community members to come together to plan contextually sensitive responses with the support of researchers and to help provide space for critical reflection and research-informed action.

The doctoral studentship for the Development and Research Partnership between the Centre for Equity in Education and Weston Academy was therefore an exciting prospect despite not envisaging or considering myself as the 'kind of person to do a PhD'. Previously, I had put off doing a doctorate since it seemed to me that such a route would offer little in terms of community interaction or change. However, the research partnership was designed in such a way that would involve the development of close relationships with a range of different community players while the data was expected to be used to inform practice. I was interested in Weston Academy since the approach aimed to overcome many of the frustrations I had previously experienced as part of my work in deprived communities. I felt a strong conviction to make the partnership work.

Navigating my journey

To begin with, the Development and Research partnership fulfilled my expectations. The innovative ideas of the executive board made me confident about the future of Weston Academy. I felt fortunate to be part of a team of academics with a wide range of research expertise which I could learn from. The executive board of Weston Academy were receptive to a multitude of different research activities and development opportunities. My experience in working in similar contexts greatly aided my ability to build trustful relationships with various stakeholders. My knowledge of relevant literature also grew and I began to feel confident in my research skills due to the training and support I received.

Designing my doctoral research project

Due to the ease of access and established relationships with the executive board, it made sense that part of my research for my doctorate would involve tracking the development of the school from their perspective. However, I was also keen to find out the perspective of the intended beneficiaries of their efforts – the students, their families and the wider community. From the vantage point of the executive board, collecting evidence of impact would also be useful. Weston Housing Trust also had an established reputation for building a number of mechanisms to encourage community involvement and was keen to build this into the work of Weston Academy.

It was decided that I would conduct family case studies over a twelve-month period. I would track family members' interactions with Weston Academy together with signs of impact. The sample consisted of ten families who were broadly reflective of the academy's intake, occupied different types of housing tenure and included some vulnerable families. The families were purposively selected, but they were also recruited under the guise that the executive board was keen to hear their views. In addition to this, they were also informed that the research partnership would enable their views to be regularly fed back and used in future plans. Such considerations were important to me as I wished to ensure that the research was meaningful. I also had strong beliefs that community involvement is vital for genuinely innovative work. There was also a significant gap in the literature of beneficiaries' experiences of community-oriented schools as well as a growing concern that attempts were missing the point because many had been dominated by exogenous agendas – from professionals and policymakers rather than community members themselves (Blank et al., 2003; Craig et al., 2004; Dyson et al., 2011).

A markedly different picture

Despite promising initial signs, it became apparent that this kind of innovative work would not characterize all of Weston Academy's development. There is not space to give a detailed analysis here, but, instead, a broad overview will be provided. Firstly, it became apparent that the executive board of the school found it increasingly difficult to put their vision of what they hoped the school would achieve into practice. In particular, they found it difficult to translate their ambitious ideas into a tangible strategy. Instead initiatives developed in a largely opportunistic and uncoordinated way. Secondly, in keeping with the demands of the policy context at the time, the executive board was forced to prioritize the need to improve narrowly conceived educational outcomes in terms of test results. Impending Ofsted visits, competition from other schools and tight accountability mechanisms meant that the pace of change was fast and improvement expected quickly. This situation led to the prioritization of standard school improvement strategies at the cost of the broader and more community-focused elements to the vision. In addition to this, Weston Housing Trust, as the sponsor, had limited expertise in such areas of school improvement, and began to take more of a back seat in the development of the school. This powerful combination of factors meant that it became increasingly apparent that the need to improve standards dominated while the more distinctive elements of the school's vision in terms of community development faded further into the background.

Unsurprisingly, there was limited evidence of substantial impact within the family case studies. Some positive impact was found in terms of academic results, but this seemed to be concentrated upon students who were already likely to achieve. There were some promising developments for particularly vulnerable families in receipt of direct interventions, though this seemed more on account of the dedication of particular individuals rather than the result of a coordinated multi-agency strategy. Such examples of impact also tended to be fairly isolated. Overall, the resulting picture was markedly different from the original vision of what the executive board hoped Weston Academy would achieve.

Balancing the need to support and challenge

At first, the Development and Research partnership concentrated on trying to support the executive board to translate their vision into practice. For example, in an effort to encourage them to make their vision more explicit, we adopted a *theory of change* approach (Connell and Kubisch, 1998; Anderson, 2005; Dyson and Todd, 2010). In brief, this approach sought to elicit a theory which explained what broad actions the executive board planned to employ and what outcomes they hoped would materialize. The theory was co-constructed through an iterative process between the research team and executive board members. It was hoped that the theory would be a useful strategic tool which could be referred to and revised in an effort to inform the development of Weston Academy. However, the increasing emphasis on the need to improve standards, and the haphazard approach to running community-focused initiatives, meant that the theory soon became redundant.

Despite our frustrations concerning the direction of the school, the research team sought to be supportive by recognizing and giving analyses of policy pressures. We encouraged the executive board to think about the difficulties in putting their policies into practice in the policy context, providing examples of interesting approaches taken by other schools from research the Centre for Equity in Education was engaged with. In some cases, visits to these schools were arranged. In spite of our efforts, the executive board found it difficult to steer the school back towards their original vision because they were fearful of taking risks that might jeopardize their efforts to improve achievement.

In line with our role as a critical friend, we tried to challenge the thinking of members of the executive board. For example, we would encourage them to reflect upon how the development of the school compared with their original vision. We provided research evidence which highlighted areas of contradiction or tension between different aspects of their work. The data collected from the family case studies were particularly useful for this purpose, since direct quotes could be used in a powerful way to demonstrate trends that we had identified.

Feelings of frustration and powerlessness

Despite our efforts, at times I felt increasingly frustrated with how the partnership worked. I became conscious of the delicate balance between support and challenge. While at times I wanted to press more for the latter, I knew that it was important that harmonious relationships were maintained. However, managing this was difficult, particularly because of the close relationships I had developed with some of the families involved with the research. For example, I repeatedly fed back data relating to how one family liaison officer was achieving excellent results but seemed over-stretched. He later suffered a heart-attack and was absent for three months. Despite highlighting concern for families who depended on his support, no alternative arrangements were made during his absence or additional officers employed when he returned. Instead, as one executive board member commented when considering the liaison officer's role, 'it's considered as additional, if we need another maths teacher that's what the money will spent on'. Incidentally, during this time, one of the students who was part of the sample and had previously received extensive support was permanently excluded from the school. The student left with no qualifications and was classed as 'NEET' (Not in Employment, Education or Training) by the age of 15, which his mother felt was a product of the lack of alternative arrangements that had been made.

Such incidents were especially troubling in light of the guise that families had been recruited for the research and the emphasis which was placed upon the importance of hearing their voices, and incorporating them into the development of the school. Although some members of the executive board strongly believed in that aspiration, they found balancing feedback from the families with other external pressures difficult. I found myself in a difficult situation that was very different from my original aspirations. I became increasingly aware of the limited power we had as researchers to affect change in the school and to prevent what, on occasion, I felt were questionable practices. Instead, for most of the time, we had little choice but to sit back and watch events unfold. Although the situation still made for an interesting research project, it was not how I hoped the partnership would evolve.

The lack of influence the research was able to have upon practice also made me question whether being an academic fitted with my own convictions and my hopes for my future career. This in turn made me feel uncomfortable in the world of academia. I found being confident both in my interactions with academics and in my writing difficult. Compared to my seemingly self-assured and skilled colleagues who displayed a strong air of conviction in what they did and the impact of their research, I felt like a phoney. This made me question my skills and wonder whether in order to survive in academia, I would have to pretend to give out a similar air as my colleagues did while questioning the value of our pursuits. This process of self-evaluation grew into a wider interest in the role of educational researchers and an attempt through the use of literature on this area to make sense of my position. This discussion will now occupy the remainder of this article.

The tasks of an educational researcher

In Michael Apple's (2013a) book *Can Education Change Society?* he sets out a number of tasks for critical scholars. The first calls for us to 'bear witness to negativity' in an effort to ensure that those in positions of power do not get away with the lies that they tell. In these neo-liberal times, where educational policy and practice are closely connected to the relations of exploitation and domination, he argues a powerful case that such injustices and inequalities need to be recorded. Such ideas are closely related to Bourdieu's (1990, p. 16) claims about the role of critical research when he said: 'I think that enlightenment is on the side of those who turn their spotlight on our blinkers.' In this sense, educational researchers need to act as 'critical secretaries' to expose the struggles of those living in societies characterized by inequality and to overcome the tyranny of common sense (Apple et al., 2009; Apple, 2010).

As Apple (2013a) recognizes, the majority of critical educational policy work falls into this category and it is something which the community does relatively well. The same can be said for the work of the Development and Research partnership between Weston Academy and the University of Manchester and, indeed, for my own PhD. For example, a large part of my critical work sought to analyse the policy context within which Weston Academy was forced to work and how a number of pressures and contradictions ultimately restricted what they were able to achieve. I was also able to relate these policy discourses to wider debates on the relationship between poverty and inequality in order to conceptualize the role of schools in combating the effects of deprivation in deprived areas (Rowley, 2013).

However, as Gunter (2009) claims, doing critical work in these neo-liberal times has become increasingly difficult. At best, an academic is positioned as a 'necessary eccentric' or at worst part of the 'hoodie research gang' (2009, p. 94). Recently, there has been somewhat of a revival of such insults as in Michael Gove (2013), who brandished a group of academics who wrote a letter criticizing his recent curriculum reforms as 'more interested in valuing Marxism, revering jargon and fighting excellence' (unpaged). Elsewhere Burawoy (2005) draws our attention to a similar issue in what he calls the 'scissor movement' which describes how as sociologists have become increasingly left-wing, the world has moved to the right. Burawoy recognizes how this presents sociologists with a paradox: the widening gap between the world which sociologists describe and mainstream common sense inspires the need for further explanation. Yet, it also creates an obstacle for public sociology. Such problems mean that critical work is frequently downcast as irrelevant and demands for academics to 'get out of their ivory towers' (Wilshaw, 2013).

However, as Gunter (2009) recognizes, such criticisms are unfair in that they do not respect the hard work that goes on: while 'doing critical work is not new or dangerous or necessarily oppositional, it is vitally important in these neo-liberal hard times' (p. 94). For Gunter (in Gunter and Fitzgerald, 2007), such work is 'necessarily subversive' and depressing because it deals with problems which cannot be solved by a list of bullet points (Gunter and Willmott, 2002). In this sense, such critical academic work 'has little to say about what to do on Monday morning' (Gunter, 2009, p. 98).

Such sentiments also connect with my frustration at the limited practical influence the research we conducted as part of the Development and Research partnership had upon Weston Academy. By its very nature, critical work often employs the use of theory to provide a conceptual explanation of a state of affairs, but sometimes this can feel removed from day-to-day reality. This meant that 'bearing witness to negativity' could sometimes be depressing, causing researchers to feel out of touch with some of the struggles which are witnessed. At the same time, such critical work occupies the bulk of writing outputs in the form of academic papers, which is what we are judged upon. What 'counts' and how 'impact' is judged, is 'channelled through a battery of disciplinary techniques' (Burawoy, 2005, p. 260) which have become increasingly narrow within neo-liberal times (Smith, 2001). Furthermore, as Burawoy (2005, pp. 260–1) recognizes, 'the original passion for social justice' is what draws many of us into sociology, and in turn this is often 'channelled into the pursuit of academic credentials'. However, 'despite the normalising pressures of careers, the originating moral impetus is rarely vanquished, the sociological spirit cannot be extinguished so easily'.

Channelling the sociological spirit by finding spaces

For Apple (2013a) in order that critical work should not lead to cynicism or despair, it is vital that the critical secretary charts progressive and counter-hegemonic actions. A shining example of such work is his research conducted on community participation in Porto Alegre and his book *Democratic Schools* (Apple and Beane, 2007; Apple, 2013a). He admits that although such examples are difficult to find in these neo-liberal times, he makes it clear that they are vitally important in order to show that there are alternatives to the prevailing discourse. Such incidents thus show that 'there are things that we can do right now' (Apple, 2013a, p. 164).

As previously mentioned, Weston Academy had rich potential. The sponsorship of the school by the local social housing provider was considered to be an ideal partnership while the community-oriented school approach in theory could 'make a major contribution to solving some of the most intractable problems that have traditionally beset disadvantaged communities and their schools' (Dyson and Raffo, 2007, p. 299). The Development and Research partnership also represented an exciting prospect for me, one which I felt would overcome my previous apprehensions of doing a doctorate. However, as previously explained, navigating the partnership and the experience of doing my PhD was at times difficult and far from my original expectations.

Despite this, as Apple (2013a) and indeed my supervisor Alan Dyson frequently reminded me that just because something does not achieve transformational impacts does not mean that these impacts are 'worthless' (Riddell and Tett, 2004, p. 227). Indeed, despite the markedly different reality of the resulting picture of the school, I was able to find a number of examples of promising impacts upon vulnerable families during my research because of the efforts of dedicated individuals. This meant that I could occupy a position of 'complex hope' described as 'an optimism of the will that recognises historical and structural difficulties which need to be overcome' (Grace, 1994, p. 59). This enables one to consider 'what *might* be done' (Dyson et al., 2010) rather than being swallowed by the depths of despair, where the only alternative to neo-liberalism is the promise that radical change may one day come.

Down from the balcony?

For Apple (2013a), a task related to the need to find such alternative spaces is the significance of learning to talk in different registers. In this sense, stepping out of traditional communication modes, such as media work, becomes necessary. In a similar vein, it is imperative to seek opportunities where pedagogic dialogue can take place with disposed peoples so 'they can talk back'. As Michael Apple's (2012b) father told him: 'you are the first generation out of the slum, your task is to tell us what you know in a way that helps our lives' (unpaged). Thus, the critical secretary needs to act in concert with progressive social movements in order to support their work. The model of 'unattached intelligentia' (Mannheim, 1936) is seen as out of date, whereas those who 'live on the balcony' as if they are the *petit bourgeois*, looking down on the streets during the carnival upon the enslaved, are misplaced (Bakhtin, 1968).

To this extent, I think that this is an area where the Development and Research could have done more. For instance, at the beginning of the partnership a number of mechanisms were set up to diversify the ways in which we carried out and fed back our research. For example, 'research champions' were created and teachers were supported to take on action-research projects and a parent participation forum was created. However, they gradually fell away and the academics involved in the research team reverted to their default position of primarily communicating with the executive board via meetings and briefing papers. Having said this, as the executive board placed increasing emphasis on the need to improve standards, such efforts were seen as peripheral. Therefore, sustaining them from our position was difficult.

However, in light of the motivations behind the partnership, and the involvement of families in the data collection, such work is vital not only for upholding good research practice but also to ensure one's 'sociological spirit' (Burawoy, 2005, p. 261) remains. Although engaging in such work is increasingly outside what is considered 'to count' in terms of how the performance of academics is judged, it is vital for the health of the academic community.

Looking to the future

Apple reminds us that the task of becoming a critical scholar is a complex one, requiring 'constant deconstruction of who we are' (Apple, 2012b, unpaged). Elsewhere, leading thinkers argue in a similar vein that becoming critical in our thinking about education is always 'work in progress' (Gunter and Fitzgerald, 2007, p. 6). The reflexivity I have tried to capture in this chapter is, it is hoped, in the spirit of this book and its contributors, my colleagues. I have sought to show some of the ways in which engagement in self-reflection became an important, and, at times, a challenging part of my journey as a an early career educational researcher.

Furthermore, reflecting upon my experiences and how the Development and Research partnership progressed, has been a vital part of my own deconstructive process of who I am and what sort of educational researcher I want to be. It is comforting to realize that one is continually 'becoming', and that the need to engage in self-evaluation is not just important in terms of 'figuring ourselves out' but also in order to maximize the impact that our research is able to have. Furthermore, while the process may raise difficult questions and induce self-doubt, Shakespeare (2005, p. 55) reminds us:

> All the world's a stage
> And all the men and women merely players
> They have their exits and their entrances
> And one man in his time plays many parts

The parts we choose to play as educational researchers are multiple and complex.

CHAPTER FOUR

School–University Partnerships: Border Crossings as 'a legal alien'

Maija Salokangas

Introduction

The question of familiarity is one that any researcher conducting ethnographic research must address. Parman (1998) articulates this dilemma in the following way:

> Each [research] setting imposes its own anthropological dilemma: first how to observe situations so familiar that it is almost impossible to extract oneself from one's own cultural assumptions and be objective; the second, how to observe situations so different from what one is used to that one responds only to differentness. (p. 305)

In educational research, a researcher may identify a setting he/she is familiar with, within an educational system he/she might even be a product of. As suggested by the quotation above, this may create what Geer (1964) has identified as a *familiarity* problem. To what extent is an ethnographer who is researching the familiar able to distance him/herself and observe the social world they are immersed in from 'a distance', as 'an outsider'? Delamont et al. (2010) have identified strategies an ethnographer may utilize in addressing the familiarity problem in their research. One of these strategies, on which this chapter focuses, is to conduct research somewhere more *exotic*, or *unfamiliar*, possibly crossing national boarders, and immersing oneself in a culture and an educational system of which the researcher has little, if any, experience. However, such an approach, as Parman (1998) suggests, is also problematic, as the dangers of misunderstanding and misinterpretation are *amplified* within an unfamiliar setting.

The focus of this chapter

During my PhD research, I had to confront these questions of unfamiliarity and interpretation as I chose to conduct ethnographically informed research in a country (England) different to that of my origin (Finland). In doing this, I had to make an attempt to understand an unfamiliar social world. In this chapter, I first discuss the ways in which I began to make sense of the unfamiliar social world of the case-study school and describe some of the navigation tools I developed to understand this unfamiliarity. Secondly, I reflect on how I handled aspects of this unfamiliarity. My observations, and the conceptualizations of the data I generated, are guiding themes throughout the chapter. Finally, after reflections on my research process, I argue that although it is a challenging and somewhat problematic approach to research, the examination of others' education policy, and its implications on practitioners can equip the researcher with competencies that help him/her in contributing to international and cross-cultural education debates.

Although the 'alien' in this chapter is a PhD student conducting research in a country different to her origin, some of the reflections may mirror the experiences of researchers conducting ethnographic research closer to home. Crossing organizational borders, albeit while remaining in a familiar national and/or cultural setting, may also give rise to experiences of 'alienation'. The researcher must learn the often unarticulated organizational practices and traditions as well as the symbolic systems of their research participants. As such, the account provided in this chapter may also resonate with the experiences of 'aliens' conducting research closer to home.

Researching the unfamiliar

For my research topic, I examined the enactment of the policy of secondary schools transforming into Academies within a case-study school (Salokangas, 2013). More specifically, my research focused on the relationship between a multi-academy sponsor, *Education for Future Trust* (EfFT) and the case-study school, Northern Academy (both pseudonyms). A central aspect of the investigation was to develop understanding of the ways in which the sponsor was involved in the local Academy-level decision-making and teaching practices. Throughout the research process, I was 'embedded' (McGinity and Salokangas, 2012) in the Academy as I had a regular presence in the school during the academic years 2010–2011 and 2011–2012. The embedded arrangement guaranteed me open access to the school, and I was able to observe the daily life of the Academy for a long period of time. I could be 'there and then' in the classrooms, corridors, dinner hall and staff rooms, immersed in the dynamic life of the school. This privileged access encouraged me to conduct ethnographically informed research.

In ethnographic research, the researcher is considered as the main instrument for interpreting and understanding the social reality of the people in focus (Erickson, 1984). As such, the experiences and motives of the researcher are considered to influence and steer the decisions made throughout the research process (Hammersley and Atkinson, 2007; Duggan, in this book). Therefore, in order to be able to reflect on the research process, and on how I began to understand the unfamiliar, I attempt here to drop what Lerum (2001) describes as 'academic armour' (p. 466) and to reveal my subjectivity through discussing key aspects of my researcher identity. I will then move on to describe how such research identity was simultaneously unhelpful and helpful in making sense of Northern Academy.

Researcher know yourself...

During the research process, it became evident that most central characteristics of my identity could be encapsulated within the identity of a Finnish teacher. This is a combination of three things: being a foreigner; a teacher; and being a foreign teacher. Firstly, my foreign identity had a significant impact on the ways in which I made sense of the social world around me. I began my research in Northern Academy in 2010, but I had lived in England for two years before this. Although I had become used to the ways in which the country operates through my reading (e.g. Fox, 2004) and the experiences I had gained working in schools, a significant feature of my identity at Northern Academy was my *immigrant status*.

I was very aware of being immersed in a new culture and of attempting to understand the unfamiliar. Generally, the research participants had very little interest in my cultural background, and apart from a few questions asked about Finland's success in international league tables of achievements in schools by some of the teaching staff, they were more tuned into broader educational debates, or a few holiday stories that participants shared from their visit to Santa Claus in Lapland! I was very much left in peace with my 'Finnishness'. Partly due to the multicultural nature of the school in which students spoke as many as sixty different languages, I fitted in well to such a diverse environment. Although there was no need to articulate my Finnish identity in such an environment externally, a process of internal reflection was ongoing throughout the research process as I attempted to understand cultural differences in school life as well as in the surrounding society.

Secondly, my *teacher identity* was a result of having trained as a teacher and having gained teaching experience in schools in Finland, England and Switzerland. Due to these experiences, I felt that I remained sensitive to the reality of teaching practice throughout the research. I often caught myself reflecting on how I would react to something I had observed in the Academy if I been working there as a teacher. According to understandings I had developed of education, I considered the most crucial interaction of any educational institution to be that between the teacher and the learner. It was these considerations that encouraged me to remain close to pedagogical practice in Northern Academy during my research project.

A final feature of my identity, and possibly the most significant one in terms of shaping the research, was my *Finnish teacher identity*. This may sound like a combination of the first two features; but, in addition, it encompasses layers of meaning folded within. I had been through a five-year combined BA and MA degree in primary teacher training in Finland. Throughout this process, my understanding of education, its purposes, functions and connection to the surrounding society and community it serves, defined my understanding of education. That understanding was affected by my experience of teaching in a variety of Finnish schools. This understanding of education became a powerful source for contextualizing Northern Academy in broader national and local structures, as well as in identifying a focus for the research and in interpreting the social world and day-to-day realities of Northern Academy.

Reading into ethnographic work

In order to best prepare myself for conducting ethnographic research in an English school, I read the work of earlier generations of British school ethnographers. The work, for example, of Hargreaves (1967), Lacey (1970) and Ball (1981) was influential. However, although their work greatly developed my understanding of various aspects of the English education system, as well as the process of conducting school ethnography, they left some important questions unanswered. I made the same observation as Delamont and Atkinson (1980) that the English ethnographic tradition was heavily grounded in the sociological tradition. As such, to a great extent it was conducted by researchers observing a system with which they were familiar, and to some extent shaped by. For someone like me, who was approaching the English educational system from outside, such perspectives were not quite sufficient. For that reason, I had to seek assistance elsewhere to better understand how to approach an English secondary school as an unfamiliar social world.

Anthropological methods and approaches have been somewhat contested and ignored in the British ethnographic research tradition (Delamont and Atkinson, 1980). The future of the discipline has been questioned due to its uncomfortable associations with the colonial project; the effects of globalization; and the loss of its distinctive concepts (Comaroff, 2010). My argument that certain methods more closely associated with this unfashionable *anthropological* approach assisted me where sociological ethnography could not (Rivoal and Salazar, 2013). In what follows I illustrate this 'turn' towards certain methodological approaches from anthropology in discussing some methods I used in my attempts to make sense of an English secondary school.

Observing the unfamiliar

Conducting school-based ethnography in an unfamiliar environment imposed certain challenges to my research. Firstly, conducting an ethnographic study in a second language brought an additional level of challenge to the research. In order to overcome these linguistic challenges, I developed a set of tools that I used throughout the research. It was during the process of developing my language tools that I found work conducted in the anthropological research tradition particularly helpful, as the tradition emphasizes the importance of *language* in the research process:

> Anthropologists of education study interconnections between education and the social and cultural contexts that shape and are shaped by it. Given the importance of language to these interconnections, anthropologists of education need to understand how educational language use presupposes and transforms social relations, and how educational actions are influenced by ideologies and language use. (Wortham and Reys, 2011, p. 137)

However, prior to being able to observe how language is used in such educational social processes (Baquendano-Lopez and Hernandez, 2011), I would argue that a researcher examining a school in a different country of their origin must become fluent in different layers of the unfamiliar language. The researcher must master his or her skills in: the language spoken in the country, the language of the general education discourse used in the country as well as the language (or dialects) used in the particular school they are researching. To illustrate the different layers of this symbolic system, I will list a selection of acronyms associated with English secondary education, some of which are impossible even for native English speakers with no professional experience of education to penetrate: A-Level, AT, CAT, CEG, CPA, CPD, CTC, DCS, DfE, DfES, EFA, EFL, GCE, GCSE, GNVQ, GTC, IEP, INSET, ITT, KS, LA, LEA, NASUWT, NQT, Ofsted, PE, PGCE, PSHE, QA, QTA, QTS, SEN! Many of them have been assimilated to the educational discourse to the extent that they are better known by the acronym than the actual combination of words. These acronyms alone reveal the depth of symbolic systems that a researcher immersed in the unfamiliar must come to terms with. The ways in which educational vocabulary is applied at national and local levels may vary. Indeed, according to my experience, different schools may have different dialects of such an educational lexicon. Northern Academy had adopted a rather distinctive educational dialect and, as a result, created a vast amount of EfFT and Northern Academy–specific vocabulary. To mention some examples, teaching assistants were called Curriculum Area Assistants (CAAs), Heads of departments were Curriculum Area Leaders (CALs) and members of staff were rarely referred to by their names in the official documentation, preferring instead abbreviations based loosely on their initials, such as MSA, in my own case.

In order to grasp the meanings, nuances and connotations of these languages, dialects and symbolic systems, I often asked my participants to explain how they understood certain terms they used. This exercise had a dual purpose as while it assisted my sense-making, it also generated rich data. I collated the various explanations of terminology provided by my participants, as well as other forms of translations I came across, into a research dictionary, which I wrote for myself and updated regularly. This set of field notes became a powerful source for understanding connections and structures in place in the Academy and a tool for communicating with participants as well as one to help me engage with academic literature. The dictionary contained Northern Academy– and EfFT-specific expressions and symbols, regional dialects used by staff and students as well as more general English education vocabulary. This aspect of my research resonated strongly with the descriptions anthropologists researching unfamiliar cultures and languages have provided of their fieldwork. Although conducting ethnographic research in an English inner-city secondary school does not quite compare with the experiences of the early anthropologists (such as Levi Strauss' (1997) accounts from Mato Grosso in the 1930s), the methods relating to language and to the social systems of the Academy which were the focus of my study, resonate with these anthropological descriptions.

As my understanding of and sensitivity to these different languages and symbolic systems developed, I began to better understand the historical contexts from which Northern Academy emerged. Much educational vocabulary has layers of connotations grounded in them. As such, they are tightly anchored in history and policy (MacLure, 2003). Many terms are confusing for a second language speaker. A 'public school', provides an excellent example of educational terminology that has a political/historical etymology revealing wider historical contexts, though their literal translations would not lend themselves logically to such labels. For the purposes of my research, I considered it crucial to develop my historical understanding of English education in general. This process led to the emergence and expansion of my understanding of the Academies programme and to an understanding of Northern Academy's more specific and localized history. This historical sensitivity provided a frame in which the Academy could be investigated. The developments within that institution could be seen as steps in a longer continuum.

Like any researcher conducting a case study, I had to understand the local and national structures in which Northern Academy was located. Only after such understandings were developed was I able to draw case specific conclusions (Simons, 2009; Yin, 2009). As someone entering the country from elsewhere, it was crucial to distinguish which features of Northern Academy were specific to the English school system, and which to the Academy system and which to the school itself. To illustrate the process, I refer to an excerpt from my PhD thesis in which I describe my first visit to the Academy. Some of the words in the excerpt are in italics to illustrate some differences I observed in Northern Academy which compared with my previous experiences of secondary education. These differences reveal many of the structures in which Northern Academy is located:

> The first thing I noticed as I stepped into the Academy building through the *visitors entrance*, was a large *sponsor logo* woven on the carpet of the *registration office*, surrounded by matching coloured carpet and chairs. From the registration office, us interview candidates were taken for a walk around the school by one of the *assistant principals* during which we visited classrooms in different *departments*. Some observations I made during the tour was the excellent behaviour of students, the high standard to which the Academy was equipped and how clean and tidy the Academy was ... Another observation I made was that the *sponsor* had a rather visible presence in the Academy, giving a distinctive flavour to the material environment. The interior design in the Academy: the chairs and carpets, matched the corporate colours of the sponsor, as did *student uniforms*. (Salokangas, 2013, p. 82)

Some of these features, or points of interest, are possibly rather insignificant for a 'native' researcher, but for somebody researching the unfamiliar, these observations are revelations of the highly complex social system in which Northern Academy was located. Of the key words highlighted in the excerpt, *visitor entrance* and *registration office* offer examples of features which a 'native' researcher could easily sideline, but someone coming from a different system found instantly confusing. In Finland, such entrance etiquette would feature in very few (if any) schools. These apparently minor observations reveal much of the significance about the broader national structures in which schools operate. For example, the Health and Safety guidance regarding visitor registration are features a researcher must engage with in order to be able understand the broader structures surrounding their case. Other revealing key words in the excerpt are the following: *departments*, *assistant principals* and *uniforms*, all of which denote the hierarchical structures of English schools more generally; among these, secondary schools tend to be sectioned into linear structures consisting of several leadership roles as well as horizontal structures such as subject area departments. Another feature of this tendency to sectioning and hierarchy is the student uniform policy widely in use across the country (DfE, 2012). As suggested earlier, these are examples of features of the broader national education system which are likely to be obvious and 'in-built' for a native researcher but something a researcher immersed in the unfamiliar must come to terms with in order to be able to contextualize their case. The terms *sponsor* and *logo* again in the excerpt refer to Academy-specific structures. As with various different sectors in England, sponsored academies are associated with non-profit sponsors who are sometimes entering the sector from commercial, industrial, religious or military spheres. This was yet another alien feature of English education for somebody whose background is in a heavily state-subsidized system.

Conceptualizing the unfamiliar

Researching an unfamiliar system also had implications to the ways in which I conceptualized and theorized the observations from Northern Academy. I would argue that my 'legal alien' status assisted me in identifying a conflict in English policy and practice, with which to anchor my research. This conflict arose from the definitions and interpretations of the term 'autonomy' – a central concept in the Academies discourse since these schools were first introduced (DfES, 2002; DfE, 2010; Adonis, 2012). I observed that there was a serious conflict in the way autonomy was described in the Academies policy rhetoric, and in the professional practice of the Northern Academy staff. Furthermore, I had my own understandings of what the concept of 'autonomy' was. These understandings were based on my experiences within the Finnish educational system which to a great extent embraces teachers' professional autonomy (Klette, 2002; Simola, 2005; Nummenmaa and Välijärvi, 2006; Hargreaves, Halaz and Pont, 2007). There is a clear illustration of this conflict in the Foreword of *The Importance of Teaching: The Schools White Paper* (DfE, 2010) in which the writers of this policy text compare the autonomy of Finnish teachers and head teachers to the ones of English academies:

> The OECD has shown that countries which give the most autonomy to head teachers and teachers are the ones that do best. Finland and South Korea – the highest performing countries in PISA – have clearly defined and challenging universal standards, along with individual school autonomy. In this country we have seen the success over the past two decades of the City Technology Colleges (CTCs) and then the Academies programme. This week's Ofsted Annual Report confirms their success – explaining that their freedoms allow them to innovate and 'ensure that educationalists can concentrate on education'. This White Paper, for the

first time, offers these freedoms to all schools in a way that encourages them to work with each other to improve. (DfE, 2010, pp. 3–4)

There are several interesting observations in this excerpt, but, for the purposes of this chapter, I focus solely on the strikingly direct comparison they make regarding the levels of teachers' and head teachers' autonomy in Finnish schools and English academies. I would argue that these systems have emerged and developed in differing historical, social and cultural contexts, in which school autonomy means very different things. I agree, however, with their observations regarding the significant levels of autonomy enjoyed by professionals working in Finnish schools. Prior to beginning my research in Northern Academy, I had worked in Finnish schools in which teachers wrote the curriculum and were designated to determine student assessment (as opposed to entering them into national exams) and in which interventions to teacher's practice in the form of observations simply did not take place (Simola, 2005; Hargreaves et al., 2007; Sahlberg, 2011). With a background in such a system that, to my mind, acknowledges and accommodates the professional autonomy of its teachers, I became fascinated by the autonomy rhetoric associated with English academies where I saw significantly less autonomy exercised by education professionals. In English academies, inspections of different forms were a common practice; and pedagogical decision-making was heavily steered by national assessment (Salokangas, 2013).

This conflict between the rhetoric and reality of autonomy remained at the heart of my research, as I wanted to understand what autonomy meant to those involved in Northern Academy. Throughout the research process, I engaged with social theories and organizational theories concerning autonomy, power and control. But in doing so I made a conscious decision to remain sensitive to my case, and allow it 'to speak for itself', rather than force it into a predetermined or programmatic theory. As such, the research was flexible by nature, as I attempted to study the social life of Northern Academy with an 'open heart and open mind'. I was particularly sensitive to this as I remained immersed in the unfamiliar. I did not want to rush into any conceptual conclusions, thereby increasing the chances of misinterpretation or cultural confusion.

As the conceptual framework of my thesis developed through a reflexive process of engaging with theory and data, I made a continuous effort to articulate my conceptual considerations to various audiences in order to test their legitimacy. I was researching in an English school and was therefore keen to articulate and reflect my findings before English academic audiences. In addition to discussing theory with my supervisor and my PhD colleagues, I attended several English education conferences, seminars and workshops that provided me with opportunities to articulate my conceptualizations to fellow researchers, many of them more familiar with English education than I was. In addition to English academic audiences, I also attended Finnish educational conferences, which proved helpful in sharpening my conceptual framework. Last but not least, I discussed my conceptualization as well as my interpretations of data with participants of the research, and their contributions also pushed my conceptualization forward. Discussing theory with participants, as well as with English and Finnish academic audiences, greatly assisted me in the challenging task of developing a legitimate and appropriate conceptual framework through which to examine and better understand the unfamiliar.

Approaches for addressing the problem of familiarity

As discussed briefly at the beginning of this chapter, conducting school ethnography in a country different to the researcher's place of origin provides the researcher with a way to address the problem of familiarity. However, for those researchers who decide to remain in a more familiar environment, there are other ways to confront the dilemma. Delamont et al. (2010) have listed some of these ways, for example, suggesting a focus on individuals in educational settings who are less familiar to the researcher and may represent a different social class, gender or maybe sexual orientation than that of the researcher. Another way to create distance between the researcher and the ones who are the focus of the research would be to study schools that the researcher has none or little previous experience of. Or, to examine schools that follow an alternative pedagogy, unfamiliar to the researcher (such as Montessori or Steiner), or those catering to particular groups of students with whom the researcher is less familiar. Focusing on actors other than teachers and students such as pastoral care staff, classroom assistants or administrative staff could help in addressing issues related to familiarity and provide alternative and fresh perspectives. My colleague Armstrong's account of his research with business managers is reported in this book – and is a good example of dealing with under-researched groups in schooling. Next, I present some reasons as to why the approaches I argue for can have value in education policy research.

Intercultural/cross-cultural research and knowledge production

An appropriate angle through which to approach the issues of unfamiliarity that I have discussed is through that of *globalized knowledge production* and the potential role of researchers within it. Researching education policy and practice in the unfamiliar, I would argue, enables a researcher to develop skills and capacities required in discussing education and 'translating' it to international audiences. As Nerad (2010) put it:

> New PhDs are expected to be competent writers, speakers, managers, and team members so they can communicate research goals and results effectively inside and outside the university. These skills are called professional or transferable skills…However, translational skills are an even more appropriate term as these skills are not only transferable but also necessary to translate research findings to social applications. (p. 6)

Even though the statement could be aimed at several types of research, it resonates strongly with the role of researchers involved in and researching global educational trends in specific settings. In recent years, we have witnessed the ways in which globalized knowledge is being produced by large scale international agencies such as OECD, as well as the ways in which transnational policy trends have gained momentum, as interpretations and versions of similar policy initiatives have been applied to national education policy in countries across the world (Grek et al., 2009; Grek, 2010).

Beware: Policy 'tourism' at work

Earlier in this chapter, I quoted an English government policy text referring to this stream of knowledge and its application to national education policy in England (DfE, 2010). I also pointed out some serious faults in the comparison they make between English and Finnish education systems, utilizing what Nerad (2010, 2011) would call 'intercultural competencies' in 'translating' educational research, policy and practice. The analogy of translation is a useful one. For, like language systems, education systems are highly complex and have emerged from and exist in very different social and cultural contexts. It can take years to learn an in-depth knowledge of them. While translating, a deep cultural understanding of these systems, and of how they relate to others, is necessary in order to explain nuances and subtleties. As with language, unthinking policy 'tourism' and policy 'borrowing' has severe limitations. There are many other related examples of the perils of surface-level engagements with unfamiliar education systems (Phillips and Ochs, 2004; Grek, 2010).

As a Finnish researcher with good English and international contacts, I have received several requests in recent years to guide tourists around Finnish schools and teacher training institutions. Recently, in February 2011, a group of English school leaders nominated me as their guide for their three-day visit to Finland. Whatever we think of the usefulness of these exercises (for either party involved), I would argue that when visiting other countries, and viewing their schooling systems, attention should not only be paid to visible surface differences (e.g. in Finnish schools, cross-country skiing trips and no shoes-policy in classrooms). There needs also to be focus on deeper systemic and cultural issues which may well account for better attainments in schools (e.g. the housing planning policies which affect schools' pupil intake; the impact of comprehensive education reform in the 1970s etc.).

Conclusion: 'intercultural education translators'?

An understanding of the political, historical, economic and social contexts in which others' education systems have emerged and developed can be much more instructive than the adoption of quick policy travel and 'fixes'. I would argue that a role for education policy research at a time of rapid reforms is one of exploring more critically the complexities that international educational comparisons hold. In the era of global knowledge production, there is a space for intercultural education translators, who hold an in-depth understanding of more than one educational system. These translators should be able to traverse and observe, and to have the capacity not only to translate but also to *comment and critique transnational policy processes*, either those already enacted or in development elsewhere.

Those of us who are 'newly minted PhD' scholars, as my colleague Duggan terms them in this book, could take a lead in playing such roles. For building the capacity to develop these roles, there are now good critical ethnographies of education policy implementation research (e.g. Hamann and Rosen, 2011; Lopez et al., 2011), providing route maps for learning about the education cultures of 'the others' as well as research-based accounts giving evidence of ways in which transnational policy exchanges and reforms *can* materialize at the grassroots, in very fruitful and productive ways.

PART TWO

Insider and Outsider Researchers

CHAPTER FIVE

Negotiating Trust: Researching the Practice of School Business Managers

Paul Armstrong

Introduction

This chapter focuses on a single yet central aspect of the research process, one that is particularly crucial to studies of a qualitative and longitudinal nature: the nature, the establishment and the maintenance of relations between researcher and participant, specifically the development and cultivation of *trust*. As the title indicates, the members of the school workforce with whom the research in question was conducted are important, coming as they do from a somewhat marginalized group categorized as 'school support staff'. As such, the development of trusting relations between these individuals and myself as researcher required an approach that was sensitive to, and appreciative of, their collective and individual professional experiences.

I begin the chapter with a brief outline of the context of the research. I go on to discuss the processes of accessing and recruiting a sample. The next section explores the negotiation of mutually positive and productive relations between researcher and participant, in so doing highlighting some of the tensions, dilemmas and enabling factors that emerged during this process. The chapter concludes with some personal reflections on aspects of the research. Like my colleagues and co-authors in this book, I draw upon personal observations and considerations surrounding a specific study in ways that hopefully prove insightful to those thinking of undertaking research in broadly similar circumstances. I build on my reading of theories and theoretical perspectives on trust, particularly those of Rousseau et al. (1998) and of Bottery (2003), in order to frame my discussion and my reflections.

A context

It is well documented that the pace and intensity of educational reform over the past quarter of a century has seen wholesale changes to the nature and organization of schooling. Increased autonomy, and greater control over finances and strategic planning, has necessitated an increased requirement for financial management and administration at senior leadership level in schools. The nature and organization of schooling has been fundamentally transformed through wholesale changes to the school workforce as well as a widening of the range of services offered by schools (Chapman and Gunter, 2009; Rowley, in this book). Consequently, the role of the school leader has been altered dramatically, with increasingly burdensome workloads for head teachers blamed for a decline in their numbers and for problems with recruitment (PricewaterhouseCoopers, 2001, 2007; Whitaker, 2003).

Since 2002, largely in response to these concerns, successive and cross-party governments have invested in national programmes to strengthen the potential of the *school business manager* (SBM). The justifications for this investment have been framed in terms of employing people who have skills, knowledge and experience that are well-suited to building capacity as well as to reduce the workload of head teachers in the operational, administrative and financial functions of schools (Woods et al., 2012). Just over a decade on, there are thought to be approximately 13,000 SBMs posts across the country (Education Executive, 2011), thus forming an integral part of the school workforce. Yet, there remains a paucity of independent educational research, and a subsequent gap in the academic literature regarding SBMs (Woods, 2009; Mertkan, 2011; Woods et al., 2012).

The lack of scholarly attention paid to SBMs provided the impetus for the research discussed in this chapter. During a three year doctoral study, I explored the emergence, impact and influence of school business management and the composition of the SBM role, taking an interpretivist perspective (Hussey and Hussey, 1997; Crotty, 1998). A multi-perspective case-study design (Stake, 1995) was employed to ascertain the sphere of professional activity of the SBM at six sites across a range of geographical, social and economic contexts. The sample included single and multi-school settings of different types and phases. Differing methods of data collection were utilized to gather documentary, survey and interview evidence from a number of sources and educational stakeholders.

Finding 'a way in': Accessing a sample

In May 2008, I was recruited to a team of researchers at the University of Manchester to work on an externally funded research project established to develop practical knowledge about how schools could benefit from shared business management expertise. Part of this project's brief was to widen the availability of such expertise to schools. The project involved thirty-five case studies, from a range of geographical and socio-economical contexts across England, each consisting of groups of schools (both primary and secondary) and outside agencies working collaboratively to develop innovative approaches to shared business management. The team from the University of Manchester was commissioned to evaluate the cases individually and collectively, so as to develop knowledge that would benefit the wider national system of school business management. The studies were divided among the members of the University of Manchester research team, with each member taking responsibility for data collection at their allocated sites.

Involvement in this research study is significant as it provided the foundations for my interest in the emergent profession of school business management as well as the means by which I was able to develop my knowledge and understanding in this area. Furthermore, conducting research on this funded study afforded me valuable school-based experience of working with SBMs as well as access to a large population of potential participants when I initiated my own independent doctoral research with this section of the school workforce.

Gaining access

One of the challenges for any researcher at the outset of their project is accessing and securing a sample of participants from which to gather meaningful evidence to address their aims. For the novice researcher, this can prove a particularly tricky hurdle to overcome. Schools are busy places. Those who work within them often have little time or energy for research commitments, particularly with research students (though experienced academics can also have difficulty securing an adequate sample for their requirements). As such, my prior experience on the larger funded study involving SBMs placed me in a favourable position with regard to gaining access to a ready population. Such opportunity sampling, where the researcher draws on their existing knowledge and/or past experience to access participants for their study (Brady, 2006), is often viewed as the least rigorous (and most desirable) form of sampling. There are elements of it in many qualitative research projects (Marshall, 1996). It is also a strategy commonly adopted by those working within an interpretivist paradigm (Mertens, 2005).

Having gained access to this population, it was then left to me to select and recruit an appropriate sample of participants, a potentially problematic undertaking given their existing involvement in a large-scale research study and the associated risk that the schools, and the SBMs in particular, would be overburdened with research commitments. Further, this situation raised concerns regarding possible conflicts of interest between the original project and my own study – a common obstacle to gaining access to schools that quite often receive numerous requests to participate in a range of potentially conflicting research projects (Mertens, 2005). In fact, the very opposite seemed to occur in that their involvement in the larger, funded research appeared to increase their eagerness to participate in my own study. As a consequence, I was able to secure the commitment and participation of SBMs and other key stakeholders from *six* case-study sites that included a single primary school; a formal federation of two primary schools; a formal federation of one secondary and two primary schools; a single secondary school; and two separate secondary schools working in informal collaborative arrangements with a group of local primary schools.

Such willingness to participate might be attributed to the positive working relationships fostered between myself, as researcher, and the participants during the year I had already spent on the earlier project. A level of mutual familiarity and trust had been cultivated that might otherwise have taken time to develop. Alternatively, perhaps as an underresearched group of a sector that otherwise receives a considerable volume of scholarly attention (Woods, 2009), they reacted positively to the heightened interest being shown in their emerging profession, coupled with a desire to tell *their* story. It was certainly the case that the SBMs who participated in both my doctoral project, and the earlier research, were keen to highlight the impact they were making in their respective schools and to emphasize the breadth and depth of their roles within the context of the wider emerging profession to which they belonged. Hailing from a previously fragmented section of the school workforce made up of bursars, clerks, secretaries and clerical assistants, whose primary purpose centred on school finances and office support, the SBMs welcomed the opportunity to demonstrate their widening organizational management remit and broader range of responsibility (Southworth, 2010).

It is worth emphasizing that the key points relating to securing a sample have no specific association with the subtleties of the emerging profession of school business management. Rather, these points are important because they illustrate some of the potential benefits of conducting research with underresearched populations who, as a consequence, may be more enthused to participate than those groups that have previously received more attention from the academic research community.

Defining, establishing and maintaining trust in research

Once a sample has been accessed and secured, the researcher finds him/ herself in a privileged position. If such a position is to be taken advantage of, this requires the creation of certain conditions favourable to, and respectful of, participants. These conditions will hopefully generate richer and more meaningful data. Before focusing on aspects of the research process relating to *establishing* and *maintaining* trusting relations between a researcher and participants, I will first identify a definition of trust within such relationships.

Defining trust

A central component of the relationship between researcher and participant is trust, the existence of which is logically assumed to facilitate positive and productive relations between both parties. These relationships will, it is hoped, result in honest and open dialogue as well as the generation of robust and meaningful data (DiCicco-Bloom and Crabtree, 2006). Yet, while trust is often mentioned within the context of conducting research there is less discussion surrounding *what we actually mean by it*. This is perhaps unsurprising, given the precise meaning of the concept is disputed territory in the academic literature both within and across disciplines (see Rousseau et al.,1998). While there is consensus surrounding trust as a relational construct, it is variably associated with a number of additional constructs. For example, some scholars discuss *confidence* as a necessary prerequisite to trust (Deutsch, 1960; Cook and Wall, 1980) whereas others, such as Luhmann (1988), distinguish between the two by suggesting that confidence implies an absence of risk whereas trust does not. *Predictability* is also commonly cited as a key component of trust (Gabarro, 1978; Gambetta, 1988) but, like confidence, predictability alleviates risk making it less about trust and more about *cooperation* (Mayer et al., 1995), yet another construct that is often associated with trust.

Bottery (2003) suggests that trust 'originates at a deep, basic and unthinking primordial level and is critically linked with the evolution of cooperative behaviour' (Bottery, 2003, p. 249). Yet, while accepting that trust often leads to cooperative actions, Mayer et al. (1995) believe that 'trust is not a necessary condition for cooperation to occur, *because cooperation does not necessarily put a party at risk*' (p. 712, emphasis in original). It appears, then, that while these different constructs are closely related to trust, they are insufficient in providing a universal definition. However, as is clear from this discussion, one construct that appears consistent with many descriptions of trust is *risk*. According to Mayer et al. (1995), risk forms an 'essential component of a model of trust' (p. 724), indeed they define trust as a 'willingness to take risk' (p. 712). Similarly, Rousseau et al. (1998) adopted a multi-disciplinary perspective on trust to generate the following definition:

> Trust is a psychological state comprising the intention to accept vulnerability based upon positive expectations of the intentions or behavior of another.
>
> (p. 395)

Bottery (2003) develops the concept of trust further by proposing a hierarchical model within which the notion of risk exists, yet becomes progressively less prominent as the level of trust deepens:

(a) *Calculative trust* whereby an initial decision to trust is based upon a calculation of potential risk.

(b) *Practice trust* whereby 'continued interaction' or 'repeated encounters' (p. 251) increase the level of knowledge of and familiarity with an individual, creating 'a new form of trust, because they facilitate the development of interpersonal bonds in relationships' (p. 251) and foster a mutual respect for integrity.

(c) *Role trust* whereby the process of calculation is hastened if the trustee belongs to a particular organization or group (e.g. a profession) underpinned by a set of common values and ethics (e.g. doctor).

(d) *Identificatory trust* whereby individuals have worked together for an extended period such that minimal calculation is required, as they have 'grown to know each other so well that they feel that they can intuitively trust one another' (p. 253).

In applying this model to the context of developing productive and positive relations between researcher and participant research, the mutual benefits to both parties of establishing a strong bond of trust become apparent. However, it is also clear that the nature of the relationship and the level of trust are inextricably linked.

Establishing trust

According to Bottery (2003), it is not always necessary, possible or even appropriate to strive for the deepest form of trust within every relationship as 'many will be conducted at the calculative or practice level, and that level of trust may be quite sufficient to ensure the fulfilment of the reason the relationship was entered into in the first place' (Bottery, 2003, p. 253). In conducting longitudinal case study research of the nature discussed in this chapter, it was necessary to develop trust *at the practice level* considering the length of the study, the amount of time that would be spent with participants and the depth of data gathered. In fact, the time I had already spent with these individuals in their schools as part of the earlier project had facilitated a mutual familiarity and a movement through the calculative trust level towards the establishment of practice trust. Consequently, the successive case-study site visits or 'repeated encounters' that formed the basis of my own research design only served to strengthen this existing bond of trust. As Sixsmith et al. (2003) suggest, gaining the trust and respect of participants involves building a rapport through immersing oneself at the research site, spending time with participants in their context and becoming known to them and their colleagues. Yet, while the establishment of practice trust was more than sufficient for the purposes of this research, the notion of role trust would also simultaneously emerge, as the next section explains.

Maintaining trust

Once trust has been established, it must be maintained. As Christopher et al. (2008) suggest, 'trust building and trust maintaining is a never-ending process' (p. 9). To this end, I return to the earlier point regarding the participants themselves, and the specific sector of the school workforce to whom they belong. The educational research community has traditionally showed more interest in those staff members directly involved in the education of students, such as teachers and school leaders, rather than the staff members who support the operational functioning of the school. This group are commonly collectively referred to as *support staff*, a broad term encapsulating many different roles including caretakers, administrators, lunchtime staff, technicians, teaching assistants and financial or business managers. This lack of scholarly attention is understandable as schools are primarily concerned with the education of young people, an area in which teachers and school leaders have the greatest influence (Leithwood et al., 2006; Printy, 2010). Yet, modern schools are large, multi-faceted operations that cannot function effectively and successfully without the hard work, knowledge and expertise of their support staff each of whom have a crucial role to play (Butt and Lance, 2005; Blatchford et al., 2009). In many ways, SBMs inhabit a somewhat unique position in the ecosystem of the school system. Not being qualified educationalists means they are generally classed as support staff, a group they often line manage and advocate for; yet they are just as likely to be members of the senior leadership team where their financial and business acumen is seen as vital to the strategic leadership and operation of the school. As such, their role is often positioned between the teaching and non-teaching staff, a kind of conduit between the two without being a genuine member of either group. In a similar way to the head teacher, the SBM role is often cited as a lonely position (Armstrong, 2012).

It is frequently the case that their role is not always fully understood, or appreciated, by some educational stakeholders or by those with an interest in education (Woods et al., 2013). Indeed on one visit to a case-study school, I was informed by the SBM that an earlier research project that she and her team of support staff had been involved with had ended somewhat acrimoniously. The researchers in question had repeatedly portrayed them in a negative light, displaying a lack of understanding of their contribution to the school and leaving them feeling underappreciated and reluctant to participate in any further research. The notion of *role trust* emerges here whereby the SBM and her support staff had placed a considerable amount of faith in the integrity and professionalism of these researchers, allowing them access to their workplace to conduct their study. Subsequently, their sense of betrayal was heightened when relations broke down over what they believed to be an inaccurate portrayal of their role within the school. As Bottery (2003) suggests:

> While the further a trust relationship evolves, the more valuable and significant such a relationship becomes, it also means that violations of such levels of trust are the most hurtful and damaging.
>
> (p. 254)

It was therefore important to distance myself from the perspectives of these previous researchers and show both an awareness of and respect for the important role played by the SBMs in their schools. As Mertens (2005) highlights, in educational settings (though the point extends to all research contexts), prospective participants may resist involvement in a study if they believe it may prove detrimental to how they are perceived. Moreover, Adler and Adler (2001) underscore the importance of 'equalising the status differentials and power inequalities' between participant and researcher and of interviewers not positioning themselves as 'overly above or below' respondents as key ingredients to positive and productive researcher/participant relations. They also talk of 'relational groundwork' whereby the researcher takes the time to get to know those from whom they are collecting data which 'enhances their access to study populations' and 'based on depth, commitment and trust... may lead to research that yields richer portraits of the subjects' (p. 527). Similarly, from their experience of conducting research with community partners, Christopher et al. (2008) propose a number of recommendations for establishing trust that are equally valid for longitudinal case study research. These include: (a) the acknowledgement of personal histories; (b) understanding the historical context of past research in the setting; (c) maintaining a presence in the research setting to speak with participants and their colleagues; (d) acknowledging the expertise and experience of participants; and (e) demonstrating clarity of purpose as to intentions and expectations of the research.

The means by which points (b) and (c) were addressed in this research have already been discussed above while point (d) is attended to in the next section on *credibility*. However, the two remaining recommendations are equally important to the development of trusting relations between researcher and participant. First, point (a) concerns the acknowledgement of personal histories and the idea that as researchers we are influenced by our backgrounds and values which we carry with us when we enter into research with a new community or organization. While we cannot expect to ever fully disregard our own personal histories, being aware that they colour much of our thoughts and considerations and working towards self-reflection at various junctures throughout the research process will help to alleviate researcher bias and portray a more accurate depiction of our participant's experiences thus reinforcing the bond of trust between the two parties. My own approach to this was to re-read and re-examine interview transcripts and written case reports to ensure the voices of my participants were being truthfully represented, while final drafts of case reports were also sent to participants for their comments to ensure they were happy with how they were being portrayed. Second, point (e) concerns the clarity of purpose as to the intentions of the research and the expectations of the participants. A large proportion of this relates to research ethics and following a code of sound ethical practice whereby participants fully understand what is expected of them and what they can expect from the researcher. Needless to say, it is beyond the scope of this chapter to discuss the details of such ethical considerations, aside from making the point that adhering to such considerations and being upfront and honest with participants from the start of the research process, can only serve to facilitate trust.

Credibility and trust

Closely linked to trust is the notion of *credibility*, another key element of the relationship between participant and researcher. If the participant perceives the researcher as credible, the participant is apt to be more forthcoming in the information they provide. They are also likely to view the researcher, and their study, with respect and authority, which again create favourable conditions for the elicitation of robust and meaningful data (Arber, 2006). The acquisition and demonstration of professional and contextual knowledge pertaining to the participants and their schools was a key means by which credibility was achieved in this research. For example, I had developed a sound knowledge of school business management through my own readings on the subject and through my work as a researcher on the previous project. This knowledge was helpful when conversing with participants about the broader issues and nuances of their profession. I also took time to develop a basic understanding of the specific school context in which the participants were operating by reading the most recent Ofsted reports and visiting the websites of the participants' schools. Developing such an understanding proved very helpful in building credibility with participants who were appreciative of the time I had taken to learn about these aspects of their working practice and local context. Moreover, taking such steps to ensure credibility promoted the level of professionalism with which the participants perceived me and thereby simultaneously strengthened the level of role trust between us.

Participant engagement and trust

Where gaining the trust of participants is central to obtaining an honest and open dialogue, engaging and motivating participants is vital to bring such dialogue to life, making it interesting and meaningful to the research inquiry (Dijkstra, 1987). A number of tactics were employed to achieve this objective particularly during the interviews with the participants. First, they were encouraged to reflect on their own practice during the conversations. For example, among the aims of the research was the exploration of barriers to the effectiveness of the SBM role and the impact being made by SBMs in their schools. Rather than simply asking them to talk about the barriers they faced, or the impact they were making, they were encouraged to think about how they might overcome such barriers and widen their impact. Within this context, one should not be afraid of asking potentially challenging questions, or shy away from stimulating a healthy debate. Approaching the interview in this way transforms it from a one-way data gathering exercise to a two-way developmental process, whereby both the respondent and the researcher gain something from the experience. Tierney and Dilley (2001) refer to this as the 'active respondent' approach, whereby the researcher 'will attempt to foster interview respondents' abilities to alter their personal or educational situations if they wish to do so' (p. 466). Second, the tone of the interviews was kept informal and relaxed, with priority given to the comfort of the respondent. If the respondents feel interrogated, or threatened, they are unlikely to be at ease and elicit the kind of information the researcher seeks (Charmaz, 2001). Third, I took care to listen more than talk, being mindful that the views and perspectives of the respondent were of primary importance. In this sense, I avoided cues that might have brought about specific responses (e.g. leading questions) or prompted the interviewee to give an answer they believed I required rather than an honest response (Robson, 2011). As well as increasing participant engagement, many of these strategies serve to reinforce the level of trust between researcher and participant. For example, using the interview as a developmental exercise for the respondents and providing them with the opportunity for self-reflection was tantamount to giving something to them in return and showing an appreciation for their valuable time and insights. In this sense, the research process becomes a two-way process, helping to equalize and enhance the relationship between researcher and participant which, in turn, strengthens trust. Similarly, adopting a relaxed, informal and conversational approach to the interviews placed respondents at ease and increased the likelihood of openness and honesty in their responses.

Reflections

Writing this chapter has provided an opportunity for self reflection on the aspects of the research process relating to building a sample of participants and the importance and benefits of developing and maintaining relations with those participants.

First, with regard to sample generation, the advantages of utilizing an existing research study from which to recruit participants are fairly clear not least because much of the initial recruitment has already been done leaving a ready population from which to select potential and suitable candidates. Of course, there are questions of representativeness that emerge in such a situation though for case study research such as this, such issues are of less concern. Rather, the focus is on a smaller sample of participants that will provide a means of deep and detailed exploration of a particular phenomenon. As such, the opportunity to draw from an existing sample for a research study of this nature proved extremely valuable. Furthermore, if the researcher has worked with the participants in the existing study, as was the case here, then much of the groundwork required to establish relations with participants and lay the foundations of trust should already have been done, thus positioning the researcher in a much stronger position from the start of their study. However, a caveat that comes attached to such circumstances is that the researcher must be crystal clear in their explanations and dissemination of their research as to the boundaries between their own study and that from which they have drawn their sample, particularly in research that is based on and exploring the same or similar subject matter.

Second, having a sound understanding of and an interest in the area of exploration is vital. This may seem an obvious point to make, as it is difficult to imagine anyone conducting research in an area in which they have little interest or prior knowledge. Yet, it is still worth highlighting that the researcher should be well read in the sphere in which their participants operate and be aware of the central issues, recent developments and points of contention in this area. Such knowledge will go a long way in facilitating a meaningful and insightful discussion, help strengthen your credibility as a researcher in the eyes of participants and contribute to the establishment of trust.

Third, and related to the above point, it is advantageous to have at least a basic understanding of the school level context in which your participants are situated. Where the macro level knowledge of the subject area demonstrates your interest in their profession and area of expertise, this micro level knowledge demonstrates your interest in their individual circumstances. Knowing you have taken the time to learn a little about their setting and any notable contextual information positions the researcher in a more favourable light with their participants, and this will again facilitate trust.

Conclusion

I have focused in this chapter on the centrality of *trust*, employing insights from some educational, philosophical and cross-disciplinary work on the concept of trust, in order to show how my reasoning has been informed by 'thinking with theory', a constant theme within the accounts in this book.

It is worthwhile, in conclusion, to make the distinction between *trust* and *being trusted*. As Bottery (2003) suggests, being trusted is 'likely to be seen by the recipient as an essential element in the recognition of personal integrity, its non-recognition a judgement on one's personal unworthiness' (p. 248). From the perspective of the researcher, these are key factors in the quest to develop and maintain the trust of participants. Yet, the same factors apply to the participants themselves. If genuine mutual trust is to be established, we must reciprocate the trust we work hard to gain from our participants to demonstrate our confidence in their integrity.

CHAPTER SIX

Leading Primary Schools: Adopting and Shaping Practice for a Changing Climate

Maureen E. Cain

Introduction

The purpose of this chapter is to explore my own research journey, so as to provide some illumination on the research process as a practitioner-researcher, uncovering new ways of seeing and knowing. I draw on my professional doctoral thesis which examined the leadership practices and the development of primary school leaders through case studies of the working lives and professional practices of nineteen primary school leaders from four schools in the North West of England (Cain, 2011).

Undertaking this work involved me in some complex re-workings of my thinking, not least a consideration of my status as an 'insider' and an 'outsider' to the research, its context and location. As a practitioner in primary school education and leadership, and as a former head teacher within the authority in which my research was done, I recognized the organizational practices and contexts which I researched. In that respect, I could be described as an 'insider'. Yet, as a researcher doing a doctorate, I was required to analyse the practice I was seeing and hearing about, using theoretical perspectives. I knew from my experience as a practitioner that leadership involved complex and holistic processes. My reading of the literatures taught me how to analyse those processes. So, I became an 'outsider' to the processes that I was researching. I shall return to the perspectives of an *insider/outsider* at a later stage, after sharing the focus and context of the work as well as some of the data on which I draw to make my arguments.

The focus of this chapter

Within this chapter, I focus on the story of a female deputy head, 'Karen', trying to lead school improvement and reform in challenging circumstances and continually shaping her role for new contexts and novel organizational structures. I present four extracts from interviews with Karen, using her own voice to bring the ordinary, familiar work to life and thus providing a platform for my research analysis. I engage with a selection of theoretical perspectives, which caused me to become an 'outsider', developing my thinking and my intellectual confidence. Discovering different writers, whose ideas and concepts refreshed and revitalized my thinking, represented a fundamental shift in my research 'appetite', leading to fresh insights and a new creation of knowledge for critical analysis.

Working with Karen during a process of change in her career – listening to, and analysing, the course of events and reflecting on *her* reflections – provided me with rich data. These data provide a platform for an interplay of actions and ideas for analysis, drawing both from my professional experience for interpretation as well as using theory to uncover meaning in a co-construction of knowledge (Mason, 1996; Clough, 2002; Shamir et al., 2005).

The data and the setting

This chapter identifies a particularly interesting piece from my fieldwork which unfolded as the programme progressed with unexpected outcomes both for the participant and myself. The participant, Karen, developed a completely different style of leadership and I engaged in a critical approach to this research which challenged my thinking and led to new meaning. Karen's leadership position was at Ash Grove primary school where she worked closely with 'Mark', the head teacher. Karen took on a major role in school leadership, leading innovations and improvement from her teaching role in Key Stage (KS) 2 (eight to eleven years old pupils in English schools). An Ofsted inspection report prior to the start of my research inspection placed Ash Grove in a category of 'notice to improve', identifying key issues as the improvement of academic standards as well as identifying shortcomings on the leadership and management within Key Stage (KS) 1 (five to seven years old pupils) of the school. The head, Mark, made a decision to re-organize the Senior Leadership Team (SLT) of the school, resulting in Karen being given responsibility for leading KS1. A second inspection was made during the year of my research. The category 'notice to improve' was removed from the school.

Karen's stories

In going on to draw from my data four stories from Karen, I will provide commentaries which seek to show how I was mapping my interpretations on to my reading and linking them to my 'insider' experiences.

Story one

The first of Karen's stories explains how she adapted to her new post of leadership in a large school. She experienced high levels of job satisfaction and personal fulfilment as she interpreted and enacted her leadership role. She organized tasks; introduced new systems; lead innovations; managed staff and oversaw operational functions and activities.

Karen's story 1

When I applied for this job, I was already a deputy head in a small school. I wanted experience in a large school but I really didn't want the final responsibility. My fingers are in most things, I know I take on too much but I enjoy it, I like to control things because then I know that they'll happen. I've got freedom here to set up my own systems, in meetings I'm always very active and opinionated and I make a good contribution to the discussions.

Mark is very trusting that teachers will do what he's asked but I've told him he needs to follow things through and check up that they're happening. There aren't too many systems in school and teachers have been doing their own thing, he doesn't like to impose systems on people. Since Ofsted, I've introduced new ideas for consistency and we're starting to monitor teaching and learning. I can't stand back and do nothing, so I've given everyone different coloured files and told them what they were for, pupil assessment, planning etc. I'm pretty good at organizing things and getting on with the job, my personality is one that if I know something is right I'll keep pushing for it so that eventually I can get my own way. I've done the job of deputy for a while so I don't think I need much more development now.

My commentary

Although Karen had previous experience of leadership and improving school effectiveness, differing contexts and school cultures require differing skills, experiences and aptitudes (Pascal and Ribbins, 1998). Data evidenced Mark delegating tasks, and distributing leadership roles and responsibility to Karen appropriate to her skills. This reflects findings in the literature research identifying the de-skilling of the head teacher in the classroom and a re-position in an increasingly 'chief executive' role (Hughes, 1973). This leadership culture, in which others are empowered to initiate and lead new developments, may be conditional on levels of 'trusting relationships' between people as identified by Fullan (2003, p. 45). These research findings were consistent with my own professional experience and did not represent any new intellectual challenge at this stage.

Story two

Following the first Ofsted inspection, Karen was directed by the head to lead the KS1 team, teaching children from aged five to seven, although her teaching experience was solely in KS2. Data evidenced findings that her preferred, directional approach to managing change provoked unexpected responses within the KS1 team, requiring her to re-appraise her leadership style.

Karen's story 2

When Ofsted had made their judgements, we all felt very flat and despondent. They'd knocked the stuffing out of us. I knew I'd been putting all my attention into KS2 and had taken my eye off the KS1 ball so I felt responsible. Then I took over the leadership of KS1. That was really difficult, probably the most challenging thing I've ever done. Everyone was very hostile to me because they were bruised and loyal to Jenny (*previous KS1 leader*). I wanted to go in and put everything right and when I tried to do that it fell flat on its face.

The team felt we hadn't supported them but they didn't know the flack we'd taken behind closed doors with the inspector. I remember one meeting which turned really nasty. They were twisting things I said and I couldn't believe that they were seeing me in this way, they were attacking me personally, not me as a leader, and it really upset me.

But I suppose I had to build my reputation with them. They didn't really know me because I'd spent so much time in KS2 and I'd had a lot of personal problems that they didn't know about. As a leader, sometimes I think you have to show that you are human and you can't take all the responsibility away from others. But at the same time I feel that I am paid a lot of money to take this responsibility, it's difficult. I feel as if I'm back again to learning how to be a leader.

My commentary

Karen's new professional role raised significant issues for her and I considered these elements within a framework of power and micro-political strategies. Any action, behaviour and use of language may be seen within a context of power and as being motivated by a range of differing influences, connected to organizational goals and individual agency (Foucault, 1977). School leaders use strategies to achieve their preferred ends, which Greenfield (1984) describes as 'persuasion, calculation, guile, persistence, threat or sheer force' (p. 166). The importance of flexibility and adaptability in leaders to develop new strategies to meet new demands is identified by McCall (1998). Southworth (2002), advises that a change of context enables leaders to 'deepen their knowledge in tasks which are a puzzle to them' (p. 86). The lack of trust between Karen and the KS1 team was identified in the empirical data and Karen stated the importance of building respect and trusting relationships for her leadership, identified in the literature (Fullan, 2001, 2006; Bryk and Schneider, 2002). Data showed Karen's knowledge of the need to gain KS1 staff commitment to the school goal, to meet the Ofsted requirements, and she positioned this within her own leadership as an area for development. Thus the 'arena of struggle' (Ball 1987, p. 19) provided the change of context to mobilize new leadership practice and development. My analysis of the data was starting to be influenced by different authors and I positioned leadership practice in an emerging informed context of power.

Story three

Karen now realized that she needed to build her relationships with the KS1 team and she reflected on a different leadership approach. Feedback from the head teacher stated that Karen had a tendency to 'drive' the staff and needed to learn how to 'pace herself'.

Karen's story 3

I had to do a lot of listening and not be defensive. I knew I had to see it from their point of view, but it was hard. I know I was pushing the team, and I didn't take time to recognize how far they'd moved on. In meetings they had little ploys to disrupt the agenda; they kept taking me down blind alleys and I got very frustrated with them. I told Mark 'it's like World War 3 in there' and I asked him to come into a meeting and give me some advice. He told me I was trying to do too much and he advised me to go more slowly with one or two targets, which I've found has worked better, but its hard when there is so much to do.

I've realized that I'm learning more about leading people from this new experience, I'm having to adapt to them and change the style of language I use. I knew I had to build my reputation with them, so we started with the reading and I explained about the systems for matching reading books to levels of attainment and I modelled reading sessions for them because it wasn't happening.

Mark and I decided what we needed to do after Ofsted. We wrote a new School Development Plan and then we took our decisions to the staff. I've realized that I would have lots of discussions with Mark and then the ideas would go to the Senior Leadership Team and then to staff, so I would have had time to think about the ideas and embed my thinking. I wondered why staff didn't make these ideas happen but they hadn't lived and breathed it for six weeks, they'd only heard it once. So I need to think about that very carefully.

My commentary

Karen's view was that KS1 staff was actively using strategies to affirm their own positions and agency within school, subverting attempts to impose new systems. The power that is structured within all activities and relations in organizations may be tied to authority and status but may also be used covertly to resist and produce discord (Foucault, 1977). Although Karen had the legitimate authority to impose new educational practice in KS1, and to monitor standards of academic achievement, she recognized the need to counter resisters and build solidarity in the team (Parsons, 2002). This imperative provided the motivation to explore, adapt and shape different leadership strategies to negotiate with the teachers and to build a new professional culture in KS1. The leadership decision to use her teaching expertise as a source of influence in her 'modelling' of good reading lessons may be identified as a micro-political 'force(s) at play', designed to promote a unified commitment to the organizational purpose (Mawhinney, 1999, p. 160). Research literature identifies the importance of the 'authentic involvement of teachers' (Blasé and Blasé, 1994, p. 18) and Karen used her own power as a practitioner as she selected strategies to involve teachers in raising and sustaining levels of pupil achievement (Anheier, 2005).

Karen selected leadership styles and approaches suitable to the context, and she used strategies of emotional intelligence to recognize and manage her own, and the group's emotions (Cherniss, 2002; Goleman et al., 2002). Certain emotional intelligence skills and characteristics have been mapped to leadership models (Higgs and Dulewicz, 1999) and provided me with a construct to describe and to analyse Karen's actions and behaviour within a frame of micro-politics. She demonstrated inter-personal sensitivity in understanding and empathizing with the group, while continuing to pursue the organizational goals (Bar-On and Parker, 2000, p. 4). Karen demonstrated high levels of emotional resilience when faced with challenge, derision and rejection and was able to motivate herself, using intuition with insight and interaction to influence others, persuading them to change their views and demonstrate commitment to a new course of action for the benefit of the pupils and the organization (Higgs and Dulewicz, 1999, pp. 7–8).

I became aware at this stage in my research that my analysis was moving into the *outsider* position while retaining a full *insider* understanding of the situation. I was able to describe and explain the actions from a theoretical perspective and provide a critical analysis of my data, while retaining my 'insider's' feel for the business of primary schooling.

Story four

Karen provided many examples of her leadership in enabling and encouraging others to negotiate outcomes and develop their skills in challenging situations. She considered this was significant personal and professional development for her. I posited that she was identifying new leadership skills for a changing context. At this stage of the fieldwork, a new head teacher had been appointed which impacted on Karen's leadership.

Karen's story 4

This year has been such a journey of developing my leadership styles, it isn't directive anymore and I realize I needed to stop controlling everything and everyone. I'm constantly getting phone calls and texts from staff about school matters and medical issues. They've got into a habit of always running things by me.

I've had a very difficult situation recently. The new head came in and I was dealing with the discipline and behaviour all over the school and there were kids kicking off here, there and everywhere. The new head said 'you're doing too much' and Mark said 'Yes you do, Karen but it's your own fault, you take it all on board.' I couldn't believe it that he was saying that in front of the new head. That really upset me, I thought I was doing the right thing and I've never been told that I shouldn't deal with the discipline. To-day teachers have sent children to me who they can't manage, I can't say to them 'sorry not my problem' and walk away.

Before the new head started, we had a meeting and he told me that he wanted to take over some of the work I'd been doing which I found devastating. I thought he wasn't trusting me to do my job. But I'm learning to accept that I can't do everything properly and I'm starting to empower people now, getting them to work out their own solutions rather than telling them how to do their jobs. I can see the benefits in that.

My commentary

Karen had developed her own public leadership persona as a deputy head who could be relied upon to support everyone and 'do the right thing'. Data evidenced her high levels of anxiety which Allix (2000) warns may be associated with leaders' behaviour in 'mobilizing motivational forces' for 'higher and higher searches for individual fulfilment' (p. 12). Karen's high levels of commitment and responsibility may also be viewed within a lens of *over-responsibility*. Fullan (2003) draws from Martin (2003) in describing powerful leaders who assume too much responsibility due to their impatience and sense of urgency for completion. This over-responsibility 'causes other members to assume minimal responsibility themselves' (Fullan, 2003, p. 67). Data I analysed showed Karen beginning to conceive a new leadership role for herself in empowering and developing others, affecting not only her own but also colleagues' expectations with the potential for productive and trusting relationships (Blasé and Blasé, 1994). Episode four provides interesting data for evidence on the importance of building trusting relationships in leadership, both for personal and professional fulfilment.

In presenting a model of developmental democracy, Woods (2005) provides a useful perspective from which to analyse this leadership practice regarding the expression of human potential. Whatever the purpose for the relayed discussion between the former and new head teachers, the outcome led to a dispirited deputy head who considered the comments impacted on her personal and professional identity, self-respect and integrity. The situation caused her to question the deeper values of truth, honesty and trust within a moral imperative (Fullan, 2003). Her reflections provide a link between leadership development and personal growth and authenticity, confirming findings in the literature regarding the leader as agent in their own developing practice (Boyatzis, 2006).

What I felt was happening at this stage was that I was combining my insider and outsider identities. I knew Karen well and was trusted in the school. Yet, my analysis of the situation was moving securely into a theoretical frame as I became increasingly confident in my capacity as a researcher on an interesting journey. The focus of my thesis was the development of my framework for understanding the data. It is to this I now turn for further critical analysis.

A theoretical framing

The scholarly work I engaged with supported an integrated, holistic framework of leadership around a central core of educative leadership. This framework is my conceptualization of leadership which I entitle PIVOT, developed through a process of intellectualizing the full research data (Cain and Gunter, 2012). The framework encloses a central space representing the core of the leadership practice, a mental model of school leadership for intellectualizing, theorizing and mediating for balanced decision-making. PIVOT is an original acronym and represents the Purpose, Identity, Values, Options and Trust as issues associated with leadership to which I make reference in my analysis.

The central space of the PIVOT framework is conceptualized and informed by a model of developmental democracy (Woods, 2005). I began my exploration with the notion of a leader having a sense of **Purpose** within a concept of leadership as planning, setting direction and influencing change for an identifiable outcome (Gronn, 2003). I then considered the importance of the **Identity** of the leader, drawing from Bottery (2004) with considerations of the character, personality, background, experience, intellect and influence of the person, or group, taking a leadership role. The importance of the alignment of **Values** was privileged in the literature (Grace, 2000) as an integral part of a leaders' work, giving attention to ethical and moral issues of fairness, honesty, justice and respect for their own sake. Values would also be addressed within contested issues of power and authority in which leaders act as examplars of the historical and cultural values of the organization. I intellectualized the concept of leadership as decision-making with full regard for the opportunities and **Options** for different priorities, identified by Woods (2005) as a check and challenge to power and authority structures. The literature identified the importance of leaders gaining the **Trust** of their 'followers' which encompassed responsibility and accountability to others for actions and behaviours practised in their leadership (Fullan, 2006). This central core of the PIVOT framework is representative of my immersion in the full research programme using literature to inform my critical thinking, develop my intellectual capacity and is representative of a scholarly study.

Emerging issues

The key issues for this chapter may be explored within the conceptualization of the professional-researcher as an insider/outsider. My own professional experience as a primary school head teacher and consultant, trainer and assessor in leadership programmes provided a background and frame of reference from which I could read, interpret and make meaning of my research. I had access to schools and my epistemological privilege was fundamental to the empirical data collection programme. Using a range of strategies to probe and prompt participants' thinking, I uncovered meaning constructed by the 'knowers' in a 'dialectical process' associated with a professional conversation, described by Mason (1996, p. 141). I found this experience both stimulating and motivating as I listened to school leaders' stories using a subjective lens and 'seeing' myself in these roles and situations. As a practitioner-researcher I had a compelling research interest in how primary school leaders develop their own leadership practice and my 'insider' knowledge of the story helped to build relationships of trust and credibility (Pascal and Ribbins, 1998).

The interpretation of the field-research presented an intellectual challenge associated with the insider/outsider perspective. A description and analysis of the data could be presented through my subjective lens, largely informed by Government ideologies and policies (e.g. DfES, 2004). For example, as a head teacher I had introduced the concepts and strategies of emotional intelligence and distributed leadership which had been promoted by Government. A body of literature identifies the importance of these strategies, with resonance for the functional work of practitioners (e.g. Day et al., 2000; Bennett et al., 2003; Leithwood et al., 2006). My familiarity and acceptance of these concepts and ideologies within a pragmatic, common-sense approach from official sources led to an initial, non-critical perspective.

However, my intellectual enquiry as a researcher took other paths and I was sensitively guided to examine different sources of knowledge particularly associated with theories of power, democracy and micro-politics (e.g. Bottery, 1992; Hoyle, 1999; Mawhinney, 1999; Grace, 2000; Gunter, 2001; Gronn, 2003). Immersion in this literature moved my thinking forward and I gradually re-adjusted my research approach to that of an 'outsider'. The empirical data was the same but I read and interpreted it differently as I began to conduct an analysis both as an insider and outsider, ultimately leading to a richer description for a critical theoretical analysis.

Why do these issues matter?

These issues matter because they have the capacity to move the professional discussion from a reductionist, functional model into an intellectual, uncensored arena with wide-ranging and informed views offering alternative representations. Woods (2005) considers the limitations of the instruments of the 'new managerialism' (p. 24) which resonated with my emerging, broader and more open approach. Woods' differing models of democracy offered an alternative way of 'seeing' and understanding, using the insider/outsider conceptualization.

The professional practice in schools is represented in much of the literature through a functional and behaviourist lens (e.g. Harris et al., 2003; Ofsted, 2003). However, this body of literature does not fully describe and explain the complexity of such practice as the school leader gains compliance to her goals and unifies staff commitment. In a sense, my listening to Karen's everyday stories did not lead me away from theory. Theory enabled me to understand the practice more fully. I needed a new approach for deeper intellectual thinking, locating practice as a site of power, influencing, motivating and mobilizing others from a position of organizational knowledge and personal status. Thus, I found the literature on theories of power and micro-politics helped me to build a framework from which I could analyse and describe the work of senior leaders in schools (e.g. Ball, 1987; Parsons, 2002; Anheier, 2005).

As my journey continued, I uncovered significant issues in the literature affecting my thinking and strengthening my argument, relating to human development and educational leadership (e.g. Grace, 1995; Bottery, 2004; Woods, 2005). For example, Woods (2005) describes a wider view of leadership development as the 'texture of relationships... a sense of mutual identity and support, feelings of empowerment, social and interpersonal capabilities... (but) not as amenable to measurement' (p. 72). The notion that certain attributes may not be measured provided the scholarly challenge, to identify what matters and has meaning in the personal and professional growth of school leaders. That kind of theoretical knowledge helped me in understanding Karen, her work and her world.

These research issues matter because, other than the head teacher, there is very little known about the reality of primary school leaders as they exercise and develop their leadership and become the educational leaders of the future. The research also matters as it gives credence to Mawhinney's (1999) argument to examine the different 'forces at play' in order to discover the 'micro realities' of school leadership cultures (p. 160).

Insider? Outsider?

As an 'insider' I was able to recognize and describe Karen's leadership as an example of a strong leader reflecting, adapting and changing her style for the context. But it is the theoretical immersion which provided the language and conceptualization for this rich analysis of the fieldwork as a site of power. This deeper and informed thinking moves the practice of the profession into a professional practice in which knowledge is derived from differing sources of expertise in order to influence the intellectual and ideological discourse. That is an educative experience.

From a practitioner and 'insider' perspective, I would suggest that Karen's story is representative of many primary school deputy heads. She is an important member of the leadership culture, trying her best to be an exemplar role model and encouraged by all, using value-laden language, to give more of herself. Karen's voice needs to be heard as she reveals her ordinary, familiar work and shares her concerns with an honesty that was my privilege to hear.

As a researcher and 'outsider', it was the scholarly immersion in the literature which affected progress in my intellectual journey. As I moved through the literature, and explored aspects of micro-politics with models of power and democracy, I learnt more about the research process and about myself as a researcher. I clarified what counted as useful data and carefully selected theoretical resources, though not dismissing the likelihood of serendipitous findings. This research process matters hugely as an opportunity to investigate the apparently ordinary experiences of leaders' working lives, and it places these in a theoretical context both for a richer understanding of the extra-ordinariness of school leaders' practice and development and as a *check* and a *challenge* to power and authority structures.

Conclusion

I have presented an aspect of my research as a scholarly process using empirical and literature research findings in a gradually unfolding intellectual practice of critical analysis. The main thrust of this chapter has been to establish the importance of integrating the research literature with the fieldwork for an informed, thoughtful and well-judged analysis. I did not seek to prove any previous theories but rather to professionally explore a current issue in my field and research the academic knowledge in a concurrent, iterative process to seek collateral relations for meaning-making to build knowledge.

CHAPTER SEVEN

Promoting Researcher Well-being: Emerging and Changing Identities

Carl Emery

Introduction

I sat physically shivering and pale faced in a cold sweat. I felt dizzy, fragile and scared. The raucous laughter and chatter of the students passing through to the canteen left me fearful and anxious. (Personal notes, 2007)

In this chapter, I reflect on my journey as an educational researcher in the field of *Social and Emotional Wellbeing* (SEWB). Three sets of conceptual 'tools' help my reflections. First, *autoethnography*, defined by Allen, as the bringing together of lived experience and analysis (Ellis et al., 2011). Second, I use concept/s identified by several of my colleagues in this book as that of the *insider/outsider* in policy research. Third, I employ the concept of *New Managerialism* (NM), a concept also utilized by colleagues. Here, I wish to apply it in order to identify and analyse NM's influence on knowledge and practices within SEWB.

I also draw on concepts from critical discourse analysis (CDA), a field explicitly interested in investigating 'critically social inequality as it is expressed, constituted, legitimized, and so on, by language use (or in discourse)' (Wodak and Meyer, 2001, p. 2).

Defining/applying conceptual tools in research

In applying an autoethnogaphic lens to explore policy processes, I identify a moment of *epiphany* regarding my identity within the SEWB community. I draw on the work of Denzin, who asserts '…epiphanies are interactional moments and experiences which leave marks on people's lives. In them, personal character is manifested. They are often moments of crisis' (Denzin, 1989, p. 70). Ellis et al. (2011) state that most autoethnographers talk about epiphanies, remembered moments perceived to have impacted on the trajectory of a person's life. I go on to explore the impact of this epiphany and my resultant shift from SEWB 'expert' to critical researcher. The quotation heading this chapter is taken from notes made at this critical moment in my professional life.

Insider/outsider status, in particular the interplay between status, language and discourse (Naples, 1996; Kanuha, 2000), is pivotal to my discussion here. As an *insider*, I had understood SEWB discourse; but as an *outsider*, I sought a distance from the subject through which to engage in critique. Like several of my colleagues, I aim to contribute to the dialogue within the Critical Policy community that relates to one's own experiences and outlook. In particular, I investigate the multiple dimensions of the insider/outsider continuum (Mercer, 2007). Sharing with my colleagues a will to resist the temptation to close off the 'hidden ethical and methodological dilemmas of insiderness' (Labaree, 2002, p. 109), I draw on experience of working within the government to analyse how this 'insiderness' can both facilitate and inhibit the aims of research.

The third key theme, NM, is threaded through the chapter. According to Farrell and Morris (2003), NM refers to the ways in which private sector ideology and practices were applied to public sector activity. This brought with it a discourse of efficiency, standards and accountability, applied through techniques such as benchmarking, strategic planning and mission statements. Others in this book investigate the impact of NM. Duggan shows that, although there is no one unitary definition of New Managerialism, one can view it in essence as management through ideology, above and beyond any professional knowledge and understanding.

Autoethnography: An insider? an outsider?

I critique education policy about SEWB in English and Welsh schools from the vantage point of someone with a long history within the area. I worked on the formation of policy, including the rise of SEAL (Social and Emotional Aspects of Learning) (DFES, 2005b) as both a policy driver and an enactor (Ball et al., 2012). From 1995 to 2008, I was as an education consultant closely connected to the New Labour education agenda (Fairclough, 2000).

I specialized in SEWB and conflict resolution and played a role in the development of SEAL. I drew on my classroom experience working with disengaged learners and I wrote and implemented activities for the SEAL framework. (For a fuller discussion of SEAL see Watson et al., 2012, Humphrey et al., 2008, 2010, and QCA, 2008b). I was active in writing and implementing a local education authority's *Behaviour for Learning* Scheme; the Qualification and Curriculum Authority's (QCA) *Personal Learning and Thinking Skills* (QCA, 2008a) and *Future Curriculum* (QCA, 2005) initiatives, as well as being an advisor to the QCA for the personalized learning element of the National Diploma (QCA, 2008a). (For a full account of my position and publications, see Watson et al., 2012).

The knowledge and experience I brought to these roles led me to co-create a SEWB assessment tool in 2006 with a University and a further education institution. This tool entered the National Qualifications Framework. These processes demanded that I work closely with managers from QCA and the Department for Education and Skills, as it was then called. These Government agencies were keen to support and promote the programme. The assessment tool was built on performance and connoisseurship, similar to graded examinations undertaken for piano or dance. Essentially, a group of experts defined what good social and emotional skills would look like when performed at a variety of progressive grades. Near to the end of the programme, I was also approached by the Welsh Assembly Government (WAG) to act as an advisor on the development of a national framework for young people. *Demonstrating Success* ran from 2008 to 2011 and resulted in the creation of Welsh guidelines for assessing SEWB (WAG, 2009).

New managerialism, knowledge and SEWB

My colleagues at Manchester have attempted to show how managerialism makes changes in the nature of knowledge in schooling. For example, in the shaping of 'school leadership' (Gunter, 2012a); practices of 'school improvement' and of a subject such as literacy, which gets 'recontextualised' from disciplines into school classrooms in particular ways (Gunter, Hall and Mills, 2012). In this book, McGinity teases out the ways in which a school's trajectory, as well as the ambitions of critical research such as hers, can be altered (and distorted?) by a set of external managerial practices. This relationship between modes of management and knowledge is a key theme in sociological thought (e.g. Bernstein, 2000; Popkewitz, 2000) that is being explored in developing depth within the Critical Policy community (e.g. Ward, 2012).

I draw on the perspectives of Apple (2007) when he defines NM as the underpinning of the neo-liberal marketization of education. The prevalence of such 'technologies' as accountability, assessment, measurement and audit has been tracked back to managerialism by both policy scholars (e.g. Ball, 2008) and by discourse analysts (e.g. Fairclough, 2000). Initially an ally and agent of the New Managerialism, I am now a Critical Policy commentator challenging both the commodification of children's social and emotional states (Timimi, 2011) and the processes whereby the market place and 'common sense' has captured the SEWB discourse.

Indeed, I argue that the current deficit-based, operational and normative model of SEWB (Watson et al., 2012), dominant across Western Europe, America and Australia, is, in essence, a model demanding *compliance*. It is also a model requiring surveillance of its practitioners and of learners. To this extent, the model is emblematic of neo-liberal education. Olssen, reflecting on neo-liberalism's effect on schooling, claims that 'The perceived possibilities of slothful indolence create necessities for new forms of vigilance, surveillance and performance assessment' (Olssen, 1996, p. 340). In my PhD study, and in other work, I have attempted to move the dominant discourses *away* from the marketplace so as to relocate it back into the community (Konu and Rimpela, 2002). In doing this, I draw upon others' work on both the power of language, and of its controlling force in perpetuating dominant hegemony about what is 'right' within schooling (Fairclough, 1992). I recognize in telling my own story that education policy research is sometimes a painful process.

My epiphany

In 2007, I was working on finalizing the assessment tool for the *National Qualifications Framework*. This process involved meetings with senior representatives of a government agency at their London headquarters. From here, a short tube journey took me to the *Department for Education and Skills* offices where I was contributing to *National Diploma* developments and placing my programme at the heart of the Diploma's Generic *Learning Content*. I had access to, and a voice within, the twin pillars of the UK education system. I was pleased with the reception my work was getting, particularly my articles in government-sponsored magazines and websites. I was receiving invitations to present my ideas to colleagues in senior positions. I had given no thought to any alternative version to the theoretical model of SEWB I was promoting. I recognize that I was perpetuating the discourse of *common sense* through which SEWB could be operationalized and measured I was at this point an insider, participating in a discourse that was in my interests.

I had reached this position driven by various motivations: opportunity, space, finance and status. The *opportunity* this work afforded me was to build on my projects with disengaged pupils and place greater emphasis on relationships and communication. Much of the content in the SEWB assessment tool I was designing came from my direct practice with programmes such as the *School Non Attenders Programme (SNAP)* and the piloting of SEAL. *Space* was provided by the possibilities which SEAL seemed to offer of alternative activities, away from the constrictions of the National Curriculum and the literacy and numeracy agendas. The third factor, finance, was quite simply that I was often paid more for a day's consultancy work than a week's teaching. Finally, *status* was an important motivation to me. I believed that, as chief examiner and author for my own course, my ideas were valued and would be acted on. I had the identity of an education consultant specializing in SEWB. This, along with a strong network of influential colleagues, and the ear of senior policymakers, gave me a sense of privileged status.

Before my moment of epiphany came milder feelings of unease. As Corbin Dwyer and Buckle (2009) note, membership of a group does not denote sameness within that group. Over time, I became increasingly ill at ease with the ways in which the assessment tool was developing. What had been intended as a mechanism to support young people disassociated from mainstream education was being shaped by somewhat different forces and intentions, driven, as I perceived it, by economic profit and by a need for the managerial control of teachers and learners.

Two specific events spurred on my reassessment. First, I was introduced to a business manager who duly informed me that I would complete daily sheets, monitoring my time and actions. I was expected to attend meetings with potential business partners to pitch my 'product' to them. What had been a creative and free space had become a 'sell'. Second, I was informed that a series of projects working with young people not in education, employment or training (NEETS) would be funded *only* if their participants were assessed using the tool I had designed. Both the assessment tool and I were being *commodified* to fit the market and tied in with institutionalized grant giving criteria. My knowledge and skills were being marketized in ways that (I now realize) are a strong feature of what Ward (2012) calls the 'neoliberalisation' of knowledge.

If New Managerialism is a governance structure in the sense of an agent that controls people and institutions by rules of the market, I was being asked to take on a particular role by virtue of my intellectual work and labour. The assessment tool was being positioned as a vehicle for compulsory measurement. Young people's social and emotional 'skills' were being audited on behalf of an organization keen to secure lucrative contracts. This auditing would be mandatory and would be a mode of assessment of students' (and their teachers') inner selves and their social encounters.

The moment of epiphany came as I left a management group meeting on 'qualification development' at an organization where I was working. As I walked out of the room, I felt lost and excluded from the very piece of work I had developed. Outside the meeting room, were a couple of chairs used as a waiting area and I dropped myself into one of these. I felt a determination not to let them get away with this. It was ethically wrong.

I resigned my position and sold my copyright to the qualification I had created. At that moment, I lost 70 per cent of my income.

From reflexivity ...

Looking back, I can see four factors that drove my reorientation from New Managerial advocate to Critical Policy commentator. First, I was uncomfortable with what Apple (2012a) terms as the 'thinness' of the new version of my work. As the qualification became better known, and the more colleagues and I talked about what SEWB looked like in practice, the less I recognized it. I felt that the participants, or 'consumers', the teachers and the students, were being asked to become agents of their own surveillance (Foucault, 1995). A second issue was my concern with the commodification of knowledge and the fact that my role had become one of a facilitator of the 'consumption' of my work (Rutherford, 2005). I was 'touting' my product around a series of educational and employment clients, including a high street bank and an international airport. A third factor, one related to the thinness identified above, was a realization that I was compliant in a kind of misrepresentation. As the programme was driven into the market place, its achievements were being described in ways which exaggerated the status of the qualification. The discourse was transforming into one about students' 'outcomes' and 'contracts agreed'. Presentation after presentation to educational organizations, public and private, located our 'product' as a solution to 'problems' of behaviour, attendance, employability – and many other social functions. Schools or colleges could 'purchase' our product assuming that by doing so they were meeting the criteria by which their success in school inspections could be achieved. Finally, the change from a voluntary to a mandatory programme created a context where, the student is defined as an economic unit, governed by self-interest (Lynch, 2010; Giroux, 2012). This also related to how I was beginning to see my own work. As long as the economic reward was big enough, it was assumed that my self-interest would ensure that I would still do that work.

Into Critical Policy research

Each of these factors contributed towards my decision to undertake Critical Policy work for my PhD research. I had no desire to be part of this co-opting of my work. But I wanted my voice to be heard. Drawing on Romanyshyn's (2007) notion of the 'wounded researcher', my research was driven by feelings of anger and injustice. Taking this a stage further, my determination to voice and make real a version of SEWB built upon subjectivity and relationships was, in essence, my attempting to fix the wounds of my own schooling. I was an angry and confused teenager, desperately seeking support and understanding. I found these things absent from my schooling. I left my English comprehensive school with no qualifications. It was only on entering further education to retake my qualifications, and meeting an educationalist who grounded his role in social and emotional understanding, that I felt safe and able to engage with learning.

I have given the background of my study through using the tools of autoethnography. I have described the journey that led me from policy formation and enactment to critical research. I now draw on my notion of insider/outsiders, using the concepts of 'position' and 'voice' from critical discourse analysis to reflect on an aspect of my research – the interviews and engagement with policymakers. In doing this, I acknowledge the debt that I, and other contributors to this book, owe to Anyon et al. (2009) concept of 'putting theory to work' in our research.

Position and voice in policy research

Fairclough (2003) and other theorists consider that critical discourse analysis starts with the awareness of a social problem and the desire to overcome it. For instance, Corson (2000) states his aims as being concerned with 'uncovering inequality, power relationships, injustices, discrimination, bias, etc.' (p. 95). The concepts of *'position'* and *'voice'* are both key focuses in the analysis of discourse. Both Rogers (2004) and Fairclough (1989) consider that the analysis of discourse processes is an insider's, or member's task, while Haig considers that the 'analyst needs to be simultaneously an outsider and an insider to the discourse processes taking place' (Haig, 2004, unnumbered page). The insider/outsider issue is as key to a sociology of knowledge (Merton, 1972) as it is to the arguments of this chapter and to those of others in this book (e.g. Davies' chapter).

From my own vantage point, it was only by being an insider that I gained access to, participated in and understood the SEWB discourse processes in England during the New Labour era. Yet, it was fundamental to my research methodology that I entered the sphere of the outsider, both as the researcher peering inside in order to analyse and understand and also in occupying a space where I no longer shared many of the characteristics of the SEWB community from which I came. Indeed, my position involved being both insider and outsider; a shapeshifter, moving 'back and forth across different boundaries' of class, values and geography (Griffith, 1998).

With other practitioners of CDA, I adopt a critical view of *common sense* within language and discourse (Fairclough, 2003). The current neo-liberal agenda, and the economic infrastructures it operates through, have changed our understanding of common sense as well as our use of language and discourse. As Fairclough (2000) identifies, we are in a period where we talk into being a series of universal truths with no space for any alternative versions. For example, in England, parental choice and published school league tables are ubiquitously presented as a positive development (Lupton, 2011). For a localized view of the neo-liberalization of education and, in particular, the ways in which discourse shapes the challenges faced by SEWB practitioners, see Emery (2013).

Putting theory to work in 'interviewing the powerful'

I interviewed policymakers in the hope of identifying the dominant discourses in play in SEWB policy, particularly in regard to national identity, power and cultural beliefs. For discussion here, I have changed identifying personal characteristics. Those I approached for interviews included a former UK Government minister, a representative in the Welsh Assembly Government and a high profile English academic working in the field of SEWB policy. As a researcher with inside experience, I had an understanding of the best avenues for approaching interviewees (Griffiths, 1985). I was knowledgeable of practices and language from SEWB and thought that these factors would increase the likelihood of my gaining interviews.

I ensured that my email communication to the Minister was respectful, giving evidence of my credibility. I referred to the Minister's work and made links to my own. I set out my status (a researcher at a University) and clarified the aims of my research. Looking back, I see I drew on my experience of the *New Labour* agenda to communicate in the language used by politicians (Fairclough, 2000). I was marketing myself through a discourse understood by the subject. By contrast, my initial email to the representative of the Welsh government took a friendly rather than formal approach. There was less declared evidence of my credibility and status. All communication was direct rather than through a third party. We had worked together, and I assumed a shared political position, grounded in our mutual commitment to Welsh devolution as well as to a model of education promoting social justice and comprehensive values. Such values, I knew, were central to the Welsh SEWB community.

I did not anticipate that access to the academic would be difficult owing to my inside knowledge and my connections. In fact, it proved impossible. This person's email address had already appeared in group emails when I had conducted previous work. When seeking the interview, I was aware that my writing, critical of English SEWB development, had been seen by the academic. I was nervous in making contact. On reflection, I see that I was already placing myself in an outsider's space in relation to this interviewee. Yet, I hoped that my insider history would give me access. Our relationship was familiar but not intimate. The process of seeking this interview took a twist when the person appeared unexpectedly in a social situation. This presents a challenge for an autoethnographic narrative as it raises questions of privacy and incidental data. Our exchange in this social forum, uncomfortable and heated, was not part of my official research process. Therefore, I do not wish to use it as data. I had considered how I would cope with a situation where a familiar/intimate subject challenged my critical position but I had not considered how I would manage this in a setting outside the official process. This was somewhat naïve, as the SEWB community is not a particularly large one. It was likely that this kind of meeting would occur, through conferences, and the like.

Following this informal meeting, I emailed again, making reference to our previous encounter, setting a positive tone and expressing the aims of the study. I explicitly asked this interviewee for their voice to be present in my research. However, they refused. I wonder if this person now saw me as a threat to the SEWB community, someone with insider knowledge and history, yet simultaneously occupying an outsider status. It could well be that by appearing to ask critical questions about what normally is assumed to be 'common sense' in my publications (in this case an objective list model of SEWB), I was being assumed to have shifted to outsider status (D'Cruz and Jones, 2004).

The physical settings were influential on the interviews and interactions. In the case of the minister, I had no prior direct contact. All communication was through a secretary. This distance continued in the physical access, which was time-limited and conducted on the subject's own territory, the daunting physical setting of the Houses of Parliament. Fitz and Halpin (1994) discuss power asymmetry in the interview process, claiming that situations place the researcher in the position of a supplicant so grateful to obtain an interview that he or she is unwilling to ask critical or demanding questions. My interview was preceded by a search of myself and my belongings by armed police! Being physically searched before entering a seat of national power places huge challenges on the researcher to maintain a clear and enquiring mind. The location cast me as an outsider from the start, albeit an officially sanctioned one, having had to apply for a pass to enter the building.

With the government minister, my name had some credibility. My work appeared to be known, though I do not believe they were aware of my critical stance. During the interview, it emerged that two older members of our families had known each other well. This added an intimate dimension that was probably advantageous, perhaps engendering a greater degree of trust. Mercer (2007, p. 7) cites Dimmock (2005) who challenges this kind of association, considering that such intimacy could disadvantage an interviewer through a possible reluctance to share information. This was not my experience. Drever (1995) posits that 'people's willingness to talk to you, and what people say to you, is influenced by who they think you are' (p. 31). I believe that I was seen as a 'safe pair of hands', someone whose family name was known to them and who had operated successfully within the same subject field, essentially an insider. Perhaps, as the interview developed, this resulted in perceived loyalties at the political, familial and the subject levels. Ball (1994) shares similar insights on the politics of interviewing politically powerful informants.

The representative of the Welsh government, by contrast, chose to meet with an open time limit at a venue suitable for both of us – more a relationship of equals or friends, reflecting the points made by Simmons (2007) cited in Burns et al. (2012) that insider status eases access and rapport. In the terms expressed by Ellis et al. (2011), this interview would have been 'intimate'. The identity this person ascribed to me, a familiar ally, clearly influenced the interview process (Drever, 1995). The Welsh interviewee was someone with whom I had previously worked and built a relationship. We were familiar to each other. Access was straightforward and informal. An email request was sent setting out the aims and schedule of the research and inviting the subject to take part. For much of my working relationship with this person, I would have appeared as an insider.

In my time with the Welsh Assembly I had helped create a national framework for measuring SEWB. Therefore, one could argue, I had helped to maintain New Managerialism. However, the cultural identity and context of a devolved Welsh Government made this position more of a problematic and complex concept. The tools of New Managerialism (accountability, assessment, measurement and audit) can only be utilized in a suitable space, such as the English education system (Lupton, 2011). Wales was not such a space during my time there. Welsh SEWB did not use an objective list model. It was underpinned by the UN Convention on the Rights of the Child and by a cultural identity grounded in concepts of social justice and communitarianism (Watson et al., 2012). The Welsh educational system was, and is still, comprehensive. It was therefore a very different cultural context from England, one that shunned much of the New Managerialism agenda.

This discomfort with a marketized version of SEWB, particularly the English version, gave me the status of an *insider* in Wales, though, geographically and linguistically, I was a clear *outsider*. Conversely, in England, the critiques I had made publically of SEWB – when participants were aware of them – could identify me as an *outsider* whilst, geographically and linguistically, I was an *insider*. Interestingly, my relationships in Wales were often defined by myself and by others by my opposition to the English SEWB model. My relationships in England were often also similarly defined by my opposition to the English SEWB model.

This shifting status during interviews was shared by interviewees. SEWB is not a static subject. It is constantly developing with new knowledge, voices and versions of the field fluctuating between policy actors. Indeed, Humphrey (2012) has called it a 'fuzzy and intangible concept'. This in itself is problematic when locating insider/outsider status as it became apparent during the interviews with both the minister and the civil servant that the version of SEWB they were discussing had in fact changed for them during the period of their policy activity. My perception of the assumed positionality of the participants as insiders, attached to a particular way of thinking and seeing SEWB, was in fact oversimple. Both interviewees discussed here said that their own status as insiders had in fact moved towards elements of outsider status as the policies they were connected to changed shape, form and function. Indeed, the minister made it very clear that the version of SEWB they were developing when in government was *not* the same as the version that appeared in policy guidance or practice. As previous commentators have noted, policy 'is really just process…none of the initiatives in these fields stay fixed for very long because the problems themselves keep moving and changing' (Considine, 1994, p. 3). Insider/outsider status bears similar comparison: it is heavily defined by process, as we are all moving and changing.

Conclusion

Having journeyed from being a school-based practitioner to an actor in the formation of policy, I now find myself as a critical educational researcher. In this role, I am persuaded to pursue Loughlin's (2004) version of an academic, believing that 'It is our *job* to think, to question, to expose faulty reasoning, to demand and scrutinize evidence' (p. 721). This stance led me to question my place in the creation of a social and emotional 'qualification' and within New Managerialism structures. Yet, Darbyshire (2008) adds a possibly uncomfortable addition to Loughlin's claims, adding that the critical thinking advocated by Loughlin is seen as dangerous if it 'risks disrupting the smooth functioning or in any way challenging the air-brushed, public relations persona of our own organisations' (p. 37).

Writing this chapter has convinced me that such dilemmas about 'disruption' and risk still exist for me. Critical thinking about policy is exciting but potentially risky. I anonymized and watered down particular details within this account for fear of legal and professional ramifications. For me, insider/outsider status is complicated, with many shades intermingling and drifting in and across my research, clearly affecting how I was viewed by interviewees and how I perceived them. When conducting my interviews, the traces of the 'insider' me were still present in a certain capacity. Also, a second wave of identity, growing in momentum, was forming and building a critical framework for viewing and understanding my experiences – the 'outsider' me. 'Differences [between insider and outsider] are not conceived as absolute, and consequently the relation between them is not one of utter antagonism' (Fay, 1996, p. 224). Researchers can be insiders, outsiders or both. Throughout this research my status was flowing and shifting: I was an insider and outsider, and often both at the same time.

Recourse to theory does not solve these conflicts and dilemmas. But the tools and concepts I have referred to (autoethnography; insider/outside status; understandings about the influence of New Managerialism) as well as concepts derived from the critical discourse community such as position and voice, can help us in identifying and beginning to live with those dilemmas.

CHAPTER EIGHT

New Teachers and Master's-level Study: Researching Tensions in the Policy–Practice Interface

Cate Goodlad and John Hull

Introduction

We are two members of The Manchester Institute of Education team teaching the MA Education (Teach First Leadership) programme, a substantial element of which involves engagement with research and the production of a dissertation. We take a lead in preparing the participants to produce their dissertations. Interestingly, from the standpoint of this book, we are researchers who teach other teachers to research.

We believe ourselves privileged to be working with these talented master's students: newly qualified teachers who have entered the profession through *Teach First* as a 'new route' that has been hailed by both New Labour (*1997–2010*) and the Coalition governments (*2010–to date*). This charity places high achieving graduates in schools in challenging circumstances and has the dual purposes of (i) reducing the gap between high and low achievers; and of (ii) raising the status of the teaching profession. New Labour and Coalition policies placed these new teachers in the schools where we help them to understand and to develop practice. We are working with students at the interface of policy and practice.

The focus of this chapter

In this chapter, we reflect on a small research project that we undertook in order to investigate what value and benefits these teachers identified from their master's study. As we reflect, we are aware of many connections with the themes addressed by several of our colleagues in this book. We promote critical reflection and research in our teaching. Yet we are aware that *we* work in an education policy environment in which standardized solutions to the problems of teaching, learning and pedagogy are often privileged. This, of course, is the same context in which those that we try to help become critical researchers also work.

Our project addressed the question of how the students' own educational research dissertations impact on their practices and their understandings when they are working 'on the frontline' of the policy–practice interface. In reporting our study, we also reflect on the position in which *our* researcher roles place *us*. We are acutely conscious of some tensions within those roles. They connect with several of our colleagues' discussions in this book of 'insider' and 'outsider' tensions in their work. Though we both have extensive experience of schooling and teaching, we are now 'outsiders' to these demanding frontline contexts. However, as we support the processes of research and writing, we become informed 'insiders', co-working with these developing practitioners and helping them in their reflections and reflexivity about processes in schools of which we are no longer a part. In our research project, we found that participants valued the master's study for the way that it allowed them to engage with wider debates within education. Through that debate, they develop a greater understanding of the context of their schools and of classrooms. Such debate also allows them to develop resilience to cope with the tensions that they were experiencing day-to-day within their classrooms. However, more importantly, it allows teachers in 'challenging' schools to open up spaces for critical reflection. This, we shall argue, is why educational research matters.

As we now write about a research project delving into the value of the research process, a number of different aspects of research emerge. These aspects include: the experience of research for the participants themselves; for our involvement as tutors; and for our experience as researchers. 'Formal' research reflections within textbooks often deal with issues such as the development of good research practices or of ethical protocols and procedures. We will focus more here on implicit aspects of research, including the *relationships* between ourselves as researchers and the participants, our students.

The policy context of the master's programme

The editors argue in the introduction to this book that for the last thirty years policymakers have sought to improve education through the implementation of centralized performance regimes and decentralized marketization policies. Successive governments have built on previous regimes' policies and ideas. Continuity has often been a striking feature. Here, we wish to highlight only those aspects of policy that have particular pertinence for this discussion. Efforts to 'modernise' the teaching profession have resulted in a noticeable shift from a largely autonomous profession to one subject to markets, control and surveillance (Mahoney and Hextall, 2000).

A feature of this policy landscape has been the strong controls over Initial Teacher Training (ITT) so that it has been described as becoming 'detheorised, non-egalitarian and technicist' (Hill, 2007, p. 204); subject to 'reductionist discourses' (Slee, 1998, p. 255), with a reduced role for Higher Education and the introduction of 'new routes' to teaching. The effects of this centralization on ITT have been well summarized by McNamara (2009) as resulting in 'short-termism'; the training of teachers has been subject to the 'vagaries of political whim' (p. 103). The development of a 'performative' culture linked to targets, league tables and performance management has, according to Ball (2003), replaced 'co-operation and older forms of collaboration' (p. 219). Critics of the policy agenda describe such policy shifts as 'de-professionalising': the insistence of 'standardised solutions' to problems in practice reducing the 'complexity of what teachers do' (Ozga, 2000b, p. 224).

The tight linkage by successive governments of the purpose of education to economic imperatives has, according to Ozga (2000b, p. 233), brought about a risk of neglecting human and social development. Others have argued that current improvement strategies based on this technicist model of teaching lead to a 'plateau problem' (Chapman and Fullan, 2007, p. 208) and a problem of 'reach' (Dyson, 2006, p. 123). Taken together, this suggests a 'stalling' of the school improvement agenda, in that without the development of practical new ideas and pedagogical strategies, schools are unlikely to raise students' attainment and engagement, especially with those young people who are hardest to reach, often in more disadvantaged areas. Would those whom we had taught to research, we wondered, see in their master's work, the early development of the ideas and strategies necessary to overcome this stalling? These 'modernising' reforms are designed to control and conform both new and existing teachers and, as Hill argues the 'spaces for "critical reflection" have been virtually squeezed out' (2007, p. 214). He asserts that in ITT we are left with a 'safe, sanitised and de-theorised education' (Hill, 2007, p. 213) which 'prepares student teachers to uncritically "deliver" the existing National Curriculum' (Hill, 2007, p. 214). In Hill's view, teacher education has been seen as simply too important to be left to teachers and educational professionals in the context of global capitalism.

According to Pring (1999), the previously strong involvement of universities in teacher training incorporated three all too often taken for granted assumptions that were rarely spelled out. First, that teachers should be 'initiated into a form of intellectual life at a relatively demanding level'; that 'systematic improvement in teaching should be based on research'; and that the 'critical faculties' of teachers should be developed (Pring, 1999, pp. 290–1). Pring developed an argument about the distinctive knowledge that teachers need by claiming that:

> It is neither the purely theoretical knowledge developed and expounded through foundation disciplines, nor the purely practical knowledge in lists of competencies that can be acquired simply by doing. It is much more the kind of *practical wisdom* born of deliberation, shaped by critical discussion in the context of the practical, informed by relevant theoretical perspectives which, however, by themselves entail no one set of practices. (Pring, 1999, p. 305; our emphasis)

While Pring recognized the contribution of schools to initial teacher training, he was concerned to remind us of the 'distinctive contribution' higher education might make. While his focus was on initial teacher training, our interest lies in working with recently qualified teachers who have entered the profession via one of the 'new routes' to teaching. We suggest, however, that Pring's claim for a 'distinctive contribution' from higher education applies, possibly even more closely, to teacher development of which master's courses have formed an important avenue.

The master's qualification: A policy anomaly?

The strong consistent cross-party consensus aligning the imperative for modernization of the education system in line with the country's economic needs has been remarkably sustained. However, policy proposals develop in debate and occasionally they survive even where the policy context has moved on. This, we suggest, is true of the discussion around teacher qualification and development, and in particular the debate around teaching becoming a master's-level profession. In the 2007 *Children's Plan: Building Brighter Futures*, the following proposal was included:

> To help fulfil our high ambitions for all children, and to boost the status of teaching still further, we now want it to become a Masters level profession. (DCSF, 2007, p. 88)

The Children's Plan proposed a new master's qualification, with the expectation that 'every teacher will now be engaged in high quality performance management linked to continued practical professional development from when they first start teaching'. The reasoning behind this was to bring the English system in line with other very high performing education systems worldwide. However, the proposal that teaching become a master's-level profession was short-lived. Given the nature of a policy thrust which was distancing teachers' training, qualification and development from higher education providers and which promoted, within schools, technical management and a belief in standardized solutions, the idea was a policy anomaly. The new Coalition government (2010), while promoting the idea of teachers' collaborative practices and development of academic knowledge in its White Paper *The Importance of Teaching*, saw this being achieved through the development of a 'national network of new Teaching Schools to lead and develop sustainable approaches to teacher development' (DfE, 2010, p. 23). In this White Paper, the only reference to the role of higher education was to the development of University Training Schools as a means of training teachers in practice. Shortly after, in March 2011, the government announced that funding was to be withdrawn from the master's in Teaching and Learning (MTL), the qualification established as a result of the Children's Plan (DfE, 2011, p. 3). However, government support for master's study has not ended there.

Teach First: A policy 'fit'?

Teach First is a charity whose stated mission is 'to end inequality in education by building a community of exceptional leaders' (Teach First, 2013a). It promises to 'train and support committed individuals to become inspirational classroom leaders in low-income communities across England and Wales' (Teach First, 2013a). *Teach First* sets as a 'minimum requirement' that recruits hold a '2.1 degree or above, 300 UCAS points or equivalent (excluding General Studies)' (Teach First, 2013b). Since its founding in 2002, it has placed 2,520 teachers into 'challenging' schools and has been voted third in *The Times Top 100 Graduate Employers* (Teach First, 2013c). In the White Paper, *The Importance of Teaching* (DfE, 2010, p. 21), the coalition committed to 'provide funding to more than double the size of *Teach First* from 560 new teachers to 1,140 each year by the end of this Parliament'. *Teach First* fits well into the 'modernisation' project, providing a 'new route' to teaching; recruiting outstanding graduates and placing them in challenging contexts to raise attainment and aspiration; and it is part of the third sector. With strong business backing, *Teach First* has won support from both New Labour and the Coalition Secretaries of State. However, while *Teach First* is a very good 'fit' with the modernization policy, it also represents an exception in that it remains committed to master's-level training. The master's qualification is promoted as an opportunity for participants 'to further develop their abilities to be effective leaders in schools' (Teach First, 2013d).

Teach First encourages master's study because the 'qualification will be valuable in any future career and will enhance your status and mobility both in the UK and beyond' (Teach First, 2013d). These statements declare a strong commitment to developing leadership potential, a central *Teach First* tenet. Less explicit, is the hope that master's study will positively influence participants' classroom practice.

Our research project sought to illuminate the extent to which these newly qualified professionals value the experience of critical discussion within a supportive community of study, the significance of research as part of their dissertation, and the impact of these on their practice and commitment.

The research project

The project focused on a selection of graduates emerging from the MA Education (Teach First Leadership). We set this study against a policy context that we have argued tends to promote standardized solutions to issues of practice and to assume that technical management models are effective. We suggest that shifting patterns of 'centralised' ITT are seeking to sideline higher education institutions' contributions.

The programme we worked on had twenty-two people graduating from the first full cycle in 2011. All the graduates were invited to take part in our research. Ten of them volunteered to take part in semi-structured interviews that took place by telephone or Skype. The interviews lasted between thirty minutes and an hour and were audio-recorded. Transcripts were later shared with participants to ensure accuracy and clarity. Discussion topics included their experience of undertaking the master's; what they had found useful or less helpful; their views of 'professionalism'; and the impact of their master's-level study on their teaching practices.

Of the ten who volunteered, three were still in their original *Teach First* placement school; two had moved to other state schools; one was now working in further education; three in the Independent sector. One had left teaching to work for a management consultancy business. This profile of the participants is comparable with the whole of the *Teach First* cohort for the North West of England region in that year. From thirty-eight in the regional cohort, twenty-eight opted to undertake the master's programme. In 2012, four years after commencing their training with *Teach First*, twenty-six (68 per cent) were still working in teaching, sixteen (42 per cent) of whom were in *Teach First* schools; and five (13 per cent) were in teaching related professions.

All the participants we interviewed had taken a 'traditional' route through education, attending some of the most highly regarded universities in the country and achieving extremely good degrees. They had been successful in a rigorous selection process and accepted onto the *Teach First* programme.

Following a six-week induction course, they were placed in schools in challenging circumstances. During their first year of teaching, they studied for a PGCE, opting to study for the master's qualification during their second year. At the time of the interviews (Summer 2012), the participants had graduated from the programme and were approaching the end of their fourth year in teaching.

Next, we explain what our research project revealed about the experience of research for the participants. Then, we reflect on our involvement as tutors, before finally making conclusions about what this says about the role of research in the development of novice teachers – and in that of their tutors.

On doing research: 'just seeping its way into your everyday practice'

Our project led us to two key findings. The first was that the participants found value in their engagement with debates and contexts and saw relationships between their study and their work and progress in schools. All the participants we interviewed expressed the view that the master's had been worthwhile and that they had derived personal benefits from it. Some placed equal value on engaging with educational research through the taught sessions as well as the practical research element of the dissertation. For others, the process of doing the research-based dissertation was the most valuable.

For some, there had been a direct impact on their practice:

> The dissertation was most useful for the impact it has made to progression and performance. It had direct relevance for teaching practice and my role as literacy co-ordinator. (Liz)
>
> I chose to do my master's on a practical application in the classroom ... it has impacted on my teaching quite a lot. It's co-operative learning and it's something I teach other teachers about. (Georgina)

Georgina further expressed the value of classroom research. She stated:

> I realised it's absolutely important to have people doing research in education in the classroom and not just doing the same thing that's always been done. I realised that it can be done and there's no reason it can't be done more often. (Georgina)

The comment by Georgina suggests that engaging in research could help to overcome some of the problems of 'stalling improvement' by developing new ways of working. Others found that while they enjoyed the dissertation and found it useful at the time, they found it had less direct relevance at the time of their interviews due to changes in their role, Matthew, for instance, focused on the value of 'work experience' for developing 'employability skills' but had now changed role, stating: 'others have read it but I don't think it's made any difference to practice'. Similarly, Danny suggested that his dissertation 'was practical at the time' for the pastoral role he had carried out previously. However, at the time of his interview, as a departmental head, it was less directly relevant, but 'probably helps in the wider sense'. Danny also noted that little came of the research due to his school's changed priorities and to a change in leadership.

However, a few of the participants found it more difficult to quantify what they had learned through the process of doing research. In cultures obsessed with measurement, more qualitative shifts are difficult to define:

> I find it hard to quantify in terms of practical impact but it has changed the way I do things. It's more subtle than like 'before I did this, now I do that'.... It has helped me see things from other perspectives especially the Bourdieu thing and my dissertation. I understand more of the pressures on boys – society's perceptions and their friends'. They exert such an influence on them. (Hannah)
>
> I found anyway, and other people that I've spoken to have found, that it's just seeping its way into your everyday practice...you are more engaged in evaluating your actions and you are more engaged in, you know, the theory behind it as well which has made me a much better teacher. (Sam)

Impact at the classroom level featured strongly, though as Hannah and Sam suggested above, this relationship between master's-level study and practice was very subtle. One participant suggested that her notion of what a 'good' teacher changed because of her master's study:

> At first, I had a very naïve view in that 'good' teaching was all about lesson planning and the focus on teaching. But as you progress you realise it's not all about teaching and learning as there are so many things outside of school which impact on performance. (Liz)

The comments here suggest that engaging teachers with higher education can help to develop a deeper understanding of the circumstances in which children learn. Liz's initial view of 'good' teaching perhaps reflects the detheorized, technicist and reductionist views of teacher education put forward by Hill (2007) and Slee (1998). As she engaged with literature and with research, her view of 'good' teaching came to acknowledge a much wider set of influences. Pring (1999, p. 305) has drawn attention to the importance of 'critical discussion' in developing the 'practical wisdom' of the teacher. Here, we perceive in our listening to voices such as Liz's, the development of this wisdom brought about by her master's study. Pring further hoped that these processes might lead to 'systematic improvement' in teaching (Pring, 1999, pp. 290–1). Taking the opportunity to update Pring's hope, we entertain the belief that this 'good' teaching, critically informed by a wider set of influences, may help overcome the 'stalling' and 'plateau' problems which we noted earlier (Chapman and Fullan, 2007, p. 208).

The value of master's study for developing practice was articulated in the majority of the interviews. However, there was little challenge to the educational system of targets and performance management other than that from Rebecca who had had a particularly bad experience of teaching in two schools where she felt unsupported and undervalued. Her frustrations resulted in her eventual leaving of the profession. She reflected:

> You know when you're at the 'coal face' as it were, working away, that unbelievable feeling of pressure and stress that you're under to follow policy and deal with the challenges, and deal with the kids, find some semblance of control with your classroom, while also trying to get towards targets that were set and by which a lot of teachers – their whole work is revolving around targets and tests. It puts a huge amount of strain on teachers who ultimately can not control these things but I've seen how all this has driven all the work that goes on in school and I think the most interesting thing for me was it [the master's] provided an opportunity to step back and reflect upon 'ok, so what are we doing here? Is it really helping the kids learn? And if not, why is it not helping?' I think that was the most helpful. (Rebecca)

She further stated:

> It is difficult, because it takes someone exceptionally brave to kind of 'buck the trend' and think about *learning* as opposed to spoon feeding or cramming students with the curriculum...you don't have much control in that situation. (Rebecca)

The suggestion that the focus should be on learning rather than grades or targets suggests a wish for reduced prescription over the working environment of teachers and a greater agency as teachers. The concept of autonomy did not feature as part of the participants' views of 'professionalism'. We suggest that this probably reflects the technical 'how to' stance of contemporary teacher training.

Developing resilience: 'the way you think about how you teach'

Our second key finding was that through study and research, the teachers developed resilience through their engagement with research. This resilience appeared to help them in understanding and overcoming tensions. The pressures of everyday 'performativity' featured strongly in their discussions. Targets, grades and outcomes were consistent features of the discourse:

> It's very, very difficult because you are under so much pressure to meet targets and you've got students who are not likely to meet those targets at such a late stage in the game, I think that's one of the frustrating things…and there's so much pressure on teachers from above to show that initiatives are in place, to deliver this huge curriculum within a short timescale to students who are switched off because they know that all they've got to do is get grades and it's really boring. (Rebecca)

Such pressures are well documented (Ball, 2003). Engagement with research appeared to help individuals to deal with their day-to-day realities and contextualize what is happening:

> It's very easy to be bogged down in day-to-day life. Master's helps you really focus on how you are doing it. It helps you understand what the students are going through and why they are the way they are. That will affect you in the way that you respond to them and the way you think about how you teach. (Georgina)

Matthew suggested that the master's could help to balance some of these tensions:

> You can learn the background through the Master's but then return to school and have a greater understanding of what you are doing. There is an element of teaching to the test and having to jump through hoops but the Master's helps you to cope with that better and achieve policy goals. (Matthew)

These comments suggest that there is a place for post-graduate study in developing the resilience of teachers, in particular those teachers in schools in challenging and difficult circumstances. With resilience, they may be able to reflect and understand complexities within the situations in which they find themselves. Policymakers may be wary of teachers' critical engagement with higher education (Hill, 2007). However, master's study with a focus on research enables teachers to develop what might be termed, following Pring (1999), a 'practical wisdom'. We found that this enabled many to begin to better deal with tensions between policy and practice in the context of the dominant performative cultures alive in policy and schools.

Reflecting on our roles: Researching our research

We are researchers who teach teachers to research. In this complex position, we now reflect on the project and its meaning for us. Therefore, a little about ourselves might be relevant here. One of us is an ex-headteacher (whose work in that role was in challenging schools), ex-advisor and ex-consultant. The other came to education through a non-traditional route, and worked in a school and further education college in challenging circumstances, before moving into higher education. We have first-hand understanding of contexts like the *Teach First* schools within which our students work. We have respect for, and empathy with, those whose research we supervise.

It seems to us that, working with these new teachers and reflecting on the process of research and dissertation production, we are both 'outsiders' and 'insiders', able to share the perspectives of our colleagues who write here. As 'outsiders', we adopt a detached stance to pose hard questions concerning the form and development of the research. For example: how is the literature review constructed so that it is comprehensive and establishes a chosen focus? is the methodology appropriate?; is its timely completion practicable? Contrastingly, in discussing findings we may become 'insiders'. We know contexts like theirs: we agree on the potential value of their focus and we want to help them capture the meanings of what they have researched. Advising on recommendations, we are cast in both roles. As 'insiders' we hope that what is recommended has the potential to improve practice and raise attainment in the location under study, thus contributing to reducing inequality in educational outcomes. As research-experienced 'outsiders', we urge that recommendations note what is still uncertain, suggest how greater clarity might be achieved and identify learning that might be useful in other schools. In line with the views of Mercer (2007), we see this *insider/outsider* distinction as being part of a continuum with the two positions being at opposite ends of the spectrum. There is therefore a degree of fluidity between the two positions while we move between insider and outsider, as we are never fully one nor the other (Bauman, 2000; Thomson and Gunter, 2011). Indeed, even when we describe ourselves as insiders due to intimate knowledge of contexts similar to those within which our students work, there is still an element of being an outsider, as this is not *our* lived experience. This degree of detachment, or 'outsiderness', can also help to guide the students in their analysis by asking those difficult questions about what is being achieved.

In this complex relationship with the researched, we should also examine our own positions. We admire the expressed philosophy and aims of *Teach First* in tackling educational inequality. However, we also appreciate that this is not easy to achieve. Our scholarship teaches us that underachievement is an enduring problem. It is a 'problem', but one highly sensitive to specific contexts, and in need of a range of different policies, and players in the game. In helping students to do research for a dissertation, we require a critical understanding. However, in the thinking that we provoke in the students, do we become too negatively controversial? We endeavour to create spaces for students to reflect with criticality upon what they do, and on how their work can be theorized and explained within a performative regime. We therefore encourage them to go beyond reductionist and technicist teaching practices and to explore the potential of research for developing new ways of working. By engaging with students, we are able to encourage them through their engagement with research to ask questions about how their practice is conceptualized and positioned within the education system.

There is one aspect of our relationship with these new teachers that we think important. These relationships are forged in a university. With reference to Pring's argument for university involvement, these new teachers have been 'initiated into a form of intellectual life at a relatively demanding level' and their 'critical faculties' have been developed (Pring, 1999, pp. 290–1). Only in a setting with staff who know, as 'insiders', the teachers' contexts, and who can, as 'outsiders', bring challenge and contact with the literature, is this possible. Universities are such settings.

Conclusion

Our research project with new teachers who have obtained a master's qualification within three years of their career suggests that they deemed the experience of becoming researchers valuable in terms of their opportunities to engage with issues, debates and contexts. Most strikingly for us, it also suggests that the experience helped them to build a resilience to deal with pressures and to overcome tensions within a performative culture.

Our reflections, supported by Pring's (1999) insights, lead us to claim that these teachers develop a 'practical wisdom' within a university setting. That wisdom may have the potential to equip teachers to raise the attainment of their students thus addressing concerns of a 'plateau problem' and of limited improvement 'reach'. Perhaps more important, in our view, is that the experience of becoming a researcher and master's graduate builds the resilience of these talented young teachers. Equipped with such resilience, they are far more likely to continue to work effectively in their challenging schools. There, they will open up spaces for different ways of working and begin to challenge systemic inequalities. We would claim that those ways of working are ways that the young people who attend these *Teach First* schools both need and deserve.

PART THREE

Researchers as Theorizers

CHAPTER NINE

School–University Research Partnerships: Knowledge Production and the Impact of Rapid Reform

Ruth McGinity

Introduction

The purpose of this chapter is to provide an analytical account of the ongoing and multifaceted research relationship between Kingswood School, an eleven-to-eighteen secondary school in the north west of England, and the University of Manchester, during a period of rapid reform in English educational policymaking. The period, between 2004 and 2013, saw a number of significant reforms within the field of educational policy, highlighting the cross-party political consensus of and commitment to the re-articulation of the purposes and values of schooling in late twentieth- and early twenty-first-century England along neo-liberal lines. Throughout this chapter, I deploy the term 'neo-liberal policy complex' to refer to the development of a complex public policy context in England 'premised on the extension of market relationships' (Larner, 2000, p. 5) to the work and to the organization of schools.

In particular, I focus upon two main policy areas that have had significant impact upon the development of the school's agenda setting, as well as upon the research relationship between the school and the university. Each of these policy areas is connected to the firmly established position of the 'standards agenda' within the neo-liberal policy complex identified above.

Kingswood: A specialist school

The *first* of these areas is the *Specialist School's Programme*, a policy introduced by the Conservative government in 1993, and subsequently adopted – and expanded – under New Labour from 1997, only to be discarded by the Conservative-led coalition in 2010. Through this programme, schools could apply to become 'specialist' in particular curriculum areas, the objective being to further the diversity of educational provision in England, as a mechanism for driving up standards (DfES, 2001; Bell and West, 2003; Exley, 2012). Under this policy, Kingswood successfully applied to become a specialist school and this process was marked by the inception of the university and school partnership as Helen Gunter (University of Manchester) and Pat Thomson (University of Nottingham) were funded by the now privatized Innovations Unit at the then Department for Education and Skills (DfES) to undertake an evaluation study of the school's emphasis on 'internal research as a method for renewing purposes and developing organisational processes' (McGinity and Gunter, 2012, p. 2).

Kingswood: An academy

The *second* area is related to the introduction of the Academies Act (2010). Again, in keeping with the 'codification' of the neo-liberal policy complex, this was part of a reform trajectory introduced by the Conservatives in the early 1990's, adopted but adjusted by New Labour in the early part of the millennium, and accelerated under the current Conservative-led coalition government in 2010, leading to the legislative framing of the policy as the Academies Act in 2010 (Thomson, 2010a). The programme, in its various guises, also purported to raise standards through diversifying provision in England, enabling schools to become autonomous institutions, with 'new freedoms' from local authority control (DfE, 2010/2011). It was during my year as an ESRC funded doctoral researcher that the school successfully applied and converted to become an academy. As such, this move had a significant effect upon the collaborative research trajectory.

Research partnerships: A rationale

I argue in this chapter that researching the localized enactments of these significant reform processes highlights the criticality of developing collaborative research relationships between schools and higher educational institutions. This is important in order to provide spaces in which professionals can reflect upon *how* schools are engaging with, and articulating, their *purposes* and *values* within a neo-liberal policy complex, as a part of a wider discourse of knowledge production. But I am reflexive and critical about such endeavours. For, the data I generated and analysed also suggest that the *power* of the neo-liberal policy complex over both school organization, and the subjectivities of professionals working within them, are such that the capacity of schools to provide alternatives is restricted by their need to 'play the game' (Bourdieu, 1990).

Localized policy processes are, I argue, framed in such a way that 'misrecognize' this restricted capacity as a necessity to survive in an increasingly centralized, regulated and market-driven landscape (Bourdieu and Wacquant, 1992). The impact of these restrictive capacities upon the model of collaborative research partnerships for the development of knowledge production between schools and universities is subsequently critiqued.

Contextualizing research partnerships

The process of developing collaborative research partnerships between schools and universities has been taken up in a number of guises in England. Researchers have worked on funded projects in collaboration with schools in areas relating to teachers' work, professional development and developing teachers-as-researchers (Little and McLaughlin, 1993; Zeichner, 1995; McLaughlin et al., 2004; Gunter et al., 2005; Day, 2008). There is also a large body of literature that has been produced as a result of the school effectiveness and school improvement movement (Teddlie and Reynolds 2000). Many of these studies have been developed as a means of *evaluating* the impact of policies on working lives in schools and as a means of *critiquing* professional and organizational practices (Fielding, 2000; Smyth, 2007; McGinity and Gunter, 2012).

With the advent of government accredited qualifications entering the field of school leadership (e.g. National Professional Qualification for Headship), the movement of teacher education into schools (Schools Direct), and school practitioners undertaking postgraduate qualifications, many practitioners undertake small-scale research projects within their school settings as part of their professional development pathways. As such, the practice of research within the teaching profession in collaboration with, or under supervision from, a higher educational institute has become commonplace (Carr and Kemmis, 1986; Gunter, 2001; Gunter and Forrester, 2009).

While these varied forms of school and university research partnerships have undoubtedly contributed to the development of a rich landscape of knowledge production in the field of educational research, criticism has been levelled at the lack of impact that research outcomes have on teaching practices (Hargreaves, 1996; McIntyre, 2005). In developing an argument from Hargreaves (1996), McIntyre (2005, p. 358) posits that the shaping of research agendas often come from researchers themselves, rather than from practitioners in schools.

However, the socio-political and economic territory of research agenda setting within the neo-liberal policy complex is a far more knotty landscape than this argument allows for. Writing on models of collaboration in universities in the UK, David Smith (2001, p. 132) postulates that research agenda setting is increasingly beset by a 'paradigm shift from discovery to utility' in which increasingly universities research agendas are being narrowed by the neo-liberal discourse of efficiency, accountability and effectiveness:

> there are also deeper shifts in the organisational, epistemological and functional bases of research. Increasingly, the academic model is being replaced by what Ziman terms an 'industrialised' or 'post-academic science'. It is marked by regulation, accountability, contracts and the decline of autonomy. (p. 136)

In this context then, educational researchers working with schools to develop collaborative research agendas are also tightly bound up with the challenge of operating within an increasingly restrictive capacity in which competition, performativity and accountability are also the established and legitimate cornerstones of activity within *universities* (Giroux, 2002). In fact, such conditions mirror well the circumstances in which many practitioners in schools have to function. As such, this mirroring provides an urgent reason for universities and schools to create research partnerships which look to critique, and to challenge, these restrictive positions.

The research partnership between Kingswood and the University of Manchester is a good example of the challenges that face collaborative agenda setting under such circumstances. Such practices provide important spaces for academics and practitioners to come together to reflect and analyse the impact of the neo-liberal policy complex on both the professional practice and the research relationship. This reflection and analysis in turn can identify jointly the restrictive capacity such complexes may actually have on how schools 'do' policy (Ball et al., 2012).

In this respect, there is an important call for collaboration between schools and universities to undertake research which challenges the orthodoxies under which the neo-liberal policy complex operates. In doing so, such work provides the evidence for developing research-based agenda setting as a means of contributing a 'democratic project in education, which in turn contributes to democracy as the creation of an informed, active citizenry, supported as Dewey (1916) imagined, by an informed, activated system of public education' (Ozga, 2000a, p. 2). I shall now illustrate some of the potential for, as well as some of the challenges of, the collaborative activities with which I have been closely involved.

Kingswood

Kingswood High School (as it was until April 2012) is a school in a small and seemingly affluent market town. It is the only secondary school in the town, attracting students from a large and diverse catchment area. This area includes the town itself and surrounding villages and towns. There are also large numbers of students from a neighbouring metropolitan borough that operates the 11+ system. The head teacher was employed in his current role in 1997. Since then, the school has witnessed rises in attainment as measured by the percentage of students achieving 5 A*–C Grades (including English and Maths) in their General Certificate of Secondary Education (GCSE). Between 1999 and 2002, the students' attainment increased from 47 per cent to 66 per cent, compared to national figures of 48 per cent and 52 per cent respectively. As such, under the leadership of the current head teacher, the school has a 'successful' track record, as measured by the performativity and accountability mechanisms embedded within the neo-liberal policy complex.

Where policy and practice meet research

In 2002 the school applied for, and was successful in achieving, specialist school status under the specialist schools programme (DfES, 2001). As a result of this nomenclature, the school also underwent a process of significant restructuring. The head teacher and the leadership team introduced a number of changes to the curriculum and to pedagogical and organizational structures within the school. Along with the specialization, these changes were in response to New Labour's commitment to the personalization of public services (Leadbeater, 2004; Miliband, 2004; Rogers in this book). Significant changes adopted by the head included the introduction of a project-based, cross-curricular learning module for students in years seven and eight as well as a broad choice agenda for students in year nine to 'specialize' in curriculum areas in which they were particularly interested. There was also the collaborative development of a '*Learning Policy*' (McGinity and Gunter, 2012).

These reforms reflected New Labour's commitment to the place that personalization could have in the modernization of public services, a development that my colleague, Stephen Rogers, critiques elsewhere in this book. This discourse about 'personalization', while limited in the realization of policy developments under New Labour, further indicated the commitment to the discourse of choice and competition within the lexicon of the neo-liberal policy complex (Johnson, 2004). Kingswood's implementation of curriculum reform based upon some of the core principles behind the personalization agenda, along with the 'successful' results and the entry into the specialist schools programme, led the school to the attention of and a subsequent grant from the Innovation Unit at the (then named) DfES in 2004. Thus, the inception of a decade long research partnership with the University of Manchester began. The head teacher described this period as such:

[T]hat innovation unit grant that we got was fantastic, it was an acknowledgement from central government that we were doing things really that most schools weren't in terms of personalisation. (Interview with head teacher, January 2011)

School–University research collaboration as 'symbolic capital'

Within the field of educational policymaking, such a successful track record indicates that the school, led by a strategic and deft head teacher, had efficaciously accumulated *symbolic capital*, which in turn was staked to locate the school in a favourable position within the landscape of diverse and competitive provision. Bourdieu defined symbolic capital as 'the form that the various species of capital assume when they are perceived and recognized as legitimate' (Bourdieu, 1989, p. 76). Bourdieu (1990) explained,

We have different fields where different forms of interest are constituted and expressed. This does not imply that the different fields do not have invariant properties. Among the invariant properties is the very fact that they are the site of a struggle of interests, between agents or institutions unequally endowed in specific capital. (p. 111)

The inception of the research partnership between Kingswood High School and two higher educational institutions, funded by a governmental department, arguably reflects the schools *legitimation* within the field of educational policymaking. Engaging in externally funded research in order to produce knowledge to be used for future agenda setting on policy and practice contributed to the schools' position in the policy complex under New Labour. For, New Labour explicitly linked their commitment to developing *evidence-based policymaking* as another lynchpin in their modernizing framework (Cabinet Office, 1999). However, as Exley (2009) cogently argues in relation to research into the specialist schools programme, there was evidence that in fact much commissioned research was being undertaken *for* policy as opposed to *of* policy. It is this distinction as Ozga (2000a) and Grace (1995) among others have argued, that highlights the importance of engaging with 'policy scholarship' as a means to undertake research that challenges the economizing agenda that has 'hollowed out' meanings and values from within the discourse of educational policymaking (Ozga, 2000a, pp. 6–7). In this process, it is vital that policy sociologists act as 'critical analysts of the change process' (Lieberman, 1992, p. 10) or as Apple (2010) implores, become 'critical secretaries'. It was in this tradition that the research relationship between the Universities of Manchester and Nottingham and Kingswood High School was established.

The symbolic capital accumulated by Kingswood with regards to the school's success in relation to the 'Standards Agenda' in the run up to the development of this research relationship undoubtedly played a role in the successful securing of research funding to undertake an evaluation of the change processes at Kingswood (Gunter and Thomson, 2004). The research project also contributed to the accumulation of symbolic capital for the researchers, in terms of acquiring funding from a high profile external source, as required as a result of performativity 'impact' measures such as the Research Excellence Framework (Hicks, 2012). The research partnership was developed in such circumstances that allowed the researchers – and the school – to collaborate on issues relating to policy and practice. These issues were of importance to the wider field of educational policymaking as a result of the specialist school status. Researchers were enabled to delve into specific and localized areas of interest, such as student voice, students-as-researchers and bullying (Thomson and Gunter, 2006, 2007). These forms of knowledge production fed into Kingswood's position as a school committed to research as an approach to develop policy and practice (McGinity and Gunter, 2012). As such, this research further reflected the school's place within the field in line with the expressed aims of New Labour's commitment to the development of research-based policies and practices. The head teacher wrote of the partnership:

> Not only were Professors Gunter and Thomson responsible for producing a major report as requested, they maintained contact with the School for a further two years, researching student voice activity in the school … Its purposes were to aid policy development in one of the school's priority areas and to develop the school's capacity in research and evidence-based policy development. (Head teacher Interview, 2013)

It was considered by the school that the collaborative research partnership had contributed to the development of knowledge production at both local and national levels. Within this context, the core aims and purposes of undertaking such research dovetailed well with the 'modernizing' agenda of New Labour. Yet it was also able to retain the critical position of *identifying areas within the school that required analysis and critique*. The meeting of the lines between the neo-liberal policy complex (during a time of investment in public services); the localized policymaking undertaken by the school; the school's position in the field as a 'success' in relation to the Standards Agenda; and the research expertise and interests of the educational researchers combined to produce a partnership which resulted in a number of internal and external proposals regarding future agenda setting (McGinity and Gunter, 2012). In this respect, the collaborative research partnership is a good illustration of how such relationships can be used to feed into both localized decision-making as well as providing space for critical policy scholarship.

The changing landscape: Collaboration post-2010

In 2009, a successful bid was awarded from the Economic and Social Research Council (ESRC) to Gunter in order to appoint a doctoral student in collaboration with Kingswood. The award facilitated work on localized policymaking at a time of rapid reform. Arguably, the symbolic capital that had been accumulated and referred to above played a significant part in the strength of the proposal. It also provided further attestation that such collaborative arrangements may be seen as useful for schools interested in developing a capacity to undertake locally produced evidence-based policy development. Significantly, between the approval of the funding from the ESRC and entering the research site, a change of government occurred and the Conservative led coalition took power. It is the impact that the Academies Act (2010) had on the school as a site of collaborative research that I want to focus on for the purposes of this chapter.

As discussed above, the school had already accumulated significant symbolic capital and, thus, legitimacy within the field of educational policymaking as a result of the specialist schools programme under New Labour. The framing of this policy in response to the personalization agenda was further reflected in one of the original intentions to focus the attention of the collaborative research agenda towards the evolving personalization of the curriculum on policy and practice in relation to different actors positioning within the school. However, by this time the Conservative led coalition had shifted the discourse away from 'personalization' as a singularly New Labour conception, and all references to this agenda had been quietly dropped from the field. In this respect, the research agenda also shifted away from focusing on this particular policy towards a focus upon how the enactment of localized decision-making positioned actors within the school, in particular with reference to the leadership decision to convert to an academy in April 2012.

There is not room here for an analysis of the school leadership's decision to convert to an academy. This can be found in detail elsewhere (McGinity and Gunter, 2015). What *is* important to note here is that the decision reflected both the school's commitment to maintaining its place within the field of educational policymaking and the central importance of the school's need to 'play the game' in order to continue to be recognized as legitimate (Bourdieu, 1990). As the head teacher said to me:

…So the DfE wouldn't have dealt with us if we weren't converting… We've had contact with the department. We ran a big project with the innovation unit and we've had a lot of links with the specialist schools trust and done a lot with and through them. But the department as it currently is, following government policy obviously, is only interested in academies. (Interview, December 2011)

During the data collection period, it became very clear from the interviews conducted with teachers that the decision to convert engendered a range of reactions. There was a number of staff who had concerns regarding the conversion, such as these two members of staff:

So I said to [the head teacher] straight away I don't believe in it … obviously what ever you decide to do, as with everything, you have my full support, publicly. As we got on board, the next conversation I had, its like big waves at the seaside, you can either choose to surf on top of it and wind up on the beach that way and smile and be ok, or you can just be rolled over and dragged until you are beached. Yeah? You are going to end up on the beach anyway so you might as well do it. And that's the way I see it…. (Interview, 2012)

I am ideologically opposed to the academy programme, because I think what it will do is break up a national system to such a degree that we will have school pitting against school, the most difficult of schools will just lose more and more kids. They wont be able to convert [on their own terms] the poorer schools won't be able to convert, they'll be forced to convert with a whole range of things around them. (Interview, 2012)

While there is not space here to analyse the importance of what these staff members are saying with regards to the policy of academization itself, the significance of teachers having the space through the research process to reflect upon, and offer up their opinions on, significant changes happening at the school is relevant in relation to research partnerships. These members of staff were, like most of their colleagues interviewed, reflexively engaged in viewing the process of educational reform as an innately political game.

While there were instances of frustration with some staff being keen to express dissatisfaction with the restrictive capacities placed upon them professionally by policies relating back to the 'Standards Agenda', there was also a notable vein of institutional loyalty running through their professional subjectivities. By locating such complexities within a Bourdieusian analytical framework it is possible to 'attempt to understand how "objective", supra-individual social reality (cultural and institutional social structure) and the internalized "subjective" mental worlds of individuals as cultural beings and social actors are inextricably bound up together, each being a contributor to – and indeed aspect – of the other' (Jenkins, 1992, pp. 19–20).

Reading Bourdieu; reading data on school–university collaboration

In particular, there is a need to reflect upon the meaning of these complicated and multifaceted social relations and the relationship between the objective and subjective worlds in which teachers must operate. There are differences between being in a 1:1 research situation, reflecting on policy enactments with a researcher, and being in the classroom and being professionally bound to the expected performativity and accountability mechanisms associated with the neo-liberal policy complex. The data suggest that participation in research, as a result of a cross institutional and collaborative arrangement, creates important spaces where reflexive subjectivities can challenge everyday organizational practices. Yet, the data also highlight the limited capacities of the research partnership, and the teachers themselves, to challenge some of the more powerful elements of the neo-liberal policy complex within the everyday institutional spaces that they occupy.

Changes were taking place, and it was the role of the teachers to ultimately acknowledge these changes as legitimate and to get on with playing the game in order to protect both their professional interests within the school and the interests of the school within the wider field of educational policymaking. Using Bourdieu, it is possible to theorize such position-taking within the conceptual framework of a doxa of misrecognition in which:

> Social agents who occupy particular positions understand how to behave in the field, and this understanding not only feels 'natural' but can be explained using the truths, or doxa, that are common parlance within the field. The doxa misrecognises the logics of practice at work in the field, so that even when confronted with the field's social (re) productive purpose social agents are able to explain it away. (Thomson, 2008, p. 70)

Elsewhere, Thomson goes on to cogently argue that such position-taking

> ... is the failure to see not only that the game is historically rigged, but also how the struggle to do better actually reproduces and keeps intact the capital that are being struggled over. The actual contest for the prizes in the field, driven by the desire in individual agents, keeps the field and its competitive and inequitable nature intact ... The doxa of devolution corresponds to the doxa of and the desire for autonomy; it creates a drive in agents that makes them operate according to the rules of the game as they stand. It works to make agents not only manage the field, but also compete over what is at stake – not to change the rules of the game or the knowledges, dispositions and strategies that constitute its winning formulae and its contribution to the wider mission of the state and the field of power. (Thomson, 2010, p. 16)

Thus, the teachers in the study, and the localized policymaking by the leadership team, may be viewed as *misrecognizing* the power of the neo-liberal policy complex in restricting their capacity to do things differently. The research partnership has a role to play within this matrix of misrecognition. While space existed within the confines of the interview room for the process of research to enable reflective position-taking for staff, and while space existed within 'academic' outputs in which to analyse such position-taking for me as a researcher, the formal structures that had been agreed with the school, in terms of data sharing and agenda setting, were in the form of report writing. It was through the process of drafting the report that it became clear that this space was limited to the extent to which a critical analysis of such instances of misrecognition was welcome to be offered up during a time of such intense and rapid reform processes.

The school was moving onto a bid to establish a 'Studio School' by this point, another exemplar of diversification of provision as a means of driving up standards. The rapidity of the localized policy trajectory along neo-liberal lines showed no signs of abating. The place of the research partnership in addressing concerns regarding the enactment of such policies, and on the positioning of different actors within the school community, looked to be restricted. Further agenda setting along collaborative lines also appeared to be restrictive. This was particularly apparent in one of the comments made by the deputy head regarding the academy programme. He said:

> There's no direct evidence that the academies programme before this one was successful in changing outcomes across the board.

What is of pertinence here is that in a school nominally committed to externally funded research as a means of developing evidence-based policymaking, a decision to convert to academy status was taken in full acknowledgement that no 'academy affect' had been identified (PwC, 2008). In this sense, the research partnership was shown to be restrictive in its potential. In turn, this raised the question as to what the purpose of such a research partnership was, if its purpose was not to use to research as a means of evidence-based agenda setting.

Conclusion

This chapter has charted the ongoing research relationship between the University of Manchester and Kingswood Academy during a time of rapid reform by using examples of how the school has framed its organizational development through the trajectory of what I identify as a neo-liberal policy complex. In doing so, I have aimed to highlight how the earlier part of the relationship gave evidence of school and educational researchers working together to develop a research agenda which would be useful in contributing to future pedagogical developments. In the latter part of the chapter, as the neo-liberal policy complex has become further entrenched into the discourse of localized policymaking, I illustrated that despite the existence of such a research arrangement, the need to 'play the game' and maintain a legitimate position within the field of educational policymaking provided a far more powerful drive to set agendas around neo-liberal lines. The willingness of the school to employ research to produce knowledge along more democratic and collaborative lines became restricted.

In a sense, the research relationship described above identifies a need to create collaborative arrangements in which cross-institutional critical debate regarding organizational reform can occur. However, it indicates that increasingly such spaces are to be squeezed out as schools 'play the game' in order to survive in the field. The democratic spaces that collaborative research partnerships can offer in which participants may feel they can 'speak the unspeakable' (Lieberman, 1992, p. 10) are at risk of being obscured by the perceived necessity of schools to adopt certain policies as a means to 'keep one step ahead of the game' (Interview, 2012).

The challenge is how schools and universities can collaborate in order to contribute to evidence-based policymaking at a local level within the restrictive capacities of the neo-liberal policy complex. This is important because together educational researchers and school practitioners have a great potential to challenge and critique policy orthodoxies in order to effect real, collaborative and democratic change:

> Researchers, resisting prescriptive shortcuts, share their conceptual frameworks and learn about and become more sensitive to real school contexts; practitioners theorize, analyze their own work, and take charge of their own professional lives. Scholarly activity then becomes a shared enterprise. (Lieberman, 1992, p. 9)

This is particularly significant because by doing so schools and universities will be in stronger positions to resist neo-liberal policy discourses which contribute to maintaining inequalities within the system. Apple reminds us that undertaking such democratic projects are crucial because 'understanding education requires that we situate it back into both the unequal relations of power in the larger society and the relations of exploitation, dominance, and subordination – and the conflicts – that generate and are generated by these relations' (Apple, 2013, p. 5). This chapter has illustrated the complexities of such projects and also the potential value of taking up such challenges.

CHAPTER TEN

Competing Identities of the Academic Researcher in Studies of Higher Education Participation: Ambassador or Observer?

Steven Jones

Introduction

In this chapter, I reflect on the delicate process of eliciting data from young people as they consider their post-compulsory educational options in the increasingly marketized context of English higher education. At a national level, debates about how universities should be funded are high profile, with some arguing that 'cost-sharing' measures are necessary to maintain institutional competitiveness following unprecedented sector expansion (Browne, 2010; BIS, 2011), and others noting that fees for students at English universities, even if deferred and collected through a more progressive repayment mechanism, remain among the highest in the world (OECD, 2012; McGettigan, 2013). This chapter focuses on how such tensions play out at a local level, particularly among students in lower-performing urban schools. The response of such young people has important ramifications for public policy in general, and the UK's widening participation agenda in particular. It is vital to monitor the extent to which the 2012 fee-increase (and the associated changes to non-repayable financial aid packages and loan settlement mechanisms) are understood, to assess the levels of debt aversion/tolerance among those directly affected and to consider the broader implications for social mobility (Milburn, 2012).

Research findings are presented elsewhere (Jones, forthcoming); what this chapter considers is the *role of the researcher* in drawing out the views of young people when potentially life-changing educational decisions are being considered. The first section deals with the dual role of the academic researcher: on the one hand, an ambassador of the higher education sector and a 'champion' of participation; and on the other hand, a disinterested and detached scholarly investigator. The second section deals with the process and practicalities of using theoretical social science tools as a means to interpret and conceptualize frontline educational research.

Overview of research undertaken

The research discussed in this chapter involved a series of interactions with classes of high academic achievers across several low participation, urban schools in the same city. According to the Office for National Statistics Atlas of Deprivation (2010), the city falls under one of the five most deprived local authorities in England, and each school's most recent Ofsted reports noted a disproportionately high number of pupils with Free School Meals eligibility. All schools are located in areas with an above-average proportion of residents with no qualifications and, according to the Income Deprivation Affecting Children Index, all are in the top 30 per cent of deprived Local Super Output Areas in England. Access was granted to year ten and eleven students who, based on attainment scores and rankings within the year group, fall in the top 40 per cent of achievers nationally and could therefore be considered suitable for progression to higher education. Contact with the young people took the form of a one-hour class. I led the sessions, and class teachers were present at all times.

Evidence about how young people from less advantaged backgrounds respond to the prospect of higher educational debt remains inconclusive. Maringe, et al. found that as long as the repayment schedule is sufficiently generous, debt did 'not seem a big deal' (2009, p. 156) to the young people they surveyed. For Callender and Jackson (2005), however, aversion is very much a socio-economic issue, even once class-related predispositions towards higher education were controlled for. Application and entry figures are inconclusive: Boliver (2013) reports that the 2004 fee rise did not disproportionately reduce applications from lower socio-economic backgrounds and initial evidence suggests that the 2012 hike resulted only in a short-term overall fall (UCAS, 2012). However, a lack of labour market alternatives may distort the picture for less advantaged applicants, and several studies have indicated that financial costs are a key consideration (and a potential deterrent) for would-be applicants (Paulsen and St John, 2002; Sutton Trust, 2010; Caetano et al., 2011).

A possible explanation for the range of (sometimes contradictory) findings reported in this area is the particular difficulty faced by the academic researcher in eliciting relevant data. The process is incestuous because one cannot avoid being seen as a representative of the research topic being investigated: the university. This inevitably affects the validity of the data. It also creates a dilemma for the academic researcher – how to obtain meaningful data without compromising an implicit professional responsibility to promote decisions about higher education that are in the best interests of those whose views are being elicited.

Researching with multiple roles

The role of Widening Participation (WP) activity is well established in most English universities. Government rhetoric, accompanied by funding incentives, have ensured that WP is a key performance indicator, and undergraduate demographics for top universities receive broad media attention, with participation rates judged against a range of 'disadvantage' variables, from post-code data to school performance. A wide body of literature has emerged to evaluate the extent to which fairness is achieved (Ogg et al., 2009; Boliver, 2011, 2013), and parliamentary debates on the topic are common (e.g. Hansard, 2011).

For many academics, therefore, WP activity is a part of the job, whether through visits to local schools, open days for under-represented groups or one-to-one sessions with individual students as part of an access programme. The goal is to sell the idea of higher education participation to those who may be under-informed about what university involves, or culturally disinclined towards entry because of non-pecuniary 'dislocation' fears (Reay et al., 2005) and the amount of 'identity work' required to fit in (Reay et al., 2010, p. 120).

Tuition fees muddy the waters of WP. Since 2004, when fees increased from £1,000 to £3,000 per year, higher education participation has become a financial gamble for disadvantaged groups as well as a cultural gamble. In the £9,000 era, WP activity is no longer able to focus exclusively on the benefits of attending university. It must also explain the economic implications. How much debt will be accrued? How much non-repayable financial help will be available? How much can graduates expect to earn in the job market? Cheerleaders for participation have become financial advisors.

Against this backdrop, using young people for research purposes becomes even more problematic for the academic researcher. How does one elicit views about participation without influencing responses by one's very presence?

To what extent, morally, can the WP agenda be simply put aside in order to uncover extant truths and dispositions? Or, to exemplify this dilemma in practice, should the researcher correct young people's misunderstandings and provide answers to their questions or remain silent because their role is to observe, not interfere?

Complicating any data gathering process are teachers who, keen to impress on students the importance of their guest speaker, inadvertently make the academic researcher's job more difficult. For example, when a short questionnaire was distributed to classes of about thirty students, results may have been distorted by one class teacher urging students to 'try very hard to answer the questions', or by another who introduced the questionnaire with: 'and let's remember to give a good impression of the school to our important visitor'. These well-meaning directives seemed to be reflected in the questionnaires returned, with students in those groups responding very differently to some questions. For example, in one class, only two students 'admitted' to not knowing anyone that had been to university. In groups from the same school that were not prompted to give a 'good impression' by their teacher, the distribution was markedly different, with the proportion being about 50 per cent. One teacher even distributed her own reformulated version of the pre-sent questionnaire so that 'better' answers would be received. Naturally, responses had to be discounted in any quantitative analysis.

Throughout the sessions, attempts were made to keep the data collection elements of the exercise separate from the WP elements. The goal was firstly to assess students' understanding of and attitude towards higher education and secondly – quite separately – to deliver a more traditional WP talk, explaining the likely benefits of participation and the financial support available. In practice, this proved impossible. Students began raising their hands from the outset, usually to ask pointed and intelligent questions, and all plans for a neatly bifurcated encounter disappeared.

What emerged in the place of quantitative data, however, was arguably something richer. Students' discussions with each other, and sometimes with their class teacher, proved highly instructive in revealing underlying predispositions towards university. As a researcher, I began to facilitate rather than orchestrate, intervening only to arbitrate on a specific factual dispute ('no, the new fee levels will be nine thousand *per year*, not nine thousand in total') or to assess broader levels of understanding ('okay, so Mrs Hanif has just mentioned a *bursary* – hands up who knows what a *bursary* is'). In most cases, students were able to resolve issues among themselves, without my intervention. For example, a question was asked in one class about whether Muslim students were allowed to pay interest on a debt. This triggered a series of responses from around the classroom, including reassurances that such loans were considered acceptable in the absence of alternatives.

At other times, however, the very presence of an academic researcher appeared to contaminate the data. For example, it was noticeable that many students apologized before making negative comments about university ('sorry, but it's just not somewhere I want to go'). Those who had already decided against participation were particularly unforthcoming, especially when their teacher was in earshot, often responding with little more than a shrug when asked to say a little more about the decision they had made. However, such reticence was informative in itself, revealing much about those students' internal negotiation between perceived educational and societal expectations and more localized life-course narratives.

'Adapting to the flow' as a researcher

Strategies are available to counterbalance the risk of data contamination, of course. For example, it may be the case that 'insider' research would improve the validity of findings (though it is difficult to imagine how any adult could canvas views about higher education participation from young people without being seen as a role model or representative of a particular pathway). Or, it may be that the researcher needs to be flexible, and adapt to the flow of the class discussion, choosing her or his moments to intervene carefully and giving students the space to express and renegotiate their ideas. In my experience, such 'researcher invisibility' yielded the most favourable results.

A more substantial risk is that the WP aims of the higher education sector, and society at large, could be bruised by a data gathering procedure that encourages young people to speak openly about their feelings towards participation and therefore, potentially, to communicate negative messages. On occasions, some students did indeed express unconstructive views about university, whether in relation to the costs involved ('I don't get it – how can it ever be worth *that* much?') or their personal anxieties about fitting in ('it's not me though, is it?'). However, by allowing young people to speak freely, it was interesting to note how discourses evolved and student continually positioned and repositioned themselves in response to new information. Upon learning that fees would be £9,000 per year, the mood was low. Upon fully understanding that none of the debt would be repayable until earnings reached £21,000 per year, the atmosphere improved. Information about bursaries and grants helped raise spirits further (though perhaps not as much as sometimes assumed). However, deep-rooted, individualized inclinations remained stubbornly difficult to shift. For those who had simply had enough of education or whose family and friends were not assuredly pro-participation, structured interaction with more positively predisposed classmates had little impact.

Public rhetoric about participation tends to suggest that the repayment schedule for higher fees is so favourable that the only barrier to participation is ignorance (Lewis, 2012). In practice, young people wanted to know more about the system. Questions were often asked about how interest accrues, how inflation and pay rises affect projected repayments, how average graduate salaries differ by subject, and how likely students are to repay their debt in full. Brynin (2013, p. 284) has noted that 'a rising proportion of graduates receive only average pay' and students were keen to learn more about the financial gamble involved, and how the graduate premium breaks down across subject areas and institution types. Cynicism was sometimes expressed that the economic benefits of participation were exaggerated ('where do we get jobs worth that much round here?'). However, once relevant information was provided, young people (or at least those from more disadvantaged backgrounds) appeared to grow in confidence. Not all indicated that they would apply to university, but most reported the participation process to be less mystified and took a step towards having firmer ownership of the decisions that lay ahead. Because they had been allowed to discuss and share ideas openly, without the presence of an overbearing 'authority' figure, the interaction arguably served WP aims just as effectively as more traditional modes of delivery.

I now consider the extent to which theories of education accommodate the kind of responses elicited from young people facing a new funding model for higher education system. Particular attention is given to two sources: *The State Nobility*, Pierre Bourdieu's 1996 study of prize-winners in competitive examinations for French students, which shares some similarities with the research described here as young people from less advantaged backgrounds compete for limited places at top educational institutions; and *The Right to Higher Education*, Penny Jane Burke's (2012) critique of societal inequalities in the UK and the politics of misrecognition.

Thinking with theory: Bourdieu and 'playing the game'

Bourdieu's 'thinking tools' (2000) of field, habitus and capital are a useful place to begin. Here, the arena of practice (field) is higher education, young people's dispositions and tastes (habitus) are revealed through the language they use to talk about participation, and the assets available (capital) incorporate everything from students' academic ability, for which attainment is a proxy, to their family connections and extra-curricular activities.

Research into higher education access regularly draws on Bourdieu's work (e.g. Reay et al., 2005; Byrom, 2010) to expose the means by which social class structures are reinforced and reproduced. For example, students are discussed in terms of their ability and inclination to 'play the game' (Bourdieu, 2000), and the symbolic effects of different forms of capital (Bourdieu, 1997) have been drawn upon to explain why equal attainment applicants do not share the same likelihood of being offered a place at top universities (Boliver, 2013; Jones, 2013). Zimdars (2010) finds evidence of 'homophily' in her study of admission tutors, suggesting that selectors may subconsciously recruit in their own image. This recalls Bourdieu's observation that applicants must demonstrate the 'dispositions to be, and above all to become "one of us"' (Bourdieu, 2000, p. 100) and raises equity questions about the prospects of young people from disadvantaged, urban areas as they attempt to play the higher education admissions game. Of those surveyed for the research described above, few were able to self-conceptualize in academically appropriate ways. They repeatedly positioned themselves as outsiders in the schooling system, and their language betrayed a distrust of education in general and – partly because of its price – higher education in particular. Few demonstrated a familiarity with the system or the confidence and capacity to 'stand out from the crowd' (Jones, 2013).

'What new entrants must bring into the game', according to Bourdieu, 'is not only the habitus that is tacitly or explicitly demanded there but a habitus that is practically compatible, or sufficiently close, and above all malleable and capable of being converted into the required habitus' (2000, p. 100). As noted in relation to the personal statements of students from low participation schools, however, 'evidence points to great variation in habitus compatibility' (Jones, 2013). And in the classroom, a similar pattern emerges. Though all of the young people surveyed had the academic ability to participate in higher education, many expressed themselves in a deeply non-scholarly fashion, often drawing censure from class teachers who held firm views about the type of persona needed to enter and succeed in higher education. Bourdieu (2000) notes that the game is not 'rigged', but likens it to a 'handicap race' in which some applicants are more advantaged than others. Evidence pointed to students self-handicapping themselves out of contention, often weighed down by inappropriate symbolic capital and burdened with cultural misconceptions and incomplete information.

However, the main form of capital lacked by those young people surveyed remains economic. In the UK, low socio-economic status generally results in lesser academic attainment and, according to commentators such as Callender and Jackson (2005) and Voigt (2007), a more pronounced resistance to accumulating high levels of debt. Within the research, evidence of what Finnie (2002) calls 'sticker price' aversion – a reluctance to participate because the total monetary commitment is so great compared to anything previously encountered – was commonplace. Such are the levels of debt accumulated, even by students in receipt of bursaries and grants, no repayment mechanism could be sufficiently sympathetic to compensate.

Findings also confirm that social capital – including the family networks and personal connections that may help students to access work experience, receive high quality guidance about the admissions process, etc. – is not evenly distributed (Bourdieu, 1997; Dekker and Uslaner, 2001). Despite their curiosity, students' understanding of higher education generally drew on 'cold information' (Reay et al., 2005) and unreliable, localized narratives. These narratives were often communicated through extended family channels ('two of my cousin's mates went [to university] and neither of them finished') and proved difficult to correct even when fallacious ('you only get a grant if your mum and dad live in separate houses'). Cultural capital was plentiful but rarely of the kind that could be productively exchanged in higher education admissions processes. Students perceived their life experience and their extra-curricular activity to be far removed from that of campus life.

Also prevalent in the research conducted was evidence of self-exclusion resulting of academic self-doubt or intellectual under-confidence ('I don't know if I'm that good though – I'd never keep passing everything'). Bourdieu notes that the choosers offer themselves up for choosing, but 'others spontaneously exclude themselves from a competition that would exclude most of them anyway' (1996, p. 141). In the classroom, self-exclusion also manifested itself as rejection of orthodox educational systems, contempt for an undergraduate culture perceived as artificial, and a loyalty to one's own 'authentic' identity. Two male students (independently) bragged that they had already attended the 'university of life'; a third described the environment in which he grew up as a 'ghetto university'. The primary function of such comments may be to foster peer respect, but they also work to sidestep engagement with participation discourse. By casting their own life experience as an incompatible alternative to higher education, less advantaged students are able to reframe the debate in terms of conventional universities failing to accommodate or recognize their potential contribution. This rationalizes a decision to self-exclude without admitting structural injustice or personal rejection.

But why does this matter? Higher education need not be for all young people and public discourse increasingly focuses on alternatives to further learning, such as work-based apprenticeships. For Bourdieu, the consequence of unevenly distributed opportunity is a fractured society and, ultimately, the emergence of 'nobility': a privileged minority comprised of the holders and regulators of institutionalized social capital.

> When the process of social rupture and segregation that takes a set of carefully selected chosen people and forms them into a separate group is known and recognized as a legitimate form of election, it gives rise in and of itself to symbolic capital that increases with the degree of restriction and exclusivity of the group so established. The *monopoly*, when recognized, is converted into a *nobility*. (Bourdieu, 1996, p. 79)

According to many studies into higher education participation, this monopoly – and therefore nobility – arises because some young people are better inducted into the game of higher education than others. Evidence of this is ubiquitous in the research described above, from misunderstandings about the loan structure with which new entrants must engage to misconceptions about the academic requirements and cultural landscape of a university experience with which they have little familiarity. This is reminiscent of Bourdieu's (2000) observation that 'what is important…is less what is explicitly taught than what is tacitly taught' (p. 231). For many young people, the academic ability is there – albeit not always self-recognized – but rarely is it complemented by insight into the nature of the education market and awareness of how to develop and exchange appropriate forms of symbolic capital.

Thinking with theory: Burke and 'deconstructed discourse'

Burke (2012) takes Bourdieu's line of thinking further – and challenges tendencies to conceptualize under-participation in 'deficit' terms, as though it were the fault of young people themselves for not 'fitting in' – by considering the role of institutional misrecognition. She argues that judgements about candidates' potential rest on 'privileged ontological dispositions (i.e. those coded as middle class, white and heterosexual)' (2012, p. 105). Common in classroom discussions of participation was potential being expressed in alternative ways. Students did not come across as budding academics but rather as ideally placed to benefit from exposure to a broader range of teaching styles, from encouragement to think differently and critique their surroundings, and from the confidence to see and articulate themselves differently. Note that recent studies (e.g. Ogg et al., 2009) continue to suggest that undergraduates from lower socio-economic backgrounds outperform equal attainment peers from more privileged backgrounds when they complete their degree programmes at university.

Burke deconstructs discourses of participation, rejecting terms like 'barrier' and 'disadvantage' because they cast some young people as in need of remedial help from the middle classes. Her observation that 'predominantly' middle-class applicants 'talk their way on to a course' by having symbolic cultural capital (2012, p. 44) was upheld by the absence of such linguistic capital in the research described above. For Burke, the habitus of young people is central to understanding the decisions they make, though she questions the extent to which such decisions are actually the result of personal agency:

> Habitus illuminates the ways that unequal relations of power become internalized and naturalized so that decisions to participate in higher education (or not) are seen as freely made individual choices. (2012, p. 60)

The newest variable for would-be higher education applicants in England to factor is the deferred cost of participation, currently up to £9,000 per year for fees alone. Burke notes that 'willingness to accept debt as an inevitable part of the pursuit to "success" is tied to particular (white, middle class) values and dispositions, as well as certain (neoliberal) political and cultural conceptions' (2012, p. 139). Unwillingness to accept debt may therefore be tied to other values and dispositions, often the kind associated with young people from non-traditional backgrounds. Evidence of this was rife, with students incorporating non-pecuniary factors into their participation decisions and often being unconvinced (or unimpressed) by the promised gains in lifetime income associated with attending university ('no-one *guarantees* you get paid extra though, do they?'). This is particularly concerning in light of Bachan's (2013) finding that students who are pessimistic about future earnings tend to be more resistant towards student debt. The formula of risk aversion and education aversion often seemed particularly potent, with a number of students indicating that a more substantial and failsafe graduate premium was needed before they could be persuaded to stay in education for a further three years.

Why 'think with theory' in policy research?

The modes of 'thinking with educational theory' that my colleagues and I try to exemplify in this book are essential both for contextualizing data in terms of structural inequity, as Bourdieu's work (1984, 1996, 2000) helps us to do, and for reflecting on how current institutional practices and discourses may be in need of attention, as Burke (2012) argues.

The decision-making process undertaken by would-be applicants today is very different from that of previous generations. Though the broad range of cultural dispositions noted by Reay et al. (2005) are still in operation, and reproduction of class-driven behaviour still observable, the picture is complicated by the introduction of higher fees and the prospect of three decades of graduate debt repayment. Educational theory allows us to take the responses of those affected and interpret them through a social science lens. Though the context may be different, the underlying structural inequities still exert the same pressures on those in possession of the least symbolic capital.

In most cases, a key requirement of any data gathering process is that the gatherer remains objective and does not influence findings. Studies into higher education participation test this principle to the limit, the process being distorted – but also potentially enriched – by the perceived and actual identities of those involved in the research. Traditional approaches to WP place the academic as an ambassador for higher education, encouraging students to participate in order to benefit financially and culturally, both for private gain and for public good. However, the increased marketization of UK higher education problematizes this role, as participation becomes an economic gamble for almost all students as well as a cultural gamble for those from non-traditional backgrounds who fear identity loss or compromise.

Researcher neutrality is almost impossible to maintain, both in the eyes of students and teaching staff. However, strategies are available to minimize contamination and allow data to remain robust. In particular, adopting a discourse analysis approach, and positioning oneself as an informed bystander (rather than central figure of authority) allows observations to be made that, though not necessarily 'pure', are nonetheless instructive and insightful when recurring themes and dispositions are unpicked.

Thinking with social science theory enables further contextualization of the research area to facilitate researchers' interpretation of data. For example, Burke's 'take' on the educational theory outlined above is that 'at the heart of Bourdieu's work...is attention to *struggle* rather than reproduction' (2012, p. 41). Evidence of this struggle repeatedly surfaces in research into perceptions of higher education among low participation groups. Often internalized as a conflict between notions of individual authenticity and the possible pay-off from entry into a sphere to which their communities may have felt historically excluded, and culturally adrift, this struggle is both shaped by, and feeds into, wider structural issues of social class reproduction.

Conclusion

Partnerships between higher education and young people from low participation backgrounds are more vital than ever in a higher fees era. However, the nature of this partnership must evolve to meet the changing context: gathering data becomes more pragmatically challenging and widening participation more ethically complex. For students, the struggle is to better understand how higher education works, both economically (in terms of the fee structure, repayment schedule and likely graduate premium) and culturally (in terms of what university is like, how to avoid academic failure, and how to self-identify within a new and very different educational setting). Not all would-be applicants are equally equipped to understand and to weigh up these variables. Bourdieu's notion of symbolic capital allows us to better understand cultural disinclinations.

What higher education must continue bringing to the partnership is a readiness to employ the most appropriate research strategies available in order to bear witness to the ways in which public policy affects all levels of society and to press for the most incisive and evidence-based interventions. This need not be incompatible with the more traditional role of the academic to widen participation by acting as an ambassador for the sector as well as being an insider authority on the 'rules of the games'.

CHAPTER ELEVEN

Virtue and Ethics in Education Policy Research: The Case of 'Personalized Learning' and 'Voice'

Stephen Rogers

Introduction

This chapter emerges from a period of research into the New Labour government's (1997–2010) policy of personalizing public services and, specifically, the concept of *personalized learning* in English schools. My research examined the experiences of young people and their head teachers as they lived through this period of reform. I posit the link between the social imaginaries of multiple, late modernities; and examine how the personal is implicated in the processes of policymaking. The concept of the *social imaginary* (Taylor, 2007) serves to highlight how personalization acted as a rubric for a policy trajectory that connected to seemingly remote social and cultural transformations: the rise of consumerism; social media targeted at personalizing services. My claim is that personalization was grounded in New Labour's propositions about social justice and their social democratic legacy.

Personalization was a policy redolent with the promise of providing young people with some 'voice', a midwife to richer democratic relationships in public institutions such as schools. The research thus explored a number of tensions and paradoxes in policy enactment (for example, the motif of the 'citizen-consumer', Clarke et al., 2007). The research further explored how personalization can be subject to both what Paul Ricouer (1970) would term a hermeneutics of suspicion (see, for example, Baudrillard, 1988), and can also be subject to a celebration of personalization's potential to enhance the productive power of contemporary Western capitalism (see for example, Zuboff and Maxmin, 2004).

The context of the research

The research took place in three English secondary schools that had some degrees of 'leading edge typicality' (Schofield, 1993, p. 103) in that their head teachers were all active in promoting personalized learning and their student population represented diverse sets of cultural and social backgrounds. The head teachers were interviewed. Groups of young people involved in 'student voice' work participated in several focus group activities similar to those outlined by Davies in this publication. Various policymakers and head teachers of other schools were also interviewed in the course of the research.

My key research questions were to understand how policy was enacted and translated by head teachers; to assess the impact upon young peoples' sense of agency in schools; and then to make some evaluation of the potential impact upon wider questions of social justice. This chapter is not so much about the findings of the research per se. Moreover, personalizing learning, or personalization (the terms were used interchangeably), as a major policy platform for New Labour presents me with an important opportunity to *critically examine the complexities of researching in a political environment where government ministers purportedly drew upon popular imaginaries in order to effect structural changes.*

New Labour, personalization and research

New Labour's *Children's Plan* claimed that: 'In the best schools in the country, excellent classroom practice has already established a pedagogy and culture of personalized teaching and learning' (DCSF, 2007, 3.54, p. 63). But 'excellent' and 'best' are deeply normative terms, suffused with political meanings. It is in the interplay between observing, questioning and theory, that researching can make an important contribution to understanding these hidden norms and their operation. Researching in schools often skirts uneasily around normative questions of what one *ought* to do in a given practice, working in a complex interplay between describing, critiquing and posing alternatives. Public policy is always a matter of what a service, or a society in general, ought to be doing and is thus invariably a matter in which philosophical thinking should be useful.

Research is always making some form of truth claim. Given the policy claims about personalization as being a critical matter of social justice (Gilbert, 2006), educational research into these claims *must* have some reasoned arguments as to why one form of practice or one set of values is preferable to another in pursuing just outcomes. One of the policy claims, couched in terms of increasing human capital, is that greater parental choice, and increased student voice in learning, leads to more distributive justice through enhanced access to the labour market. My colleague Emery, in this book, considers the concept of 'voice' in his research through the application of tools from critical discourse analysis. I argue, in this chapter, that another way of thinking about the research dilemmas of voice in this policy context lies in the use of an ethical philosophy drawn from the work of Alasdair MacIntyre. I select this perspective as it acknowledges that philosophical thinking takes place within particular historical and social contexts and provides reasoned grounds for making ethical judgements, not in spite of, but through, this contingency (MacIntyre, 1994).

MacIntyre on moral manipulation: Ethical theory and educational research

I use some of the theoretical insights from MacIntyre's work in order to work through two, linked phases of argument in this chapter. In the first, the dilemmas of researching the agency of head teachers and young people are examined in the context of a critique of moral modes of manipulation in the political culture of English secondary education at the time of my research. Head teachers experienced particular challenges through having to deal with competing models of governance that created tensions concerning the heads' sense of agency (Newman, 2001). Some of the dilemmas in my research were age-old ones of conducting qualitative research. I was both insider and outsider to many of the people I researched with in similar ways to those described by other contributors to this book. Some of the dilemmas of educational research I experienced were, I suspect, unique to this contemporary political conjuncture, in which an ever more narrow definition of 'use value' became the 'ghost' in the research practice.

Second, I turn to MacIntyre's account of social practices to explore how reasoned ethical judgements can be made to evaluate the 'state' of student voice. In so doing, I make the case for research as a political act that can point to possibilities and alternatives. I conclude by using the ethical theory to make an assessment of the balance between optimism and pessimism as to the possibilities for witnessing some richer, more authentic person-centered as well as democratically centered forms of schooling.

Applying ethical theory to educational research

MacIntyre's work has aroused controversy, debate and much interest (for example, Knight and Blackledge, 2008). MacIntyre has frequently admitted to being on a philosophical journey, continually responding to his previous positions. I take as a starting point his arguments in *After Virtue* (1981/1994), where he outlines his concepts of 'social practices'; his reworking of Aristotelian virtue ethics; and his critique of Western modernity's forms of moral manipulation.

At the heart of *After Virtue* is, for some, the controversial and pessimistic critique of the ills of late modernity and the inability of the liberal tradition to provide rational grounds for resolving ethical conflicts and difficulties (see for example, Chappell, 2008; Feinberg, 2012). This is because contemporary moral discourse is characterized by 'emotivism' (MacIntyre, 1994, p. 11): a doctrine that, 'all moral judgements are nothing but expressions of preference' (1994, pp. 11–12). So there are no grounds for a shared moral discourse, no evaluative language for judging and agreeing upon, for example, the claims of a policy to have impacted upon social justice or to identify what such justice might even look like. This might seem like an extreme and unsustainable claim. But, when one considers the levels of disagreement and interminable circularity of much educational research, there is a suspicion that there may be some justification for the proposition.

What the above argument does point to is how contemporary policy propositions reduce what are *ethical* questions to *technical* ones, even if the propositions are couched in moral aims such as social justice. Examining the supposed expertise embodied in the 'characters' of modernity highlights the fracture between ethical and technical claims in policy. MacIntyre deliberately adopts a dramaturgical metaphor in proposing that the 'characters' of modernity (the aesthete, the manager and the therapist) embody moral modes of manipulation. The metaphor of character suggests not so much the particular roles and the activities of individuals but a generalized moral representation of a culture. The manager takes the ends of a practice as given and: 'represents in his *character* the obliteration of the distinction between manipulative and nonmanipulative social relations' (1994, p. 30, original emphasis).

The 'manager' holds authority, through expertise and the promise of effectively securing outcomes but: 'the concept of managerial effectiveness is after all one more contemporary moral fiction and perhaps the most important one' (MacIntyre, 1994, pp. 106–7). This is not because the 'manager' lacks skills and knowledge, but because the claims to expertise rest upon a number of illusions. For example, 'management expertise' imagines a mechanistic view of how humans act and behave: a corresponding 'myth' that law-like generalizations and predictions can be made by experts and that these experts can claim morally neutral knowledge. Through the appeal of a manager's authority, systematic public ethical discussion of the *telos* or *ends* of social practices are negated in favour of the technical specification of seemingly rational interventions that claim to be morally neutral and objectively appropriate.

Of course, one can object that school leaders as managers debate and talk about moral purpose, the values that brought them into their work, and labour to maintain their sense of purpose. Indeed, my research interviews were redolent with accounts of value and purpose. However, the milieu in which such values are debated and exchanged in public service takes place within competing values of governance (Newman, 2001). Hierarchical control is exerted through audit of rational goals expressed in short-term targets; a head teacher is at severe personal risk if they are not met (see Mills, 2011, for an account of primary schools head teachers' experiences of being subject to such demands). Such demands can be met through attempting to become technically proficient at meeting the narrow range of criteria that come to represent a moral manipulation of the social relations that ought to characterize education. Later in the chapter, I will use MacIntyre's (2001) distinction between goods of *effectiveness* and those of *excellence* to explore this claim a bit further.

Researching modernization in schools

At this point, I examine what it was that might have made the political climate, as well as the contemporary context of schooling at the time I was carrying out my research, different in respect to the notion of moral manipulation. I also discuss some of the consequent research dilemmas, old and new.

The New Labour governments in England (1997–2010) embarked upon a prolific policy reform of public services. Schools in particular were central to the Labour Party's restructuring process. There are arguments to be had as to whether New Labour's 'Third Way' represents an accommodation to neo-liberalism (a 'double-shuffle', Hall, 2003, unpaged web; Duggan, in this book), or is a more confused and nuanced mixture of discourses (see Newman, 2001). Either way, for many professionals reform seemed to move at an 'obsessive' and 'pathological' pace of restructuring, leaving little or no space for evaluation or consideration of the effects of this 'hyperactivity' (Pollitt, 2007, p. 531). The trajectory of the narrow range of audit measures, with their concomitant malaise of mistrust, accompanied by the grip of political party ideologies on curriculum and school structures, shows no sign of abating under the current UK coalition government. At the time of writing, the Secretary of State for Education who labels critics as 'enemies of promise' (Gove, 2013) presents simply another political version of New Labour's modernizing ideologies in that the message brooks 'no excuses' and paints the viewpoints of critics as leading to a failing of school pupils.

In this highly charged political climate of urgency, are the practices of research any different, or has it ever been thus in the education systems of late modernity? Posed in this form, the question probably has no useful or definitive answer. However, the question raises real challenges in considering *how* as a researcher one works within high stakes and fast moving audit-heavy regimes, where a head teacher's values about what ought to be done are often in conflict not only within herself but with aspects of policy.

Personalization as a policy story, in appealing to the head teacher's sense of child-centredness, certainly concentrated the potential for political compliance, undermining notions of some public telos through insinuating the language of the market and 'sweetening the pill' of orientating practices to the competitive pulls of consumer choice (Hartley, 2009).

Dilemmas for researchers: Recent and contemporary

In researching the competing values that head teachers negotiated, I experienced dilemmas in several ways. One was in worrying about whether the truthfulness of the account I could produce is undermined in any way through the relationship of researcher and 'researched'. The schools I worked in were settings that knew me from other professional experiences, and I gained access through an already established trust. In interviewing head teachers, one had a sense of how 'busy' they were and how critical their position is to policy, thereby raising a haunting question of whether their business is more important than mine as a researcher. Is there a pressure to be more utilitarian about the research account? Is it 'useful' to the heads, for example? Does it attempt to be more sympathetic to them by way of denying or downplaying their agency – seeing 'leadership' as something done to them rather than by them? 'Am I too anxious to give something back in a relationship in which I am dependent on their generosity and do not want to be seen as abusing this?' In contrast, does the research with young people tend to be overly sympathetic and privilege their voice as a valid standpoint, which then excludes other possible explanations and alternatives?

The above questions are but a few of the possible ones that the qualitative research process raises. They are not new. Nor are they unique to me, as the accounts by Duggan, Rowley and other colleagues in this book make plain.

However, what I would suspect is different in the context in which I was researching is that the dichotomy between the purposes of the researcher and those of policymakers, and practitioners, works complexly in and through very contemporary modes of *moral manipulation*. Terms such as 'modernization', 'social justice' and 'personalization' become ideological because head teachers, researchers and young people are ever more denied the ability to engage in reasoned arguments about value and purpose in relation to education and schooling. For example, the technical ability to capture the large data sets, required by approved methods of school improvement, anchors a utilitarian view of 'what works' as personalization.

To critique the unexamined political assumptions behind such data sets casts off the researcher as the potential 'enemy' of social justice. Although all the head teachers in this study described parts of their role through the metaphor of a sieve, sifting policy overload before it came into school, the values that acted as strainers were hedged in by demands for rapid short-term audit. The young people in the study saw the resulting targets as having little to do with them personally but far more about maintaining and enhancing the school's reputation and public persona.

Education research: A dialogue about practice?

The hyperactivity of educational policy-making, as well as policymakers' ideological corralling of notions such as 'excellence' and 'justice', suggests that the exchange value of one's account in making a contribution to policy debate is determined by its use value to a narrowly defined set of parameters. As a researcher, one could feel morally manipulated into being a 'useful' insider the more one is cast as the potentially 'useless outsider'. The manipulative dimension lies not only in the manner that the 'objects' of understanding, for example policy outcomes, are placed ideologically beyond critical scrutiny, but in the potential undermining of trust between education researchers and head teachers. Both share values around affecting wider human goods through learning. Both – researchers and head teachers – could otherwise share a valuable dialogue about the shape and content of educational practices.

However much one tries not to look at those you research with as 'objects', 'data sources' or 'respondents', that is what they can become as the ships of research and schooling briefly cross paths and sail off separately into the night. Perhaps a good research account requires this degree of separation. But, in a critically realist approach, it is quite possible to acknowledge the hermeneutic element of one's research work and maintain its truth making capacity (Bhaskar, 2011). The hermeneutic in this case arises in the sorts of pre-judgements (Gadamer's, 2006, notion of prejudice) that those who have worked as teachers and heads, then turn researchers, bring with them about what 'good' practice could be and against which they use research to extend their horizons. The interpretative act can carry with it a certain admiration for and willingness to trust public servants because one knows how tough the job is. Thus, following Gadamer's aphorism, if we are to understand at all, we have to understand differently, to render 'the familiar strange' (Delamont, 1981, p. 13), and to do so in the context of public service is a political act in an arena that purports to be politically neutral.

Yet, the manner in which social relations are so constituted as to enable trust in public services, and encourage the widest possible debate on, say, education, are political arrangements. In order to support ideas for alternative political arrangements, the judicious use of theory is required to be interplayed with the passionate and the dispassionate processes that researching must inevitably entail. MacIntyre's theory has been used in this chapter to explore how values and politics in contemporary discourses are effectively manipulated apart. Next, I will turn to another aspect of MacIntyre's argument in order to show how theory might work to evaluate and recover the possibilities for alternative educational ideas.

Procrustean schooling?

Methodological rules for research can help to support the truth claims that researchers can make. But the political act of researching into 'voice' will ultimately transcend such strictures; for, it brings together the interpretive world of values and human desires with theoretical reasoning. In the contemporary political climate, a passion for the virtues of justice is required more than ever. To make defendable normative claims about the organization and content of a policy is to understand something of the intrinsic purposes and the standards of excellence that contribute to wider human goods through the telos of practices in which they are enacted. A key element of MacIntyre's (1994) argument is the definition of the *internal goods* of a social practice and the *standards of excellence* that are definitive of such goods. A social practice is defined as:

> any coherent and complex form of socially established cooperative human activity through which goods internal to that form of activity are realized in the course of trying to achieve those standards of excellence which are appropriate to, and partially definitive of, that form of activity, with the result that human powers to achieve excellence, and the human conception of the ends and goods involved, are systematically extended. (MacIntyre, 1994, p. 187)

To work within social practice is to co-operatively strive towards some standards of excellence that are defined by the purpose or *telos* of the practice, *internal goods* and to whose authority I am beholden. These purposes are not aims. Aims may help us organize and understand our purposes; but the notion of systematically extending human goods is that there are no end points, just a continual process of striving for excellence. To realize and extend excellence in a practice requires the understanding, and development of, virtues: acquired qualities that are both partly definitive of standards of excellence and that are also necessary to extend those goods.

'Independent practical reasoning' and 'Just generosity' (MacIntyre, 1999, p. 121) are examples that ought to be intrinsic to the goods of schools. They are examples of virtues that contribute to the wider one of justice. Just generosity, for example, enables giving and receiving 'with a certain affectionate regard' (1999, p. 122).

If, for instance, a young person experiences and learns about such just generosity in the context of school, then that both defines and extends the goods intrinsic to teaching and learning. Therefore, such generosity ought to be reflected in the evaluation of standards of excellence in the practices of schooling. Contemporary policy, especially when it is framed as policy that develops human capital, places much emphasis on excellence as being defined by goods such as exam results. But are they intrinsic measures of the worth of learning?

Exam results might be a socially valued good of education in effecting just outcomes, and their pursuit could thus be seen to undermine the argument that they are important outcomes of schooling. But there is a distinction to be made between effectiveness in producing high standards of exam passes to meet externally imposed standards and richer notions of excellence intrinsic to learning as a human activity *in itself*. MacIntyre (2001), not entirely satisfied with his conclusions in *After Virtue*, developed the concept of goods of effectiveness and those of excellence. In the course of research into young peoples' voice within the context of personalization, it seemed that schools were more defined by effectiveness than goods of excellence (Wilcox, 1997).

Indeed, I use the analogy of Procrustes (the mythical innkeeper with an unpleasant way of fitting guests to his iron bed) to describe how young people on the whole, contrary to policymakers' claims, on the whole experienced a 'one size fits all' approach aimed at securing their compliance and enhancing the school's reputation. Excellence achieved in pursuit of the goods of effectiveness is not necessarily extending the virtues of independent reasoning or of just generosity.

'Talking about things that matter in schools'?

Research that specifies in detail how one ought to teach needs to be treated with caution, given the arguments about the myth of managerial expertise (arguments taken up by my colleague, Duggan, in this book). However, in order to contribute to 'systematically' extending human goods, the use of MacIntyre's (1994) reworked virtue ethics as a lens through which to evaluate the excellence, or not, of a practice enables one to ask reasoned and critical questions about how to seek possible alternatives. Asking of a practice, 'how it is systematically extending the virtues that form its telos', is to be puzzled and concerned about how it could be done 'better'. I use

Taylor's argument about 'horizons of significance' (2003, p. 39) to justify the concept of ethical authenticity. Thus, a researcher can bear witness to nascent possibilities for authentic voice, and significant agency, by combining ethical reasoning and testimony from the fieldwork.

For example, Carol, aged 15, during the course of the study, captured the frustration of the whole sample of young people, but in addition, put forward thoughtful alternatives. Carol said that: 'we never talk about things that matter in school'. The core purposes of school, teaching and learning, was not a dialogue they felt on the whole to be engaged in. Young people in the research felt that their voices were being trivialized. However, Carol went on to describe senior leaders and teachers who evidently engaged them in often difficult conversations about learning about their wider concerns of life; these teachers cared deeply about the young people being involved in meaningful contributions to the goods of their schools. Other young people in the study also experienced such care and concern but, in agreement with Carol, the perceptions of these students is that such experiences are isolated encounters that take place occasionally within the corridors or classrooms of their schools. They were not experienced by the young as part of the institutional 'narratives'.

Against those who might argue that such a dialogue is not the business of young people in schools, a virtue ethics viewpoint provides good reasons to argue that it is essential to hear young people's voices and their definitions of excellence in teaching and learning. Again, these are points implicit in Davies' work, in this book. If learning is to support a flourishing democracy, and to develop moral and intellectual virtues among the young, then their exclusion from the experience of such virtues poses serious questions about the instrumental means by which schools are organized and audited as 'successful'.

While pondering about the tensions in how 'voice' is, and ought to be, engaged, I was orientated to how these young people advanced not just critiques but impressively powerful ideas for the more democratic and learning orientated running of their schools. They were highly attuned to the intrinsic goods and virtues, or lack of them, in contemporary schooling. Some of the head teachers in the sample also expressed their frustrations and worries about not being able to develop a wider, meaningful institutional dialogue with young people. These heads recognized the rather utilitarian nature of their 'student voice work' to date but were striving to extend the boundaries of what was possible, because they saw this effort as not only intrinsic to the goods of learning but also to those of healthier civic encounters. As a researcher, in a period of intense pressure upon schools, I felt a constant ebb and flow between the 'inside' of concrete and difficult puzzles of the present and the 'outside' of ethical and political commitments to a different future.

Are these possibilities fragile flowers in a cold and forbidding political climate or harbingers of some more democratic spring?

Researching policy: A broader conception of its value?

On its own, the research from which this chapter has grown cannot answer that question. Misquoting Gramsci, it is possible to be intellectually pessimistic, yet to retain an optimism of the will that sees in the research process many reasons for its continued necessity. I argue that the deadweight of mistrust and compliance, exercised through the contemporary audit processes of public services, is a mode of governing head teachers that works to channel their agency into producing readily visible and technical solutions to the risks inherent in their public profile.

Taken with the ideological work done by the use of terms such as 'modernization', 'standards' and 'excellence', it all suggests that contemporary policymaking represents a morally manipulative mode in late modernity that 'hollows out' public dialogue about public services. In effect, policy work too often divorces politics, values, social purposes, pedagogical thinking and ethical dialogue from each other, rendering only the narrowest of goods available for the debate about schooling. Despite often being positioned through policy and ideology as compliant managers, head teachers do have, and do exercise, an ethical agency. They display this by telling stories of the goods in learning beyond the narrow measures of effectiveness by which they are publically judged. 'Karen', the deputy head teacher in my colleague Cain's account in this book exemplifies these kinds of stories. However, the content of, and the contexts in which, public debate about purposes and values can be conducted are increasingly narrowed.

Educational researching can be marginalized from the debate because of how the 'use value' of scholarship that looks to embody theory wisely is framed in increasingly narrow utilitarian terms. As a researcher in this context, I am left with some pessimism for the possibilities of realizing more democratic forms of justice through the institutions of schools. However, a virtue ethic account of social practices such as MacIntyre's (1994) provides resources from which to advocate for a broader conception of the value of research. Research has value if it can use theory to examine its own political nature as well as analysing the ethical relationships that suffuse practices in schools. In my own example, discussed in this chapter, the practices have centred on the nature of personalization and the value of student voice.

Although not an outcome of this chapter, the philosophical approach can propose reasoned and defendable ethical propositions for how things ought to be. If justice is to be developed through the institutions of schools, then it is utterly necessary that ethical encounters, in which each participant's voice has some authentic weighting, should be an intrinsic good of the institutional narrative. My research with head teachers and young people provided some optimism for suggesting that this necessity has some manifestations in current practice. Head teachers are worrying over the intrinsic goods of the practices that they have been tasked to manage. To 'tip' the balance in favour of one's theory is a political act of intervention; and here researchers need to learn from the theories they propose.

Conclusion

If MacIntyre's (1994, 2001) arguments about the virtues, social practices and the goods of excellence are to be used as a way of seeing and responding to the world, they must also be used to critique the research process itself. Researching ought to be a co-operative social practice, one that extends beyond the often, narrow confines of small discipline based teams or supervisory relationships. As researchers, we ought to be developing the courage to seek more just institutional and political arrangements but temper our efforts with doubt and humility where applicable. There is a difficult balance to be struck between the 'arrogance' of our theory and an open-mindedness to others, and to their voices. This requires that when working in schools, researchers need to develop the virtues of independent and bold argument – constantly developing an independent reasoning that is informed by just generosity: giving and receiving 'affectionately', alongside those with whom you are researching.

In this regard, theoretical work where moral theory is acknowledged has an important ethical contribution to make in proposing richer and more democratic narratives of learning than many young people currently experience. I sought in the research to be open enough to witness the optimism in teaching and learning practices offering glimpses and spaces for a more just schooling system, even if I found myself pessimistic in critiquing the ossification of practices that possess little scope for bringing greater justice into the world and lives of young people. Whether my research has an 'impact' beyond its own self-satisfaction is a matter for the wider practice community to judge.

CONCLUSION

Thinking and Theorizing at a Time of Rapid Reform

Helen M. Gunter, David Hall
and Colin Mills

Introduction

> And this thinking, fed by the present, works with the 'thought fragments' it can wrest from the past and gather about itself. Like a pearl diver who descends to the bottom of the sea, not to excavate the bottom and bring it to light but to pry loose the rich and the strange, the pearls and the coral in the depths and to carry them to the surface ... (Arendt, 1993, p. 205)

Each of our writers has delved deep and surfaced important issues about the lived experience of research, and through the writing process they have made this more visible and legible.

We began in our introductory chapter with the gloomy and indeed hostile context in which educational research located in the social sciences is taking place. But following Arendt's ideas we have set out to illuminate these dark times, and methodologically we have taken her thinking about this seriously. In doing so, we recognize, as others have noted (e.g. Sikes et al., 2003; Carnell et al., 2008), that writing about and for educational research is not just giving an account of the necessary technical aspects that need to be honed. It is also identity work. It is about finding a voice speaking in ways that show a commitment to values. For us, it about scholarly activism.

The 'pearls' we have brought up to the surface for ongoing examination and discussion are ones that we as individuals have recognized through group seminars, our metaphorical diving expeditions. In doing this we are sympathetic to Holligan and Wilson's (2013) challenges to the instrumentalism of capacity building and arguments for 'research cultivation' based on how 'experiences have helped create meaning and a sense of purpose in…their work' (p. 2). Consequently, the stories have provided a reflexive narrative that exposes the untidiness, the thinking and the challenges that are faced in real-life research. We are doing what Nixon and colleagues (2003) have characterized as 'thoughtful research' (p. 91). So we are focusing on what are interesting research issues and how we have to examine what is researchable within context. Following Blackmore (1999), we have troubled and continue to be troubled by the position and the positioning of the researcher. However, we have shown how we have confronted and worked our way through this through our writing: the production of a project report; feedback sessions with partners; and a new project design and/or a thesis. Our research continues outside and beyond these milestone 'markers' as research is integral to our lives. In this final chapter, we would like to identify and talk through the identification of our 'pearls'. No doubt you will have yours that sparkle in your discourse and texts.

These 'pearls' are concerned with the challenges faced in doing research in a socially unjust world and are linked to our support for public domain education and our aspirations for equity and democratic renewal. We intend examining four themes: first, we are deeply indebted to our colleague, Michael Apple, who has helped us to think about the location of the researcher within the research process, and so we draw on Apple's (2013a) arguments for researchers as 'critical secretaries' (p. 41); second, we build on this by revisiting Arendt's political analysis by invoking another metaphor: 'thinking without a bannister' (Canovan, 1995, p. 6); third, the complexity of doing research in localized real-life settings is engaged with through Thomson and Gunter's (2011) metaphor about 'liquid researchers' (p. 26); and fourth, we complete this analysis by addressing our work with theory, and so we invoke Fine's (2009) metaphor of 'kneading theory' (p. 191) as the means through which our needs as researchers are met.

Coming down off the balcony

Apple (2013a) provides nine tasks for the scholarly activist, and here we are particularly concerned with his claims that researching is about struggles over the positions taken by the self as well as the positioning that is done to us by others. As researchers, we proactively take reflexive positions in connection with professional relationships that we entered into within sites of educational activity. We are aware of how our doing this may position us with regard to the assumed authority of the university (Coburn et al., 2008). Through Apple's metaphor of *the balcony* the researcher could take the position and/or be positioned as someone who is elevated and separate, as one who literally looks down upon activity. We might imagine the researcher with her or his clip-board, writing down observations with the accompanying categorizing, counting and labelling that could generate comments from the observed, such as, 'who is he?' 'what is she doing?' and 'why have I not been asked if this is okay?'. We know from our work that standing on the outside can be important and necessary, but our reading of much of the methodological literatures assume this without troubling or examining it. We do not accept that schools, homes and streets are laboratories where the researcher is shielded from those deemed as the researched or playgrounds where the researcher indulgently plays with the researched without due respect. What adds to our concerns is that there could be confusion between the researcher and the inspector. A number of us have experienced doing research with all the research integrity protocols in place to find that professional respondents regard us and speak to us as inspectors. An Ofsted inspection is a disciplined enquiry; it is not primary research. The impact of technical accountability for data about 'outcomes' on the profession is that language and dispositions can be scripted and defensive (Courtney, 2013; Waters, 2013).

Hence we are considering the relationship between position and voice, and so, following Apple (2010), we would agree that 'we need to think *relationally*' (p. 14, original emphasis). How we have worked with this idea is through enabling the power relations within our various research sites to be opened up for scrutiny, and this has shaped the questions we have asked. For example, Armstrong enquires into the building and sustaining of trusting relationships over time. The current narrative is that researchers are not to be trusted because they ask dysfunctional questions and take no responsibility for outcomes. And yet Armstrong's account shows not only the importance of the projects he has worked on in the production of knowledge and the giving of a voice to a professional group but also how as a researcher he has responsibilities for and to respondents. What this reminder of the researcher story does is to connect our thinking to Apple's (2010) arguments for '*repositioning*... that is, we need to see the world through the eyes of the dispossessed and act against the ideological and institutional processes and forms that reproduce oppressive conditions' (p. 15, original emphasis). In coming off the balcony we not only observe what is going on but work with and for communities on how research can reveal power relations and work for a different situation. For example, a number of the accounts give voice to student voice in compulsory education, whereby Rogers reveals the silence of the pupils, Jones engages with the ways advantage and disadvantage work to construct such silence, and Davies confronts the advantaged child who is silenced in other ways.

As researchers, we have tried to articulate in these stories something more than the evidence-informed policy and the practical strategies of the past two decades. We agree with the notion that practice should be enabled by the best possible evidence about professional practices regarding teaching and learning, and we have all undertaken reviews of the evidence base that has informed our thinking and the nature of our contribution. Notwithstanding the technical problems with evidence-informed policy and practice, and the politics of whose evidence matters (see Ribbins et al., 2003), our concern is that the methodologies of systematic review are a form of functionally restricted knowledge production. In addition, as Paechter (2003) argues, the 'instantly useful' research may have short-term utility, but this could be 'at the expense of other important factors, such as ethical groundedness, rigour, clarity of approach and relation to theory' (p. 115). We have witnessed and experienced that calls for relevance in research is a power process that not only does damage to many researchers but also to those who are meant to be the beneficiaries of such research. It seems that so-called 'users' of research are positioned as empty until they are given the answers by elite data gatherers. This has veiled the policy process with a form of respectable accountability and enabled particular beliefs about education and who is capable of being educated to remain in play. We would locate ourselves with researchers who, like Apple (2010), ask:

> Whose knowledge is this? How did it become 'official'? What is the relationship between this knowledge and the ways in which it is taught and evaluated and who has cultural, social, and economic capital in this society? Who benefits from these definitions of legitimate knowledge and from the ways schooling and this society are organized and who does not? How do what are usually seen as 'reforms' actually work? What can we do as critical educators, researchers, and activists to change existing educational and social inequalities and so create curricula and teaching that are more socially just. (p. 14)

These are questions that our stories show to be pertinent. They are not always easy to ask. Following Paechter (2003) we would agree that 'we should focus on conducting good research in the field of education and trust to its utility' (p. 116), and asking such questions is consistent with this approach. Our stories illuminate that such questions enable us to develop insights, and our work with professionals shows a need for something more than functionality. For example, those researchers who are outsiders embedded within an educational setting – Duggan, McGinity, Rowley, Salokangas – give accounts about their struggles over such questions and how this impacted on their voice within the partnership process. Indeed, within the particular research sites there are compromises to make in relation to the challenges faced by our partners and respondents. There are no easy answers to this. Apple's (2013a) arguments for our role as 'critical secretaries' has been helpful, not only in creating a researcher identity that is conductive to more symmetrical research relationships within partnerships but also in giving recognition to professionals, parents and children as authentic knowers.

For Apple (2013a), coming down off the balcony means that researchers develop partnerships that do a number of things: first, work on the meaning of research, not least the pluralism within knowledge claims and methodologies as resources for intellectual work and action; second, agree projects and positioning so that relations of power are open and acknowledged; third, give recognition to the realities of doing 'non-reformist reforms' (p. 42) and how counter projects and stories can illuminate a different kind of change. This secretarial work interconnects with the other tasks for researchers recommended by Apple (2013a), not least through how data analysis is connected to responsibilities that 'point to contradictions and to spaces of possible action' (p. 41). Our stories show the ways in which this can be enabling, on the one hand all of our co-authors make contributions through revealing a situation that otherwise would be hidden, and some have used their research to enable professional development whereby Cain shows the link between her data and theorizing about school leadership. But we have also experienced challenges. For example, embedded researchers have generated data that is integral to organizational goals and professional value systems, but they have also experienced the dominance of reform agendas that have squeezed the opportunities for localized strategies. This reveals what Lather (1991) identifies as the challenges of being both 'within' and 'against' social injustice and is made complex by fears of not being seen as cooperating with what is 'for' change which can often be veneered with claims about social justice.

Holding on tight and letting go

Our stories show the necessity but dangers of thinking. Our co-authors provide a range of examples that illuminate this: Goodlad and Hull present accounts from teachers who have been enabled to think differently about professional practice through postgraduate study, in contrast to reports from Duggan, McGinity and Rowley that show professional thinking has been variously stymied by reform delivery. There are no recipe books for researchers and so thinking on your feet within the research site as well as seeking advice and talking things through within a supervision team or project advisory group becomes important. For example, Cain shows how her prior professional knowledge about people, purposes and practices of primary schools enabled her to be able to think herself into the research setting. Through doing this, the interplay between her research data and reading developed novel insights about her own and her respondents' professional identities. Her research enabled her professional role as a consultant to be developed as research informed professional practice, working with senior leaders as productive thinkers. Similarly, but more dramatically, Emery's professional identity enabled him to both develop his contribution to social and emotional well-being in schools and to break out through resignation from his job. His epiphany involves a shift from unease and disorientation into action which is based on his rejection of the commodification of his identity. These selected examples speak to Arendt's metaphor of 'thinking without a banister' (Canovan, 1995, p. 6), whereby our authors think they are stepping onto a stable and secure set of stairs with a familiar banister to hold onto. Yet, as reading and data collection progresses, the interplay between the two requires them to rethink the intellectual climb they are making. This metaphor enables thinking to take place about position-taking and positioning, and it enables repositioning to take place. Furthermore, Arendt's writing can be a stream of thought about issues and events, and as researchers such an approach to what is being witnessed and experienced is a vital part of the process. Our advice is to write and then get it right, in the sense that the events and meanings are encoded in ways that are personally intelligible and are then reworked for an external audience. Hence our chapters are based on work over the past three years and at least a year when the book has been under development. The chapters have been talked and written into existence in seminar discussions, tentative writing drafts, reworking and final text presentation, and so we would want to give recognition to how we have created stability through the banisters of writing and editing.

Such struggles are also illustrated by Duggan's account of researching within the Stockborough Challenge. Through a partnership project, and espoused methodology, the staircase is built and the banister installed in ways that are transparent. While all partners are also simultaneously on other staircases – at the time Duggan as also on the University of Manchester doctoral staircase – then the parallel nature and interconnections can be secured. However, insidious managerialist intervention means that when primary research is underway, he finds it problematic to get onto the first step of the Stockborough Challenge staircase. He makes the point, and one that we as researchers are familiar with, that important educational issues have been made impenetrable to and for research. The spaces for thinking have been boxed in. Nevertheless his own thinking about his project illustrates the validity of the Arendtian metaphor for action, through which he has identified opportunities for thinking without a banister.

Emerging from these researchers' stories is the risk-taking involved in thinking, whereby Strong (2012) articulates Arendt's methodology:

> *Thinking is*, thus, what is required by *and made possible by* the lack of a banister, for, if there are universal or transcendent categories to rely on, then there is, according to Arendt, no need to think (this does

not mean that one could not, only that our life situation does not make it necessary). Thinking without a banister thus means thinking for oneself.... (pp. 334–335)

Hence if change in education is based on common sense and/or approved of methods from non-educational settings, then there may be nothing to think about. This has huge implications for how theory is understood, not least the characterization that it is an 'it' that is to be applied. The irony that is uncovered in our stories is that reformist categories such as 'improvement' and 'standards', promoted by neo-liberal and neo-conservative popularizers, often prevent thinking. Social science theorizing is perceived as being an irrelevant category because it is characterized as incentivizing dysfunctional thinking about education and schooling. Strong (2012) shows that, in Arendt's view, truth is not an outcome of thinking: 'truth...is always the beginning of thought; thinking is result-less' (p. 339). In other words, 'science has results, philosophy never. Thinking starts after an experience of truth has struck home, so to speak' (p. 339). Our research produces robust and valid data. How we engage with that is the starting point for novel thinking. This is why we adopt the stance that our research is never finished: it reaches a stage when it is ready to be engaged with by our peers.

Swimming but not drowning

In 2004, Thomson and Gunter (2011) began a project in a high school that led them to think about position-taking and positioning as researchers. By drawing on Bauman's (2000) metaphor of liquidity, they reflected upon, and sought to make a contribution to, the 'insider-outsider' reflexive approaches. Doing insider research can mean that a person employed by the organization has understandings that an outsider may not have, a form of privileged 'in the know' access to the research site. Doing research as an outsider can mean that a person employed by another organization has understandings that an insider may not have, a form of privileged 'knowing' access to the library. The interplay between the two is crucial because the insider needs to develop outsider perspectives; the outsider needs to see the situation from an insider point of view. The shift away from the in-out binary continues to be a feature of reflexive research accounts (Sikes and Potts 2008), and as 'liquid researchers' Thomson and Gunter (2011) came to develop better understandings about what it means to re-emplot and re-identify who they were in their long-term engagement with professionals and children as well as how they came to feel comfortable with fluidity and flux. They make a very necessary point that this liquidity can be disconcerting for those working in a context that demands certainty and confidence. There could well be impatience with ideas and debate at a time when data, targets and plans are urgent. The realpolitik of research is therefore in evidence. The power dimensions of voice and contribution come to the fore, and this is interlaced with issues of identity and legality. Identity in the sense of who speaks, and when they speak about certain matters, and legality in regard to who is on the payroll with direct accountability for process and outcomes.

Our stories speak to this matter, and our co-authors tend to address it through notions of borders. The denial of the concept of the teacher as researcher in current neo-liberal and neo-conservative discourses means that the professor and/or the research student entering into an educational site can be regarded as an authoritative stranger by virtue of location but also as an ignorant stranger who does not really know because they don't do the job of a teacher, head teacher or student. Salokangas is literally crossing borders as she carries her Finnish nationality into the academy school where she undertook her research. Such borders are not only at the airport but are also visible as she enters and re-enters the university and the academy school. Such border crossings challenge the assumptions of those involved relating to what is known and needs to be known. Salokangas addresses matters of cultural and linguistic clarification that are overlooked in many research accounts. Such an addressing speaks to home-based researchers as well, helping them to negotiate research relationships that enable the obvious and the different to be captured as data. All researchers cross borders and in doing so have to negotiate access as a process rather than a one-off event.

Let us say something more about this. Liquidity enables critical research but as we have noted such activity can be *misrecognized* in regard to who we are regarded as being and what we are assumed to do (Bourdieu 2000). Furthermore, we are constructed within the current context and seemingly have the luxury to reflect upon and redesign the self through our practice, not least through exotic texts such as this one. Without such activity we could not do the research that matters. The challenges of 'doing' this liquidity are evident within the stories. For example, Rowley directly addresses Apple's tasks for critical researchers, showing the tensions and complexities in doing this at both her desk and in the site of her research. She notes how researchers are condemned for being in the ivory tower. Yet, in doing a collaborative development and research project which was designed to examine directly the role of schools in combating disadvantage, she identifies how it was families that were excluded in the development of the academy.

Doing research inside your own workplace illustrates how the challenges of liquidity operate in close-to-practice ways. Davies gives an account of undertaking action research in her own school where she had to acknowledge not only the need for 'multiple identities' but also to have an internal dialogue with herself. This careful explanation of the self became a feature of both her thesis and her professional identity. Research is not only challenging to the person who undertakes it, not least as a new doctoral student, it also can be perceived as a threat to those who work and live with the researcher. Shifting within and between identities has enabled Davies to recognize what has both limited and liberated her engagement with her professionalism. Like other authors, Davies has crossed borders by coming into the university. Like Goodlad and Hull's students, she has been able to think differently about the purposes of professional practice.

Needing theory

We take from Fine (2009) ideas about the deliberate use of theory and how in drawing together messages from theorizing by educational researchers she comments:

> Although encouraged to use theory, these writers don't simply 'begin' their chapters with famous men and women and then wander into their own analyses. They don't glibly 'authorise' their findings by locating them alongside a critical theorist in parentheses. They do not superficially 'fit' their data into a pre-existing theoretical frame. To the contrary, these writers knead theory, research and action. They engage with ideas, writers, and politics from far and near, in order to prepare conceptually the grounds in which to plant their work. (p. 191)

We would hope she would say this about our approach as well! We have taken inspiration from Jean Anyon and colleagues' book (2009) in which Fine writes. All of our chapters say something about theory and theorizing, and how its deployment enables descriptions, understandings and explanations that could not be generated otherwise. And yet there are different approaches to theorizing and how even within our research community we have talked through the ways in which some of our writers have expressed the idea that they may not be proper academics because they do not have a grand theoretical framework. Indeed, the determinism of big theories is often why theory is ridiculed and simplifications presented by what Bourdieu characterizes as *Le Fast Talkers* (see Gunter 2012b) in policy and in some parts of academia. None of our writers have codified all-encompassing theories. We don't know anyone who does! Rather we use theory as a resource for theorizing. It is how we draw on and deploy theory, and develop our ideas, that is the focus of our attention. It seems to us that theory and theorizing holds us to account in more demanding ways that targets and performance reviews cannot. Performance is about being busy doing data; theorizing is about taking action about what such data actually means, and what it obscures, and why.

Three of our co-authors are writing about their experiences of researching localized policymaking and how their analysis 'needs' theory and how, following Fine (2009), they have 'kneaded' theory, data and action. McGinity has been an embedded researcher in a high school for three years, and the explanation of academy conversion has been enabled through using Bourdieu's thinking tools of *capital*, *habitus* and *field*. By putting the academy conversion into a longer term analysis of how the school has played the national reform game locally, she reveals *misrecognition* of how the game has been rigged. Jones also uses Bourdieu's tools, examining the higher education game at a time of high fees which brings the risk of debt for children who are culturally averse to such a risk. Importantly, he examines his place in this game both as a member of staff of a university and as a researcher. Thinking with theory enables Jones to uncover meanings and explanations about how sorting and re-sorting happens through the workings of class, identity and access to higher education. This game is rigged as well, and the children, teachers and researchers know this. The role of research in opening this up is vital, not least in employing analyses such as Burke's (2012) account which shows how misrecognition is evident in the teacher and student practice.

Children feature strongly in the stories of our co-authors. They are meant to be the beneficiaries of reforms, yet they are usually treated as the objects upon which elite adults are meant to impact through performance audits. Addressing this, and rethinking the role of children and head teachers in the educational process, is what Rogers has engaged with, utilizing MacIntyre's philosophical ideas in doing this. These ideas enable him to confront issues of morality in regard to the tensions and dilemmas in the experience of teaching and learning. While our stories are concerned with researcher voice, Rogers focuses on the possibilities for student voice. He is able to show how the students moved from critique to discussions about virtues within educational organizations. He concludes that theory does something more than explain. It also acts as a resource for advocacy. Importantly this means that as researchers we must critique the research process. In Rogers' view, this takes courage and requires humility.

This is very pertinent to the endemic predicaments in which educational research is located. In 2000, Woodhead, the then HMCI (Her Majesty's Chief Inspector), described what we do as 'wacky theorizing' (Woodhead, 2000, p. 13), and more recently this has shifted to condemnation by the current Secretary of State, whereby Gove (2013) describes researchers as 'enemies of promise' (unpaged) by deliberately setting out to prevent children from achieving in education. There has been a clear shift in tone and content from impatient ridicule to denunciation. Yet, when we work with professionals and children within research partnerships, they recognize their own theorizing and relish the opportunities to make this public. So, in Rogers' terms, we need the courage to be able to work within our partnerships, yet we also need to be humble in regard to how the 'management of ignorance' (Inglis, 1985) as a policy strategy is read and engaged with locally. The problem is that like Inglis (1985) we (and our colleagues in educational organizations) know what the 'monstrous and well-named confidence trick' (p. 105) is, and in speaking about this openly (such as in letters to newspapers) we let the cat out of the bag. In short, research for policy enables the manipulation of enthusiasm for goals that cannot be questioned, whereas research about policy not only reveals this but also gives voice to alternatives.

This requires researchers to work within transparent research conduct procedures. Sikes (2012) alerts us to the situation whereby a project may have been approved through research integrity processes in the university, but the ethical issues located in doing and writing up research can be more complex in relation to how people and their work are 'written up'. She highlights the existence of nasty research and researchers, where revenge served hot off the photocopier may enable them to handle negative experiences. And so we have a duty of care to our respondents in terms of how they are included and how this inclusion interconnects with how we see the purposes of research. We must remember this when we are working on our research subjects' right to be included, not least because of the way professionals and children experience research. Negative experiences of researchers may mean that access is closed.

In raising the issue of 'nastiness' in research, Sikes (2012) leads us to some difficult questions regarding the meaning of this notion in the current policy context. Researchers, such as those included in this book, working with theories that question the hegemonic normality of neo-liberal and neo-conservative approaches to education may not always be welcome in educational institutions that have been carefully marshalled to work tightly within performative regimes where this normality has been carefully veiled through selective discursive practices (Hall, 2013). What we regard as diving for pearls might be viewed in far less favourable terms by those who may fail to see the beauty of these precious objects. In such contexts, this raises questions about the interpretation of 'nastiness' and how critical researchers may find that the distinction between robust intellectual challenge and 'nastiness' is clear neither in the mind of the researcher nor the research participants.

Overall, it seems to us that we are being explicit about research, yet we are being condemned by certain political interests for doing so. We follow Jackson (2010) in acknowledging that generating fear and fearfulness is a silencing process used by the powerful. Our approach is to be explicit about how this has become a popular and increasingly legitimate political strategy, not least because our work on policy and school leadership at Manchester shows totalitarian tendencies within education policymaking (Gunter 2014).

Metaphoric research

In paraphrasing Jane Austen, we would like to say: it is a truth universally acknowledged that the best teachers teach through stories and storytelling. Our co-authors have spoken about their research in ways that matter, and they have highlighted their learning about the research process. From these stories, our messages are that scholarly activism is simultaneously national and local; it is intellectual and practical; and it is public and private. All enquiry is underpinned by theories and uses theorizing to make sense, and we are demonstrating the complexities, tensions and challenges in doing this. It seems to us that teaching and learning in classrooms can benefit from such researcher dispositions, and we all have experiences of doing this in schools, colleges and higher education. Importantly the structures do not come tumbling down because of this, and students continue to achieve and staff continue to be accountable.

In the introduction, we began with pearl diving through deploying thinking about research in regard to the story of Martha Payne. Metaphors are storied illustrations. They generate perspectives and interpretations, where rival stories can ensure that what we leave on the seabed for now is not forgotten. One outcome of our current pearl diving is that it seems to us that many adults in elite roles need to come off the balcony in relation to experiences such as that we have storied about Martha Payne, not just in relation to a child and parent project but in relation to other adults involved. Partnerships with children and the school workforce could begin by dispensing with established categories and common sense notions of 'pupil' and 'dinner lady' and take risks in regard to building collaborative projects about food, funding and consumption. Such relationality would generate border crossings into and out of kitchens (as well as classrooms, offices and council chambers), where liquidity would generate associations with positioning and position-taking that could be what Sikes (2008) articulates as outside-insider, and inside-outsider. The conversations, the examples and the generation of plans, would inevitably be both theoretical and practical (e.g. using theories, developing theories, discounting theories and so forth). Action research could enable data gathering and analysis through which research training and development could take place. Consequently, in presenting a declaration of research as scholarly activism we would like to align with Fine (2009) regarding the importance of ideas and theories to shape and conceptualize, and converse with the lives of those who do research and those who are in our research partnerships. This is tough work. We have not resolved this here, and we did not set out to do so.

What we do want to give recognition to are projects where a range of people in the education system are involved in communicating their research at conferences and in published texts. But at the same time we would want to return to Apple's (2010) arguments about 'elite knowledge' (p. 16). There seems to be a range of political interests that would want to dispose of the types of research and theoretical knowledge that we have engaged with in this book. On the one hand neo-liberals see it as unsellable and neo-conservatives see it as disruptive of the traditional ways of being in the world. Those who may regard themselves differently to this may wish to dispense with 'elite knowledge' because it denies authentic experiences, where there are issues of class, race, gender and colonialism in its production.

We agree that such knowledge is problematic, and we side with the need to challenge the way power structures impact on what is known and deemed worth knowing and who the elite knowers are. Libraries are not necessarily beacons of democracy. At the same time, we agree with Apple (2010) that we should not commit 'intellectual suicide' (p. 16), and instead we need to critically and socially critically engage with the adoption and use of theories and how our intellectual work is by necessity disruptive of our data and identities. As Apple (2010) states:

> ...there are serious intellectual (and pedagogic) skills in dealing with the histories and debates surrounding the epistemological, political, and educational issues involved in justifying what counts as important knowledge and what counts as effective and socially just education. These are not simple and inconsequential issues, and the practical and intellectual/political skills of dealing with them have been well developed. However, they can atrophy if they are not used. We can give back these skills by employing them to assist communities in thinking about this, learning from them, and engaging in the mutually pedagogic dialogues that enable decisions to be made in terms of both the short-term and long-term interests of dispossessed peoples. (p. 16)

Recognizing and questioning the resources that children, teachers, parents and communities might have and might develop to support equitable processes and outcomes is central to scholarly activism. It is the skills and not necessarily the knowledge that are confined to elite settings and is becoming more so as our stories illuminate. Integral to research partnerships is how we frame and develop issues, how we problem-pose and not just seek to problem-solve, and as such our stories illuminate how we have developed and deployed and keep learning about research skills; and how those we work with have developed them in ways that enable their learning and professional work. What we are saying aligns with Inglis (2003) that 'intellectual method cannot promise genius, but it should at least forestall stupidity' (p. 131). Hence research is pedagogic, and we present these stories and our analysis of what they might mean as an illustration of what and how we have learned.

Like other researchers, we are deeply located in knowledge production. As developing knowers, we are concerned with issues of knowledge and knowing. We inhabit dialogic spaces: we are simultaneously in the library, in the field and at our desks staring at a screen. In this book, we have presented stories that have enabled us to reflexively engage with what it is like, what it feels like and what it means to do research in an unjust world. These stories say a lot about the researcher and research, not least the cultural vitality in which projects are developed and conducted. Following Arendt, we have recognized the endurance of dark times, and we have worked on illuminating through the flickering light of thinking, talking and writing. In mixing our metaphors we have shown how we have, in Bourdieu's words, been like a 'fish in water' (Bourdieu and Wacquant, 1992, p. 127). The interplay between agency and structure is such that we need to recognize the 'weight of the water' and how we 'take the world about itself for granted' (p. 127). We may shift ponds or seas by doing research in unfamiliar waters, with the danger of accepting the normality of what we are swimming in. Our pearl diving is necessarily in waters we come to know, but we will not know much or know what is worth knowing about unless we dive and search for pearls. In doing so, we struggle for meaning through our stories, where writing is a process through which we come to understand what we do and do not know. Our stories are never finished.

REFERENCES

Adler, P.A. and Adler, P. (2001), 'The reluctant respondent', in J.F. Gubrium and J.A. Holstein (eds), *Handbook of Interview Research: Context and Method*. London: Sage, 515–531.

Adonis, A. (2012), *Education, Education, Education: Reforming England's Schools*. London: Biteback Publishing.

Ainscow, M. (2002), 'Using research to encourage the development of inclusive practices', in P. Farrell and M. Ainscow (eds), *Making Special Education Inclusive*. London: Fulton, 25–38.

Allix, N.M. (2000), 'Transformational leadership: Democratic or despotic?' *Educational Management and Administration*, 28 (1), 7–20.

Anderson, A. (2005), 'An introduction to the theory of change'. *Evaluation Exchange*, 11 (2), 12–19.

Anderson, G.L. and Herr, K. (2009), 'Practitioner action research and educational leadership', in S. Noffke and B. Somekh (eds.), *The Sage Handbook of Educational Action Research*. London: SAGE Publications, 155–165.

Anheier, H.K. (2005), *Non-profit Organisations: Theory, Management Policy*. London: Routledge.

Anyon, J. with Dumas, M.J., Linville, D., Nolan, K., Pérez, E.T. and Weiss, J. (eds) (2009), *Theory and Educational Research*. New York: Routledge.

Apple, M.W. (2001), *Educating the 'Right' Way*. New York, NY: Routledge.

———. (2006), 'Interrupting the right: On doing critical educational work in conservative times', in G. Ladson-Billings and W.F. Tate (eds), *Education Research in the Public Interest: Social Justice, Action, and Policy*. New York, NY: Teachers College Press, 27–45.

———. (2007), 'Education, markets and an audit culture'. *International Journal of Educational Policies*, 1, 4–19.

———. (2010), 'Global crises, social justice, and education', In M.W. Apple (ed.), *Global Crises, Social Justice and Education*. New York NY: Routledge, 1–24.

———. (2012a), 'Afterword on neoliberalism, the current crisis, and the politics of hope', in M.Lall (ed.), *Policy, Discourse and Rhetoric: How New Labour Challenged Social Justice and Democracy*. Rotterdam: Sense Publishers,141–150.

———. (2012b), *The Task of the Critical Scholar/Activist in Education*, address to seminar, Institute of Education, University of London, London, England. 15th June.

———. (2013a), *Can Education Change Society?* New York: Routledge.

———. (2013b), *Knowledge, Power, and Education: The Selected Works of Michael W. Apple*. New York: Routledge.

—— and Beane, J. (eds) (2007), *Democratic Schools: Lessons in Powerful Education* (second edition). Portsmouth, NH: Heinemann.

——, Au, W. and Gandin, L.A. (eds.) (2009), *The Routledge International Handbook of Critical Education*. New York: Routledge

Arber, A. (2006), 'Reflexivity: A challenge for the researcher as practitioner?' *Journal of Research in Nursing*, 11 (2), 147–157.

Arendt, H. (1958), *The Human Condition* (second edition). Chicago, IL: The University of Chicago Press.

——. (1993), *Men in Dark Times*. San Diego, CA: Harcourt Brace & Company.

Armstrong, P. (2012), 'Managing the business of schools: Perspectives on the expansion and "professionalisation" of the school business manager role in England' paper presented at the *International Congress for School Effectiveness and School Improvement (ICSEI)*, Sweden, 5–8th January.

Audit Commission. (2008), *Are we there Yet? Improving Governance and Resource Management in Children's Trusts*. London: Audit Commission.

Bacchi, C. (2009), *Analysing Policy: What's the Problem Represented to Be?* Frenchs Forest, NSW: Pearson Education, Australia.

Bachan, R. (2013), 'Students' expectations of debt in UK higher education'. *Studies in Higher Education*, DOI:10.1080/03075079.2012.754859. (Accessed 4th December 2013), 1–26.

Bakhtin, M.M. (1968), *Rabelais and His World* (translated by H. Iswolsky). Cambridge, MA: MIT Press.

Ball, S.J. (1981), *Beachside Comprehensive*. Cambridge: Cambridge University Press.

——. (1987), *The Micro-politics of the School: Towards a Theory of School Organisation*. London: Methuen.

——. (1990), *Politics and Policy Making in Education: Explorations in Policy Sociology*. Abingdon, Oxon: Routledge.

——. (1994), 'Political interviews and the politics of interviewing', in G. Walford (ed.), *Researching the Powerful in Education*. London: UCL Press, 96–115.

——. (2003), 'The teacher's soul and the terrors of performativity'. *Journal of Education Policy*, 18 (2), 215–228.

——. (2007), *Education Plc: Understanding Private Sector Participation in Public Sector Education*. London: Routledge.

——. (2008), *The Education Debate*. Bristol: Policy Press.

——. (2012), *Global Education Inc.: New Policy Networks and the Neoliberal Imaginary*. Abingdon, Oxon: Routledge.

——, Maguire, M. and Braun, A. (2012), *How Schools Do Policy: Policy Enactments in Secondary Schools*. Abingdon, Oxon: Routledge.

Baquedano-Lopez, P. and Hernandez, S.J. (2011), 'Language socialization across educational settings', in B.A.U. Levinson and M. Pollock (eds), *A Companion to the Anthropology of Education*. Malden, MA: Blackwell Publishing, 197–211.

Barber, M. (2008), *Instruction to Deliver: Fighting to Transform Britain's Public Services*. London: Methuen Publishing.

Barnard, C.I. (1948), *The Functions of the Executive*. Cambridge, MA: Harvard University Press.

Barnet London Borough. (2010), *One Barnet Framework*, Report by Cabinet Member for Customer Access and Partnerships (Online at: http://barnet.

moderngov.co.uk/Data/Cabinet/201011291900/Agenda/Document%204.pdf)
(Accessed: 3rd October 2013).

Bar-On, R. and Parker, J.D.A. (eds). (2000), *The Handbook of Emotional Intelligence*. San Francisco: Jossey-Bass.

Baudrillard, J. (1988), 'The Consumer Society', in M. Poster (ed.), *Jean Baudrillard: Selected Writings*. Oxford: Polity/Basil Blackwell, 32–59.

Bauman, Z. (2000), *Liquid Modernity*. Cambridge: Polity Press.

Beckett, F. (2007), *The Great City Academy Fraud*. London: Continuum.

Bell, K. and West, A. (2003), 'Specialist schools: An exploration of competition and co-operation'. *Educational Studies*, 29 (2/3), 273–289.

Bennett, N., Harvey, J., Wise, C. and Woods, P. (2003), *Distributed Leadership, Full Report*. Nottingham: National College for School Leadership.

Bernstein, B. (2000), *Pedagogy, Symbolic Control and Identity: Theory, Research, Critique*. Maryland: Rowman and Littlefield.

Bevir, M. (2005), *New Labour: A Critique*. Abingdon, Oxon: Routledge.

Bhaskar, R. (2011), *Reclaiming Reality: A Critical Introduction to Contemporary Philosophy*. Abingdon: Routledge.

BIS (Department for Business, Innovation and Skills). (2011). 'Students at the Heart of the System'. https://www.gov.uk/government/uploads/system/uploads/attachment_data/file/31384/11-944-higher-education-students-at-heart-of-system.pdf.

Blackledge, P. (eds) (2008), *Revolutionary Aristotelianism: Ethics, Resistance and Utopia*. Stuttgart: Lucius & Lucius.

Blackmore, J. (1999), *Troubling Women*. Buckingham: Open University Press.

Blank, M., Melaville, A. and Shah, B. (2003), *Making the Difference: Research and Practice in Community Schools*. Washington, DC: Coalition for Community Schools, Institute for Educational Leadership.

Blasé, J. and Blasé, J. (1994), *Empowering Teachers: What Successful Principals Do*. Thousand Oaks, CA: Corwin Press/Sage.

Blatchford, P., Bassett, P., Brown, P., Martin, C., Russell, A. and Webster, R. (2009), *The Deployment and Impact of Support Staff project: Research Brief (DCSF-RB148)*. London: Department for Children, Schools and Families.

Boliver, V. (2011), 'Expansion, differentiation, and the persistence of social class inequalities in British higher education'. *Higher Education*, 61, 229–242.

———. (2013), 'How fair Is access to more prestigious UK universities?' *British Journal of Sociology*, 64 (2), 344–364.

Bottery, M. (1992), *The Ethics of Educational Management: Personal, Social and Political Perspectives on School Organisation*. London: Cassell.

———. (2003), 'The management and mismanagement of trust'. *Educational Management and Administration*, 31 (3), 245–261.

———. (2004), *The Challenges of Educational Leadership*. London: Paul Chapman Publishing.

Bourdieu, P. (1984), *Distinction: A Social Critique of the Judgment of Taste*. Cambridge: Harvard University Press.

———. (1989), 'Social space and symbolic power'. *Sociological Theory*, 7 (1), 14–25.

———. (1990), *In Other Words: Essays Towards a Reflexive Sociology*. California: Stanford University Press.

————. (1996), *The State Nobility: Elite Schools in the Field of Power* (translated by Lauretta C. Clough). Stanford: Stanford University Press.

————. (1997), 'The forms of capital', in A.H. Halsey, H. Lauder, P. Brown and A.S. Wells (eds), *Education: Culture, Economy and Society*. Oxford: Oxford University Press, 46–58.

————. (2000), *Pascalian Meditations*. Cambridge: Polity Press.

———— and Wacquant, L.J.D. (1992), *An Invitation to Reflexive Sociology*. Cambridge: Polity Press.

Boyatzis, R. (2006), *Leadership Development and Personal Effectiveness* (Online at: www.ncsl.org.uk/researchpublications) (Accessed: 12th January 2012).

Brady, A. (2006), 'Opportunity sampling', in V. Jupp (ed.), *The Sage Dictionary of Social Research Methods*. London: Sage, 205–6.

Brannick, T. and Coghlan, D. (2007), 'In defense of being "native": The case for insider academic research'. *Organizational Research Methods*, 10 (1), 59–74.

Browne, E. (2010), *Independent Review of Higher Education Funding and Student Finance* (Online at: http://webarchive.nationalarchives.gov.uk/+/hereview. independent.gov.uk/hereview/) (Accessed: 15th June 2013).

Bryk, A. and Schneider, B. (2002), *Trust in Schools*. New York: Russell Sage.

Brynin, M. (2013), 'Individual choice and risk: The case of higher education'. *Sociology*, 47 (2), 284–300.

Burawoy, M. (2005), '2004 American sociological association presidential address: For public sociology'. *The British Journal of Sociology*, 56 (2), 259–294.

Burke, P.J. (2012), *The Right to Higher Education*. London: Routledge.

Burns, E., Fenwick, J., Schmied, V. and Sheehan, A. (2012), 'Reflexivity in midwifery research: The insider/outsider debate'. *Midwifery*, 28, 52–60.

Butt, G.W. and Lance, A.C. (2005), 'Modernising the roles of support staff in primary schools: Changing focus, changing function'. *Educational Review*, 57 (2), 139–149.

Byrom, T. (2010), *The Dream of Social Flying: Education Choice and the Paradox of Widening Participation*. Saarbrücken, Germany: Lambert Academic Publishing.

Cabinet Office. (2010), *The Coalition: Our Programme for Government*. London: HMSO.

Caetano, G., Palacios, M. and Patrinos, H. (2011) *Measuring Aversion to Debt: An Experiment among Student Loan Candidates*, World Bank Policy Research Working Paper Series. (Online at: SSRN:http://ssm.com/abstract=1895966]. (Accessed: 4th December 2013).

Cain, M.E. (2011), 'Inside the primary school leadership team: An investigation into primary school leadership practice and development as an integrated process', Unpublished Ed. D. thesis, The Manchester Institute of Education, The University of Manchester.

———— and Gunter, H.M. (2012), 'An investigation into primary school leadership practice: Introducing the PIVOT framework of leadership'. *Management in Education*, 26 (4), 187–191.

Callender, C. and Jackson, J. (2005), 'Does the fear of debt deter students from higher education?' *Journal of Social Policy*, 34 (4), 509–540.

Campbell, D. (2012), 'Can Jamie's school meals revolution survive the Gove recipe?' *The Guardian*, 27th April, 14.

Canavan, J., Coen, L., and Dolan, P. (2009), 'Privileging practice: Facing the challenge of integrated working for outcomes for children', *Children and Society*, 23 (5), 2–12.

Canovan, M. (1995), *Hannah Arendt: A Reinterpretation of Her Political Thought*. Cambridge: Cambridge University Press.

Carnell, E., MacDonald, J., McCallum, B. and Scott, M. (2008), *Passion and Politics: Academics Reflect on Writing for Publication*. London: Institute of Education, University of London.

Carr, W. and Kemmis, S. (1986), *Becoming Critical: Education, Knowledge and Action Research*. Deakin: Deakin University Press.

Chapman, C. and Fullan, M. (2007), 'Collaboration and partnership for equitable improvement: Towards a networked learning system?' *School Leadership and Management*, 27 (3), 207–211.

—— and Gunter, H.M. (eds) (2009), *Radical Reforms: Perspectives on an Era of Educational Change*. London: Routledge.

Chappell, T. (2008), 'Utopias and the art of the possible', in K.Knight and P. Blackledge (eds), *Revolutionary Aristotelianism: Ethics, Resistance and Utopia*. Stuttgart: Lucius and Lucius, 179–203.

Charmaz, K. (2001), 'Qualitative interviewing and grounded theory analysis', in J.F. Gubrium and J.A. Holstein (eds), *Handbook of Interview Research: Context and Method*. Thousand Oaks: Sage, 675–695.

Cherniss, C. (2002), 'Emotional intelligence and the good community'. *American Journal of Community Psychology*, 30 (1), 1–11.

Children's Aid Society. (2001), *Building a Community School*. New York: Children's Aid Society.

Christensen, T. and Lægreid, P. (2008), 'NPM and beyond – structure, culture and demography'. *International Review of Administrative Sciences*, 74 (1), 7–23.

——. (2011), 'Post-NPM reforms: Whole of government approaches as a new trend – new steering concepts in public management'. *Research in Public Policy Analysis and Management*, 21, 11–24.

Christopher, S., Watts, V., McCormick, A.K.H.G. and Young, S. (2008), 'Building and maintaining trust in a community-based participatory research partnership'. *American Journal of Public Health*, 98 (8), 1398–1406.

Chung, J. (2010), 'Finland, PISA, and the implications of international achievement studies on education policy', in Alexander W. Wiseman (ed.), *The Impact of International Achievement Studies on National Education Policymaking*, International Perspectives on Education and Society, 13. Bingley, UK: Emerald Group Publishing Limited, 267–294.

Clarke, J., Gerwitz, S. and McLaughlin, E. (2000), 'Reinventing the welfare state', in J. Clarke, S. Gerwitz and E. McLaughlin (eds), *New Managerialism New Welfare?* London: Sage, 1–26.

—— and Newman, J. (1997), *The Managerial State: Power, Politics and Ideology in the Remaking of Social Welfare*. London: Sage.

——, Newman, J. and Westmarland, L. (2008), 'The antagonisms of choice: New Labour and the reform of public services'. *Social Policy and Society*, 7 (2), 245–253.

——, Newman, J., Smith, N., Vidler, E. and Westmarland, L. (2007), *Creating Citizen-Consumers: Changing Publics and Changing Public Services*. London: Sage.

Clough, P. (2002), 'Narratives and fictions in educational research', in P. Clough (ed.), *Doing Qualitative Research in Educational Settings*. Buckingham: Open University Press.

Coburn, C., Bae, S. and Turner, E.O. (2008), 'Authority, status, and the dynamics of insider-outsider partnerships at the district level'. *Peabody Journal of Education*, 83 (3), 364–399.

Comaroff, J. (2010), 'The end of a anthropology, again: On the future of an in/ discipline'. *American Anthropologist*, 112, 524–538.

Connell, R.W. (1983), *Which Way Is Up?: Essays on Sex, Class and Culture*. Sydney: Allen and Unwin.

Connell, J.P. and Kubisch, A.C. (1998), 'Applying a theory of change approach to the evaluation of comprehensive community initiatives: Progress, prospects and problems', in K. Fulbright-Anderson, A.C. Kubisch and J.P. Connell (eds), *New Approaches to Evaluating Community Initiatives. Volume 2: Theory, Measurement and Analysis*. Queenstown: The Aspen Institute, 15–44.

Considine, M. (1994), *Public Policy: A Critical Approach*. Melbourne: McMillan.

Cook, J. and Wall, T. (1980), 'New work attitude measures of trust, organizational commitment and personal need nonfulfilment'. *Journal of Occupational Psychology*, 53, 39–52.

Corbin Dwyer, S. and Buckle, J.L. (2009), 'The space between: On being an outsider in qualitative research'. *International Journal of Qualitative Methods*, 8 (1), 54–63.

Corson, D. (2000), 'Emancipatory leadership'. *International Journal of Leadership in Education*, 3, 93–120.

Courtney, S.J. (2013), 'Headteachers' experiences of school inspection under Ofsted's January 2012 framework'. *Management in Education*, 27 (4), 164–169.

Craig, J., Huber, J. and Lowensworth, H. (2004), *School's Out: Can Teachers, Social Workers and Health Staff Learn to Live Together?* Demos/Hay Group: London.

Crotty, M. (1998), *The Foundations of Social Research: Meaning and Perspective in the Research Process*. London: Sage.

Crowther, D., Cummings, C., Dyson, A. and Millward, A. (2003), *Schools and Area Regeneration*. Bristol: The Policy Press.

Cummings, C., Dyson, A. and Todd, L. with the Education Policy and Evaluation Unit University of Brighton. (2004), *An Evaluation of the Extended Schools Pathfinder Projects*. Research Report: 530. London: DfES.

Czerniawski, G. and Kidd, W. (eds) (2011), *The Student Voice Handbook: Bridging the Academic/Practitioner Divide*. Bingley: Emerald Group Publishing Limited.

Darbyshire, P. (2008), '"Never mind the quality, feel the width": The nonsense of "quality", "excellence", and "audit" in education, health and research'. *Collegian*, 15, 35–41.

Day, C. (2008) 'Committed for life? Variations in teachers' work, lives and effectiveness'. *Journal of Educational Change* 9 (3), 243–260.

———, Harris, A., Hadfield, M., Tolley, H. and Beresford, J. (2000), *Leading Schools in Times of Change*. Buckingham: Open University Press.

D'Cruz, H. and Jones, M. (2004), *Social Work Research: Ethical and Political Contexts*. Thousand Oaks: Sage Publications.

Dekker, P. and Uslaner, E.M. (2001), 'Introduction', in E.M. Uslaner (ed.), *Social Capital and Participation in Everyday Life*. London: Routledge, 4–11.

Delamont, S. (1981), 'All too familiar: a decade of classroom research', *Educational Analysis*, 3, (1), 69–84

—— and Atkinson, P. (1980), 'The two traditions in educational ethnography'. *British Journal of Sociology of Education*, 1 (2), 139–154.

—— and Pugsley, L. (2010), 'The concept smacks of magic: Fighting familiarity today'. *Teaching and Teacher Education*, 26, 3–10.

Denzin, N. (1989), *The Research Act: A Theoretical Introduction to Sociological Methods*. Englewood Cliffs: Prentice Hall.

Department for Business, Innovation and Skills (BIS). (2011), *Students at the Heart of the System*. London: HMSO.

——. (2008a), *Strengthening Children's Trusts: Legislative Options*. London: HMSO.

——. (2008b), *Children's Trusts: Statutory Guidance on Inter-agency Cooperation to Improve Well-being of Children, Young People and their Families*. London: HMSO.

Department for Children, Schools and Families (DCSF). (2007), *Children's Plan: Building Brighter Futures*. London: HMSO.

Department for Education (DfE). (2010), *The Importance of Teaching: The Schools White Paper*. London: HMSO.

——. (2011), *Letter from Secretary of State to the chair of the Training and Development Agency for Schools*, March 2011. (Online at: http://www.ucet.ac.uk/downloads/2763.pdf) (Accessed: 8th May 2012).

——. (2012), *School Uniform Guidance*. London: DfE.

Department for Education and Employment (DfEE). (1997), *Excellence in Schools*. London: DfEE.

——. (2000), *Influence or Irrelevance: Can Social Science Improve Government?*, Secretary of State's ESRC Lecture Speech, 2nd February. London: DfEE.

Department for Education and Skills (DfES). (2001), *Schools: Achieving Success. White Paper*. London: HMSO.

——. (2003), *Every Child Matters*. Nottingham: DfES Publications.

——. (2004), *National Standards for Headteachers, Ref: DfES/0083/2004*. Nottingham: DfES Publications.

——. (2005), *Social and Emotional Aspects of Learning*. Nottingham: DfES Publications.

Department of Education and Science (DES). (1985), *Better Schools*. London: HMSO.

Deutsch, M. (1960), 'The effect of motivational orientation upon trust and suspicion'. *Human Relations*, 13, 123–40.

Dewey, J. (1916) *Education and Democracy*. New York: Ann Arbor.

Di Cicco-Bloom, B. and Crabtree, B.F. (2006), 'The qualitative research interview'. *Medical Education*, 40 (4), 314–21.

Dijkstra, W. (1987), 'Interviewing style and respondent behavior: An experimental study of the survey-interview'. *Sociological Methods and Research*, 16 (2), 309–34.

Drever, E. (1995), *Using Semi-Structured Interviews in Small-Scale Research*. Edinburgh: The Scottish Council for Research in Education.

Dryfoos, J.G. (1994), *Full-Service Schools*. San Francisco: Jossey-Bass.

Duggan, J.R. (2012), 'A local authority initiative to foster a collaborative culture between organisations working with children and young persons'. Unpublished Ph.D. thesis, The Manchester Institute of Education, The University of Manchester.

————. (2014), 'Critical friendship and critical orphanship: Embedded research in an English local authority initiative'. *Management in Education*, 28 (1), 12–18.

Dunleavy, P., Margetts, H., Bastow, S. and Tinkler, J. (2005), *New Public Management Is Dead: Long Live Digital Era Governance*, EDS Innovation Research Programme: Discussion Paper Series (Online at: http://www.lse.ac.uk/researchAndExpertise/units/innovationResearch/pdf/EDSdp004.pdf) (Accessed: 13th October 2013).

Dyson, A. (2006), 'Beyond the school gates: Context, disadvantage and urban schools', in M. Ainscow and M. West (eds), *Improving Urban Schools: Leadership and Collaboration*. London: Open University Press, 117–129.

———— and Raffo, C. (2007), 'Education and disadvantage: The role of community-oriented schools'. *Oxford Review of Education*, 33 (3), 297–314.

———— and Todd, L. (2010), 'Dealing with complexity: Theory of change evaluation and full service extended schools initiative'. *International Journal of Research and Method in Education*, 33, 119–134.

————, Gallannaugh, F. and Kerr, K. (2011), *Conceptualising school community relations in disadvantaged areas* (Online at: http://www.ahrc.ac.uk/Funding-Opportunities/Research-funding/Connected-Communities/Scopingstudies) (Accessed: 16th October 2012).

————, Millward, A. and Todd, L. (2002), *A Study of the Extended Schools Demonstration Projects*, Research Report 381. London: DfES.

————, Raffo, C., Gunter, H., Hall, D., Jones, L. and Kamalbouka, A. (2010), 'What Is to be done? Implications for policy makers', in C. Raffo, A. Dyson, H. Gunter, D. Hall, L. Jones and A. Kalambouka (eds), *Education and Poverty in Affluent Countries*. London: Routledge, 163–177.

Easen, P., Atkins, M. and Dyson, A. (2004), 'Inter-professional collaboration and conceptualisations of practice'. *Children and Society*, 14, 355–367.

Education Executive. (2011), *Most SBMs in England Hold a Qualification* (Online at: http://www.edexec.co.uk/news/1495/most-sbms-in-england-hold-qualification-/) (Accessed: 25th September 2013).

Ellis, C., Adam, T. and Bochner, A. (2011), Autoethnography: An overview. *Forum: Qualitative Social Research*, Volume 12. (Online at: http://www.qualitative-research.net/index.php/fqs/article/view/1589/3095) (Accessed : 10th May 2013).

Ellis, S. and Moss, G. (2013), 'Ethics, education policy and research: The phonics question reconsidered'. *British Educational Research Journal*, (Online at: DOI: 10.1002/berj.3039) (Accessed: 20th June 2013).

Emery, C. (2013), 'Children's wellbeing in Wales: An ethos under attack'. *Planet*, 211, 9–17.

Erickson, F. (1984), 'What makes school ethnography "ethnographic"?' *Anthropology and Education Quarterly*, 15, 51–66.

Exley, S. R. (2009), 'Exploring pupil segregation between specialist and non specialist schools'. *Oxford Review of Education*, 35 (4), 451–470.

Exley, S. (2012), 'The politics of educational policy making under New Labour: An illustration of shifts in public service governance'. *Policy and Politics*, 40 (2), 227–244.

Exworthy, M. and Halford, S. (2002), 'Professionals and managers in a changing sector: Conflict, compromise and collaboration?', in M. Exworthy and S. Halford (eds), *Professionals and the New Managerialism in the Public Sector*. Buckingham: Open University Press, 1–17.

Fairclough, N. (1989), *Language and Power*. Edinburgh: Longman.
———. (1992), *Discourse and Social Change*. Cambridge: Policy Press.
———. (2000), *New Labour, New Language*. London: Routledge.
———. (2003), *Analysing Discourse, Textual Analysis for Social Research*. London: Routledge.
Farrell, C. and Morris, J. (2003), 'The neo-bureaucratic state: Professionals and managers and professional managers in schools, general practices and social work'. *Organisation*, 10, 129–157.
Fay, B. (1996), *Contemporary Philosophy of Social Science: A Multicultural Approach*. Cambridge: Blackwell.
Feinberg, W. (2012), 'The Idea of public education'. *Review of Research in Education*, 36 (1), 1–22.
Fergusson, R. (2000), 'Modernising managerialism in education', in J. Clarke, S. Gewirtz and E. McLaughlin (eds), *New Managerialism, New Welfare?* London: Sage, 202–221.
Fielding, M. (2000), 'Education policy and the challenge of living philosophy'. *Journal of Education Policy*, 15 (4), 397–415.
———. (2006), 'Leadership, radical student engagement and the necessity of person-centred education'. *International Journal of Leadership in Education*, 9 (4), 299–313.
Fine, M. (2009), 'Epilogue', in J. Anyon with M.J. Dumas, D. Linville, K. Nolan, E.T. Perez and J. Weiss (eds), *Theory and Educational Research*. New York: Routledge, 179–195.
Finnie, R. (2002), 'Student loans: Borrowing and burden'. *Education Quarterly Review*, 8 (4), 28–42.
Fitz, J. and Halpin, D. (1994), 'Ministers and mandarins: Educational research in elite settings', in G. Walford (ed.), *Researching the Powerful in Education*. London: UCL Press, 32–50.
Flybjerg, B. (2001), *Making Social Science Matter: Why Social Inquiry Fails and How it Can Succeed Again*. Cambridge: Cambridge University Press.
Foster, W. (1989), 'Toward a critical practice of leadership', in J. Smyth (ed.), *Critical Perspectives on Educational Leadership*. London: Falmer, 48–66.
Foucault, M. (1977), *Power/Knowledge*. New York: Pantheon Books.
———. (1994), *The Archaeology of Knowledge*. London: Routledge.
———. (1995), *Discipline and Punish: The Birth of The Prison*. New York: Vintage Books.
Fox, K. (2004), *Watching the English: The Hidden Rules of English Behaviour*. London: Hodder and Stoughton.
Fullan, M. (2001), *Leading in a Culture of Change*. San Francisco: Jossey-Bass.
———. (2003), *The Moral Imperative of School Leadership*. Ontario: Corwin Press, Inc.
———. (2006), *Primary Leadership Paper*, No. 18. West Sussex: National Association of Headteachers.
Gabarro, J. (1978), 'The development of trust, influence and expectations', in A.G. Athos and J. Gabarro (eds), *Interpersonal Behavior: Communication and Understanding in Relationships*. Englewood Cliffs, NJ: Prentice Hall, 290–303.
Gadamer, H.-G. (2006), *Truth and Method*. London: Continuum.
Gambetta, D.G. (1988), 'Can we trust trust?', in D.G. Gambetta (ed.), *Trust*. New York: Basil Blackwell, 213–237.

Garrett, P.M. (2009), *Transforming' Children's Services?: Social Work, Neoliberalism and the 'Modern' World*. Maidenhead, Berkshire: Open Univesrity Press.

Geer, B. (1964), 'First days in the field', in P. Hammond (ed.), *Sociologists at Work*. New York: Basic Books, 372–398.

Gerwirtz, S. (2001), *The Managerial School: Post-welfarism and Social Justice in Education*. London; New York: Routledge.

Gilbert, C. (2006), *A Vision for Teaching and Learning in 2020': Report of the Teaching and Learning in 2020 Review Group*. Nottingham: DfES.

Giroux, H.A. (2002), 'Neoliberalism, corporate culture, and the promise of higher education: The university as a democratic public sphere'. *Harvard Educational Review*, 72 (4), 425–464.

———. (2012), *Education and the Crisis of Public Values*. New York: Peter Lang.

Goleman, D., Boyatzis, R. and McKee, A. (2002), *The New Leaders: Emotional Intelligence at Work*. London: Little Brown, Time Warner Books U.K.

Gove, M. (2012), Speech on Academies, Haberdashers' Aske's Hatcham College, 4 January 2012 (Online at: https://www.gov.uk/government/speeches/michael-gove-speech-on-academies) (Accessed: 3rd October 2013).

———. (2013), 'I refuse to surrender to the Marxist teachers hell-bent on destroying our schools: Education Secretary berates "the new enemies of promise" for opposing his plans'. (Mail Online) (Online at: http://www.dailymail.co.uk/debate/article-2298146/I-refuse-surrender-Marxist-teachers-hell-bent-destroying-schools-Education-Secretary-berates-new-enemies-promise-opposing-plans.html) (Accessed: 27th March 2013).

Grace, G. (1994), 'Urban education and the culture of contentment: The politics, culture and economics of inner-city schooling', in N. Stromquist (ed.), *Education in Urban Areas: Cross-national Dimensions*. Westport, CT: Praeger, 45–62.

———. (1995), *School Leadership: Beyond Education Management*. London: Falmer Press.

———. (2000), 'Research and the challenges of contemporary school leadership: The contribution of critical scholarship'. *British Journal of Educational Studies*, 48 (3), 231–247.

Greenfield, T. (1984), 'Leaders and schools: Wilfulness and non-natural order in organisations', in T. Sergiovanni, and J. Corbally (eds), *Leadership and Organisational Culture: New Perspectives on Administrative Theory and Practice*. Urbana: University of Illinois Press, 142–169.

Grek, S. (2010), 'International Organisational and the shared construction of policy "problems": Problematisation and change in education governance in Europe'. *European Educational Research Journal*, 9 (3), 396–406.

———, Lawn, M., Lingard, B., Ozga, J., Rinne, R., Segerholm, C. and Simola, H. (2009), 'National policy brokering and the construction of the European education space in England, Sweden, Finland and Scotland'. *Comparative Education*, 41 (1), 5–21.

Griffiths, G. (1985), 'Doubts, dilemmas and diary-keeping: Some reflections on teacher-based research', in R. Burgess (ed.), *Issues in Educational Research: Qualitative Methods*. London: Falmer Press, 197–215.

Griffith, A. 1998. 'Insider/outsider: epistemological privilege and mothering work'. *Human Studies*, 21, 361–376.

Gronn, P. (2003), *The New Work of Educational Leaders*. London: Sage.

Gunter, H.M. (2001), *Leaders and Leadership in Education*. London: Paul Chapman Publishing.

———. (2009), 'The "C" word in educational research: An appreciative response'. *Critical Studies in Education*, 50 (1), 93–102.

———. (2012a), *Leadership and the Reform of Education*. Bristol: The Policy Press.

———. (2012b), 'Intellectual work and knowledge production', in T. Fitzgerald, J. White and H.M. Gunter (eds), *Hard Labour? Academic Work and the Changing Landscape of Higher Education*. Bingley: Emerald Group Publishing Limited, 23–40.

———. (2014) *Educational Leadership and Hannah Arendt*. Abingdon: Routledge.

Gunter, H. and Fitzgerald, T. (2007), 'The contribution of researching professionals to field development: Introduction to a special edition'. *Journal of Educational Administration and History*, 39 (1), 1–16.

——— and Forrester, G. (2009), 'School leadership and education policy-making in England'. *Policy Studies*, 30 (5), 495–511.

——— and Thomson, P. (2004), *Kingswood High School: Baseline Report 2004*. Report to the DfES Innovation Unit: London.

——— and Willmont, R. (2002), 'Biting the bullet'. *Management in Education*, 15 (5), 35–37.

———, Hall, D. and Mills, C. (2012), 'Education policy: A critical study of knowledge production and the rise of the consultocracy'. Paper presented at *Annual Policy and Politics Conference*, Bristol, 14th September 2012.

Gunter, H., Rayner, S., Thomas, H., Fielding, A., Butt, G., and Lance, A. (2005) 'Teachers, time and work: findings from the Evaluation of the Transforming the School Workforce Pathfinder Project'. *School Leadership and Management*, 25 (5), 441–454.

Haig, E. (2004), 'Some observations on the critique of critical discourse analysis'. *Studies in Language and Culture*, 25, 129–149.

Hall, D. (2013), 'Drawing a veil over managerialism: Leadership and the discursive disguise of the new public management'. *Journal of Educational Administration and History*, DOI: 10. 1080/00220620.2013.771154.

———, Gunter, H.M. and Bragg, J. (2013), 'The strange case of the emergence of distributed leadership in schools in England'. *Educational Review*, DOI: 10.1080/00131911.2012.718257.

Hall, S. (2003), *New Labour's Double-shuffle*. (Online at: http://www.lwbooks. co.uk/ReadingRoom/public/DoubleShuffle.html) (Accessed: 18th May 2011).

Hamann, E. and Rosen, L. (2011), 'What makes anthropology of educational policy implementation 'anthropological'', in B.A.U. Levinson and M. Pollock (eds), *A Companion to the Anthropology of Education*. Malden, MA: Blackwell, 461–477.

Hammersley, M. and Atkinson, P. (2007), *Ethnography: Principles in Practice* (third edition). New York, NY: Routledge.

Hansard. (2011), House of Commons, Further and Higher Education (Access) Bill, 2nd reading, 04.03.11. (Online at: http://www.publications.parliament.uk/pa/cm201011/cmhansrd/cm110304/debtext/110304-0001.htm#11030451000002) (Accessed: 24th April 2014).

Hargreaves, D. (1967), *Social Relations in a Secondary School*. London: Routledge & Kegan Paul.

———. (1996) *Teaching as a Research-based Profession*, Teacher Training Agency Annual Lecture. London: Teacher Training Agency.

Hargreaves, A., Halaz, G. and Pont, B. (2007), 'School leadership for systemic improvement in Finland: A case study report for improving school leadership'. (Online at: http://www.oecd.org/edu/school/39928629.pdf) (Accessed: 5th May 2013).

Harris, A., Muijs, D. and Crawford, M. (2003), *Deputy and Assistant Heads: Building Leadership Potential*. Summary Report. (Online at: www.ncsl.org.uk/literaturereviews) (Accessed: 14th April 2008).

Hartley, D. (2009), 'Personalisation: The nostalgic revival of child-centred education?' *Journal of Education Policy*, 24 (4), 423–434.

Harvey, D. (2007), 'Neoliberalism as creative destruction'. *The Annals of the American Academy of Political and Social Science*, 610 (1), 21–44.

Hicks, D. (2012), 'Performance-based university research funding systems'. *Research Policy*, 41 (2), 251–261.

Higgs, M.J. and Dulewicz, V. (1999), 'Can emotional intelligence be measured and developed?' *Leadership and Organisation Development Journal*, 20 (5), 6–32.

Hill, D. (2007), 'Critical teacher education, New Labour and the global project of neoliberal capital'. *Policy Futures in Education*, 5 (2), 204–225.

Hillage, J., Pearson, R., Anderson, A. and Tamkin, P. (1998), *Excellence in Research on Schools*. London: DfEE.

Hodkinson, P. (2005), ''Insider Research' in the study of youth cultures'. *Journal of Youth Studies*, 8 (2), 131–149.

Holligan, C. and Wilson, M. (2013), 'Critical incidents as formative influences on the work of educational researchers: Understanding an insider perspective through narrative enquiry'. *British Journal of Sociology of Education*, DOI: 10.1080/01425692.2013.835713.

Hood, C. and Peters, G. (2004), 'The middle ageing of new public management: Into the age of paradox?' *Journal of Public Administration Research and Theory*, 14 (3), 267–282.

Hoyle, E. (1999), 'The two faces of micropolitics'. *School Leadership and Management*, 19 (2), 213–222.

Hughes, M.G. (1973), 'The professional as administrator: The case of the secondary school head'. *Educational Administration Bulletin*, 2 (1), 11–23.

Humphrey, N. (2012), Personal communication with the author.

———, Lendrum, A. and Wigelsworth, M. (2010), *Social and Emotional Aspects of Learning (SEAL) Programme in Secondary Schools: National Evaluation*. University of Manchester and Department for Education.

———, Kalambouka, A., Bolton, J., Lendrum, A., Wigelsworth, M., Lennie, C. and Farell, P. (2008), *Primary Social and Emotional Aspects of Learning (SEAL): Evaluation of Small Group Work*. University of Manchester and Department of Schools, Families and Children.

Hussey, J. and Hussey, R. (1997), *Business Research: A Practical Guide for Undergraduate and Post-graduate Students*. London: MacMillan Press Ltd.

Inglis, F. (1985), *The Management of Ignorance*. Oxford: Basil Blackwell.

———. (2003), 'Method and morality: Practical politics and the science of human affairs', in P. Sikes, J. Nixon and W. Carr (eds), *The Moral Foundations of Educational Research: Knowledge, Inquiry and Values*. Maidenhead: Open University Press, 118–132.

Jackson, C. (2010), 'Fear in education'. *Educational Review*, 62 (1), 39–52.

Jackson, A.Y. and Mazzei, L.A. (2012), *Thinking with Theory in Qualitative Research: Viewing Data Across Multiple Perspectives*. Abingdon, Oxon: Routledge.

Jenkins, R. (1992), *Pierre Bourdieu*. London: Routledge.

Johnson, M. (2004), *Personalised Learning: An Emperor's Outfit: An Emperor's Outfit?* London: Institute for Public Policy.

Johnston, J. and Kouzmin, A. (1998), 'Who are the rent seekers?: From the Ideological attack on public officials to the "pork barrel" par excellence: privatization and out-sourcing as oligarchic corruption'. *Administrative Theory & Praxis*, 20 (4), 491–507.

Jones, S. (2013), '"Ensure that you stand out from the crowd": A corpus-based analysis of personal statements according to applicants' school type'. *Comparative Education Review*, 57 (2), 397–423.

Kanuha, V. (2000), '"Being" native versus "going native": Conducting social work research as an insider'. *Social Work*, 45, 439–447.

Klette, K. (2002), 'Reform policy and teachers professionalism in four Nordic countries'. *Journal of Educational Change*, 3, 265–282.

Knight, K. and Blackledge, P. (eds) (2008), *Revolutionary Aristotelianism: Ethics, Resistance and Utopia*. Stuttgart: Lucius and Lucius.

Konu, A. and Rimpela, M. (2002), 'Wellbeing in schools: A conceptual model'. *Health Promotion International*, 17, 79–87.

Koyama, J. (2010), *Making Failure Pay: For Profit Tutoring, High Stakes Testing and Public Schools*. Chicago: University of Chicago Press.

Labaree, R. (2002), 'The risk of "going observationalist": Negotiating the hidden dilemmas of being an insider participant observer'. *Qualitative Research*, 2, 97–122.

Lacey, C. (1970), *Hightown Grammar*. Manchester: Manchester University Press.

Larner, W. (2000), 'Neo-liberalism: Policy, ideology, governmentality'. *Studies in Political Economy*, 63, 5–25.

Lather, P. (1991), *Feminist Research in Education: Within/Against*. Geelong: Deakin University Press.

Leadbeater, C. (2004). *Personalisation through participation: a new script for public services*. London: Demos.

Leithwood, K.A., Day, C., Sammons, P., Harris, A. and Hopkins, D. (2006), *Seven Strong Claims about Effective School Leadership*. Nottingham: national College of School Leadership.

Lerum, K. (2001), 'Subjects of desire: Academic armor, intimate ethnography and the production of critical knowledge'. *Qualitative Inquiry*, 7 (4), 466–483.

Levi-Strauss, C. (1997), *Tropiikin kasvot*, Helsinki, Loki-kirjat (Translation from 1955 *Tristes Tropiques*).

Lewis, M. (2012), *You Can Afford To Go To University* (Online at: http://www.studentfinance2012.com/files/Fulltime_Guide_2013.pdf) (Accessed: 4th July 2013).

Lieberman, A. (1992), 'The meaning of scholarly activity and the building of community'. *Educational Researcher*, 21 (6), 5–12.

Little, J.W. and McLaughlin, M.W. (eds.) (1993), *Teachers' Work: Individuals, Colleagues, and Contexts*. New York: Teachers College Press.

Lopez, P., Valenzuela, A. and Garcia, E. (2011), 'The critical ethnography of public policy for social justice', in B.A.U. Levinson and M. Pollock (eds), *A Companion to the Anthropology of Education*. Malden, MA: Blackwell, 547–562.

Loughlin, M. (2004), 'Quality, control and complicity: The effortless conquest of the academy by bureaucrats'. *International Journal of the Humanities*, 2, 717–724.

Luhmann, N. (1988), 'Familiarity, confidence, trust: Problems and alternatives', in D.G. Gambetta (ed.), *Trust*. Basil Blackwell: New York, 94–107.

Lupton, R. (2011), 'No change there then (?): The onward march of school markets and competition'. *Journal of Educational Administration and History*, 43, 309–323.

Lynch, K. (2010), 'Carelessness in higher education'. *Arts and Humanities in Higher Education*, 9, 54–67.

MacIntyre, A. (1994), *After Virtue: A Study in Moral Theory*. London: Duckworth.

———. (1999), *Dependent Rational Animals*. London: Duckworth.

———. (2001), *Whose Justice? Which Rationality?* London: Duckworth.

MacLure, M. (2003), *Discourse in Educational and Social Research*. Maidenhead: Open University Press.

Mahony, P. and Hextall, I. (2000), *Reconstructing Teaching*. London: RoutledgeFalmer.

Mannheim, K. (1936), *Ideology and Utopia*. New York: Harvest Books.

Mansell, W. (2007), *Education By Numbers*. London: Politico.

Maringe, F., Foskett, N. and Roberts, D. (2009), '"I can survive on jam sandwiches for the next three years": The impact of the new fees regime on students' attitudes to HE and debt'. *International Journal of Educational Management*, 23 (2), 145–160.

Marshall, M.N. (1996), 'Sampling for qualitative research'. *Family Practice*, 13 (6), 522–525.

Martin, R. (2003), *The Responsibility Virus*. New York, NY: Perseus Publishing

Mason, J. (1996), *Qualitative Researching*. London: Sage Publications.

Mawhinney, H.B. (1999), 'Reappraisal: The problems and prospects of studying the micropolitics in reforming schools'. *School Leadership and Management*, 19 (2), 159–170.

Mayer, R.C., Davis, J.H. and Schoorman, F.D. (1995), 'An integrative model of organizational trust'. *The Academy of Management Review*, 20 (3), 709–734.

McCall, M.W. (1998), 'High flyers; developing the next generation of leaders'. *Harvard Business School Press* (Online at: http://www.ncsl.org.uk) (Accessed: 16th March 2009).

McGettigan, A. (2013), *The Great University Gamble*. London: Pluto Press.

McGinity, R. and Gunter, H.M. (2015), 'New practices and old hierarchies: Academy conversion in a successful English secondary school', In P. Thomson (ed.), *Educational Leadership and Pierre Bourdieu*. London: Routledge, In press.

———. (2012), 'Living improvement 2: A case study of a secondary school in England'. *Improving Schools*, 15 (3), 228–244.

McGinity, R. and Salokangas, M. (2012), 'What Is Embedded Research?' paper presented at conference on *Embedded Research*, University of Manchester, School of Education, 20th June.

———. (2014), 'Introduction: "embedded research" as an approach into academia for emerging researchers'. *Management in Education*, 28 (3), 3–5.

McIntyre, D. (2005), 'Bridging the gap between research and practice'. *Cambridge Journal of Education*, 35 (3), 357–382.

McLaughlin, C., Black-Hawkins, K. and McIntyre, D. (2004), *Researching Teachers, Researching Schools, Researching Networks: A Summary of the Literature*. Cambridge: University of Cambridge.

McNamara, O. (2009), 'Initial teacher education: A(nother) decade of radical reform' in radical reform', in C. Chapman and H.M. Gunter (eds), *Radical Reforms: Perspectives on an Era of Educational Change*. London: Routledge, 91–103.

Mercer, J. (2007), 'The challenges of insider research in educational institutions: Wielding a double-edged sword and resolving delicate dilemmas'. *Oxford Review of Education*, 33 (1), 1–17.

Mertens, D.M. (2005), *Research and Evaluation in Education and Psychology* (second edition). London: Sage.

Mertkan, S. (2011), 'Leadership support through public-private partnerships: Views of school leaders'. *Educational Management, Administration and Leadership*, 39 (2), 156–171.

Merton, R. (1972), 'Insiders and outsiders: A chapter in the sociology of knowledge'. *American Journal of Sociology*, 78, 9–47.

Milburn, A. (2012), *University Challenge: How Higher Education can Advance Social Mobility: A Progress Report by the Independent Reviewer on Social Mobility and Child Poverty*. London: Cabinet Office.

Miliband, D. (2004), *Personalised Learning: Building a New Relationship with Schools*. Speech by the Minister of State for School Standards to the North of England Education Conference. January 2004.

Mills, C. (2011), 'Framing literacy policy: Power and policy drivers in primary schools'. *Literacy*, 45 (3), 103–110.

Mirowski, P. (2013), *Never Let a Serious Crisis go to Waste: How Neoliberalism Survived the Financial Meltdown*. London: Verso.

Naples, N. (1996), 'A feminist revisiting of the insider/outsider debate: The "outsider phenomenon" in rural Iowa'. *Qualitative Sociology*, 19, 83–106.

Nerad, M. (2010), 'Globalisation and the internationalisation of graduate education: A macro and micro view'. *Canadian Journal of Higher Education*, 40 (1), 1–12.

———. (2011), 'It takes a global village to develop the next generation of PhDs and postdoctoral fellows', *Acta Academica Supplementum*, 2001, (2), 196–216. (http://www.ufs.ac.za/ActaAcademica). (Accessed: 5th November 2013).

Newman, J. (2001) *Modernizing Governance: New Labour, Policy and Society*, London: Sage.

Nixon, J., Walker, M. and Clough, P. (2003), 'Research as a thoughtful practice', in P. Sikes, J. Nixon and W. Carr (eds), *The Moral Foundations of Educational Research: Knowledge, Inquiry and Values*. Maidenhead: Open University Press, 86–104.

Nummenmaa, A. and Välijärvi, J. (2006), *Opettajan työ ja oppiminen*, A teacher's work and learning). Jyväskylä: Institute for Educational Research, University of Jyväskylä.

Office for National Statistics. (2010), *Atlas of Deprivation*. (Online at: http://www.ons.gov.uk/ons/dcp171780_239839.pdf) (Accessed: 3rd June 2013).

Office for Standards in Education. (2003), *Leadership and Management: What Inspection Tells Us*, HMI Report 1646. London: Ofsted Publications Centre.

Ogg, T., Zimdars, A. and Heath, A. (2009), 'Schooling effects on degree performance: A comparison of the predictive validity of aptitude testing and secondary school grades at Oxford University'. *British Educational Research Journal*, 35 (5), 781–807.

Olssen, M. (1996), 'In defence of the welfare state and publicly provided education: A New Zealand perspective'. *Journal of Educational Policy*, 11, 337–362.

Organisation for Economic Co-operation and Development. (2012), *Education at a Glance*. (Online at: http://www.oecd.org/edu/highlights.pdf) (Accessed: 14th December 2012).

Ozga, J. (2000a), *Policy Research in Educational Settings*. Buckingham: Open University Press).

———. (2000b), 'New labour, new teachers?', in J. Clarke, S. Gewirtz and E. McLaughlin (eds), *New Managerialism, New Welfare*. London: Sage, 223–235.

Paechter, C. (2003), 'On goodness and utility in educational research', in P. Sikes, J. Nixon, and W. Carr (eds), *The Moral Foundations of Educational Research: Knowledge, Inquiry and Values*. Maidenhead: Open University Press, 105–117.

Parman, S. (1998), 'Making the familiar strange: The anthropological dialogue of George and Louise Spindler', in G. Spindler and L. Spindler (eds), *Fifty Years of Anthropology and Education 1950–2000*. Mahwah, NJ: Lawrence Erlbaum, 393–416.

Parsons, T. (2002), 'On the concept of political power', in M. Haugaard (ed.), *Power: A Reader*. Manchester: Manchester University Press, 147–162.

Pascal, C. and Ribbins, P. (1998), *Understanding Primary Headteachers*. London: Cassell.

Paulsen, M.B. and St. John, E.P. (2002), 'Social class and college costs: Examining the financial nexus between college choice and persistence'. *Journal of Higher Education*, 73, 189–236.

Peck, J. (2013), *Constructions of Neoliberal Reason*. Oxford: Oxford University Press.

Phillips, D. and Ochs, K. (eds) (2004), *Educational Policy Borrowing: Historical Perspectives*. London: Symposium Books.

Platt, J. (1981), 'On interviewing one's peers'. *British Journal of Sociology*, 32 (1), 75–91.

Pollitt, C. (1995), 'Justification by works or by faith? Evaluating the new public management'. *Evaluation: The International Journal of Theory, Research and Practice*, 1 (2), 135–157.

———. (2007), 'New labour's re-disorganization'. *Public Management Review*, 9 (4), 529–543.

——— and Bouckaert, G. (2003), 'Evaluating public management reforms: An international perspective', in H. Wollmann (ed.), *Evaluation in Public Sector Reform: Concepts and Practice in International Perspective*. Cheltenham: Edward Elgar, 12–36.

Pollock, A.M., Price, D. and Player, S. (2007), 'An Examination of the UK Treasury's evidence base for cost and time overrun data in UK value-for-money policy and appraisal'. *Public Management and Money*, 27 (2), 127–134.

———, Shaoul, J. and Vickers, N. (2002), 'Private finance and "value for money" in NHS hospitals: A policy in search of a rationale?' *British Medical Journal*, 324, 1205–1209.

Popkewitz, T. (2000), 'Introduction', in T. Popkewitz (ed.), *Educational Knowledge: Changing Relationships between the State, Civil Society, and the Educational Community*. New York: State University of New York Press, 3–27.

Power, A. and Mumford, K. (1999), *The Slow Death of Great Cities? Urban Abandonment or Urban Renaissance*. York: York Publishing Services.

PricewaterhouseCoopers. (2001), *Teacher Workload Study*. London: DfES.

———. (2007), *Independent Study into School Leadership*. London: DfES.

———. (2008), *Academies Evaluation: Fifth Annual Report*. Nottingham: Department for Children, Schools and Families Publications

Pring, R. (1999), 'Universities and teacher education'. *Higher Education Quarterly*, 53 (4), 290–311.

Printy, S. (2010), 'Principals' influence on instructional quality: Insights from US schools'. *School Leadership and Management*, 30 (2), 111–126.

Qualifications and Curriculum Agency (QCA). (2005), *A Curriculum for the Future, Subjects consider the Challenge*. London: QCA.

———. (2008a), *Guidelines on Recording Personal, Learning and Thinking Skills in The Diploma*. London: QCA.

———. (2008b), *Personal Learning and Thinking Skills Framework*. London: QCA.

Ravitch, D. (2011), *Death and Life of the Great American School System: How Testing and Choice are Undermining Education*. New York: Basic Books.

Reay, D., Crozier, G. and Clayton, J. (2010), '"Fitting in" or "standing out": Working class students in UK higher education'. *British Educational Research Journal*, 32 (1), 1–19.

———, David, M. and Ball, S. (2001), 'Making a difference?: Institutional habituses and higher education choice.' Sociological Research Online. Online at: http://www.socresonline.org.uk/5/4/reay.html

——— and Ball, Stephen. (2005), *Degrees of Choice: Social Class, Race and Gender in Higher Education*. Stoke: Trentham Books.

Ribbins, P., Bates, R. and Gunter, H.M. (2003), 'Reviewing research in education in Australia and the UK: Evaluating the evaluations'. *Journal of Educational Administration*, 41 (4), 423–444.

Ricoeur, P. (1970), *Freud and Philosophy: An Essay on Interpretation*. New Haven: Yale University Press.

Riddell, S.and Tett, L. (2004), 'New community schools and inter-agency working: Assessing the effectiveness of social justice initiatives'. *London Review of Education*, 2, 219–228.

Rivoal, I. and Salazar, N.B. (2013), 'Contemporary ethnographic practice and the value of serendipity'. *Social Anthropology*, 21, 178–185.

Robson, C. (2011), *Real World Research* (third edition). Oxford: Blackwell.

Rogers, R. (ed.) (2004), *Critical Discourse Analysis in Education*. Mahwah, NJ: Lawrence Erlbaum Associates.

Romanshyn, R. (2007), *The Wounded Researcher*. New Orleans: Spring Journal Publications.

Rousseau, D., Sitkin, S.B., Burt, R.S. and Camerer, C. (1998), 'Not so different after all: A cross discipline view of trust'. *Academy of Management Review*, 23 (3), 393–404.

Rowley, H. (2013), *Schools and Deprived Communities: A Case Study of a Community-Oriented Schools*, Unpublished Ph. D thesis. The Manchester Institute of Education, University of Manchester.
———— and Dyson, A. (2011), 'Academies in the public interest – a contradiction in terms?', in H.M. Gunter (ed.), *The State and Education Policy: The Academies Programme*. London: Continuum, 79–91.
Rudduck, J. and McIntyre, D. (eds) (1998), *Challenges for Educational Research*. London: Paul Chapman Publishing.
Rutherford, J. (2005), 'Cultural studies in the corporate university'. *Cultural Studies*, 19, 297–317.
Sahlberg, P. (2011), *Finnish Lessons: What can the World Learn from Educational Change in Finland?* New York: Columbia University, Teachers College Press.
Salokangas, M. (2013), *Autonomy and Innovation in English Academies: A Case Study*, Unpublished PhD thesis. The Manchester Institute of Education, The University of Manchester.
Saltman, K.J. and Gabbard, D.A. (2011), *Education as Enforcement* (second edition.) New York, NY: Routledge.
Schofield, J.W. (1993), 'Increasing the generalizability of qualitative research', in M. Hammersley (ed.), *Educational Research: Current Issues*. Buckingham: Open University Press, 91–113.
Scottish Executive. (2006), *Getting it Right for Every Child: Implementation Plan*. Edinburgh: Scottish Executive.
Shakespeare, W. (2005), *As You Like It* (Wordsworth Classics). London: Wordsworth.
Shamir, B., Dayan-Horesh, H. and Adler, D. (2005), 'Leading by biography: Towards a life-story approach to the study of leadership'. *Leadership*, 1 (1), 13–29.
Shorthouse, R. (2013), 'A bright future:Accelerating education reform', in R. Shorthouse and G. Stagg (eds), *Tory Modernisation 2.0 – The Future of the Conservative Party*. London: Bright Blue Campaign. Conservative Party, 59–72.
Sikes, P. (2008), 'Researching research cultures: The case of new universities', in P. Sikes and A. Potts (eds), *Researching Education from the Inside*. London: Routledge, 144–158.
————. (2012), 'Some thoughts on ethics review and contemporary ethical concerns in research in education'. *Research Intelligence*, 118, 16–17.
———— and Potts, A. (eds) (2008), *Researching Education from the Inside*. London: Routledge.
————, Nixon, J. and Carr, W. (eds) (2003), *The Moral Foundations of Educational Research: Knowledge, Inquiry and Values*. Maidenhead: Open University Press.
Simons, H. (2009), *Case study research in practice*. London: SAGE publications.
Simola, H. (2005), 'The Finnish miracle of PISA: Historical and sociological remarks on teaching and teacher education'. *Comparative Education*, 41 (4), 455–470.
Sixsmith, J., Boneham, M. and Goldring, J.E. (2003), 'Accessing the community: Gaining insider perspectives from the outside'. *Qualitative Health Research*, 13 (4), 578–589.
Slee, R. (1998), 'Higher education work in the reductionist age'. *International Studies in Sociology of Education*, 8 (3), 255–269.

Smith, D. (2001), 'Collaborative research: Policy and the management of knowledge creation in UK universities'. *Higher Education Quarterly*, 55 (2), 131–157.

Smyth, J. (1998), 'Finding the "enunciative space" for teacher leadership and teacher learning in schools'. *Asia-Pacific Journal of Teacher Education*, 26 (3), 191–202.

———. (2007), 'Toward the pedagogically engaged school: Listening to student voice as a positive response to disengagement and "dropping out"', in D. Thiessen and A. Cook-Sather (eds), *International Handbook of Student Experience of Elementary and Secondary School*. Dordrecht, The Netherlands: Springer, 635–658.

Southworth, G. (2002), 'Instructional leadership in schools: Reflections and empirical evidence'. *School Leadership and Management*, 22 (1), 73–91.

———. (2010), *School Business Management: A Quiet Revolution*. Nottingham: National College for School Leadership.

Spring, J. (2012), *Education Networks*. New York, NY: Routledge.

Stake, R. (1995), *The Art of Case Research*. Thousand Oaks, CA: Sage Publications.

Stockborough Challenge. (2007), *The Stockborough Challenge: Bringing together and joining up 2008–2013: Everyone Different: Everyone Matters*, Unpublished policy document. Stockborough Children's Services.

Strong, T.B. (2012), *Politics Without Vision, Thinking Without a Banister in the Twentieth Century*. Chicago, IL: The University of Chicago Press.

Sutton Trust. (2010), *Initial Response to the Independent Review of Higher Education Funding and Student Finance*. London: Sutton Trust.

Tamboukou, M. (2012), 'Truth telling in Foucault and Arendt: Parrhesia, the pariah and academics in dark times'. *Journal of Education Policy*, 27 (6), 849–865.

Taylor, C. (2003), *The Ethics of Authenticity*. Cambridge, MA: Harvard University press.

———. (2007), *Modern Social Imaginaries*. Durham: Duke University Press.

Teach First. (2013a) *About Us* (Online at: www.teachfirst.org.uk/about) (Accessed: 14th November 2013)

———. (2013b), *Recruitment and Selection* (Online at: http://graduates.teachfirst.org.uk/recruitment/requirements/index.html) (Accessed: 14th November 2013).

———. (2013c), *How Teaching in a Low Income School Became a Prestigious Career for Graduates*. (Online at: www.teachfirst.org.uk/blog/how-teaching-low-income-school-became-prestigious-career-graduates) (Accessed: 14th November 2013).

———. (2013d), *Our LD Programme*. (Online at: http://graduates.teachfirst.org.uk/our-programme/masters-education.html) (Accessed: 14th November 2013).

Teddlie, C. and Reynolds, D. (eds) (2000), *The International Handbook of School Effectiveness Research*. London: Routledge Falmer.

Thomson, P. (2008), 'Field', in M. Grenfell (ed.), *Pierre Bourdieu: Key Concepts*. Stocksfield: Acumen, 67–81.

———. (2010a), 'Headteacher autonomy: A sketch of a Bourdieuian field analysis of position and practice'. *Critical Studies in Education*, 51 (1), 5–20.

———. (2010b), 'A critical pedagogy of global place: Regeneration in and as action', in C. Raffo, A. Dyson, H.M. Gunter, D. Hall, L. Jones and A. Kalambouka (eds), *Education and Poverty in Affluent Countries*. New York, NY: Routledge, 124–134.

—— and Gunter, H.M. (2006), 'From "consulting pupils" to "pupils as researchers": A situated case narrative'. *British Educational Research Journal*, 32 (6), 839–856.

——. (2007), 'The methodology of students-as-researchers: Valuing and using experience and expertise to develop methods'. *Discourse: Studies in the Cultural Politics of Education*, 28 (3), 327–342.

——. (2011), 'Inside, outside, upside down: The fluidity of academic researcher "identity" in working with/in school'. *International Journal of Research and Method in Education*, 34 (1), 17–30.

Tierney, W.G. and Dilley, P. (2001), 'Interviewing in education', in J.F. Gubrium and J.A. Holstein (eds), *Handbook of Interview Research: Context and Method*. London: Sage, 453–473.

Timimi, S. (2011), 'Children's mental health in the era of globalisation: neo-liberalism, commodification, McDonaldisation, and the new challenges they pose' (Online at: http://www.criticalpsychiatry.net/wp-content/uploads/2009/12/NewchapterIntech1.pdf) (Accessed: 17th October 2013).

Universities and Colleges Admissions Service. (2012), *Admissions Process Review: Findings and Recommendations*. Cheltenham: UCAS.

van Thiel, S. and Leeuw, F.L. (2002), 'The performance paradox in the public sector'. *Public Performance & Management Review*, 25 (3), 267–281.

Voigt, K. (2007), 'Individual choice and unequal participation in higher education'. *Theory and Research in Education*, 5 (1), 87–112.

Ward, S.C. (2012), *Neoliberalism and the Global Restructuring of Knowledge and Education*. New York, NY: Routledge.

Waters, M. (2013), *Thinking Allowed on Schooling*. Carmarthen: Independent Printing Press.

Watson, D., Bayliss, P. and Emery, C. (2012), *Children's Social and Emotional Wellbeing in Schools: A Critical Perspective*. Bristol: Policy Press.

Weiss, C.H. (1999), 'The interface between evaluation and public policy'. *Evaluation*, 5 (4), 468–486.

Welsh Assembly Government. (2009), *Demonstrating Success: Handbook for Practitioners*. Cardiff: Welsh Assembly.

Whitaker, K.S. (2003), 'Principal role changes and influence on principal recruitment and selection'. *Journal of Educational Administration*, 41 (1), 37–54.

Wilcox, B. (1997), 'Schooling, school improvement and the relevance of Alasdair MacIntyre'. *Cambridge Journal of Education*, 27 (2), 249–260.

Wilshaw, M. (2013), 'Get out of the ivory towers, academics told', *The Times* (Online at: http://www.thetimes.co.uk/tto/education/article3718769.ece) (Accessed: 25th March 2013).

Wodak, R. and Meyer, M. (eds) (2001), *Methods of Critical Discourse Analysis*. London: Sage.

Woods, C. (2009), 'Remodelling and distributed leadership: The case of the school business manager', in C. Chapman and H. Gunter (eds), *Radical Reforms: Perspectives on an Era of Educational Change*. London: Routledge, 80–90.

——, Armstrong, P. and Pearson, D. (2012), 'Facilitating primary head teacher succession in England: The role of the school business manager'. *School Leadership and Management*, 32 (2), 141–157.

——, Bragg, J. and Pearson, D. (2013), 'Perfect partners or uneasy bedfellows? Competing understandings of the place of business management within contemporary education partnerships'. *Educational Management Administration Leadership*, 41 (6), 751–766.

Woods, P. (2005), *Democratic Leadership in Education*. Thousand Oaks: Paul Chapman Publishing.

Woodhead, C. (2000), 'Old values for a new age'. *Times Educational Supplement*, 7th January, p. 13.

Wortham, S. and Reyes, A. (2011), 'Linguistic anthropology of education', in B.A.U. Levinson and M. Pollock (eds), *A Companion to the Anthropology of Education*. Malden, MA: Blackwell Publishing, 137–153.

Wrigley, T. Thomson, P. and Lingard, B. (eds) (2012), *Changing Schools: Alternative Ways to Make a World of Difference*. Abingdon Oxon: Routledge.

Yin, R.K. (2009), *Case Study Research: Design and Methods*, 4th Edition. London: Sage.

Zeichner, K. (1995), 'Beyond the divide of teacher research and academic research'. *Teachers and Teaching*, 1 (2), 153–72.

Zimdars, A. (2010), 'Fairness and undergraduate admission: A qualitative exploration of admissions choices at the University of Oxford'. *Oxford Review of Education*, 36 (3), 207–323.

Zuboff, S. and Maxmin, J. (2004), *The Support Economy: Why Corporations are Failing Individuals and the Next Episode of Capitalism*. New York: Penguin.

INDEX